Time and Tide
Wait for No Man

TIME AND TIDE WAIT FOR NO MAN

The Changing European Geopolitical Landscape

KAREL DE GUCHT

AND

STEPHAN KEUKELEIRE

Foreword by Valéry Giscard d'Estaing

New York
Westport, Connecticut
London

Library of Congress Cataloging-in-Publication Data

Gucht, Karel de.
    Time and tide wait for no man : the changing European geopolitical
landscape / Karel de Gucht and Stephan Keukeleire ; foreword by
Valéry Giscard d'Estaing.
        p. cm.
    Includes bibliographical references and index.
    ISBN 0–275–94062–4 (alk. paper)
    1. Europe—Politics and government—1989– 2. Geopolitics—Europe.
I. Keukeleire, Stephan. II. Title.
D2009.G83   1991
320.1′2—dc20   91–9196

British Library Cataloguing in Publication Data is available.

Library of Congress Catalog Card Number: 91–9196
ISBN: 0–275–94062–4

First published in 1991

Praeger Publishers, One Madison Avenue, New York, NY 10010
An imprint of Greenwood Publishing Group, Inc.

Printed in the United States of America

The paper used in this book complies with the
Permanent Paper Standard issued by the National
Information Standards Organization (Z39.48–1984).

10 9 8 7 6 5 4 3 2 1

Contents

Foreword *by Valéry Giscard d'Estaing*   vii

Preface   ix

Chapter 1.   Reappraising the German Identity   1

Chapter 2.   The Change in the West German Perception of Security   19

Chapter 3.   Toward a Political Interpretation of the Change in the West German Perception of Security   31

Chapter 4.   Growing Doubts about the United States and Nuclear Deterrence   47

Chapter 5.   "La mort d'une certaine conception de l'alliance"   65

Chapter 6.   French Independence in Doubt   81

Chapter 7.   Together, yet Alone   91

Chapter 8.   The Shock of Reykjavik   103

Chapter 9.   One Cheeky Bird Does Not Make a Summer   113

Chapter 10.   Erich Honecker's Visit to Bonn   133

Chapter 11.   Two Streams in One Channel   145

Chapter 12.   The Growing Political Role of the European Community   157

Chapter 13. Necessity and Conviction 173

Chapter 14. The Year of Upheaval 187

Chapter 15. L'Histoire est Libre 209

Epilogue 227

Selected Bibliography 231

Index 235

Foreword

The recent changes in Central and Eastern Europe represent a great victory for the principles that we have always defended: the values of liberal democracy with a social conscience, and the methods of the market economy.

This victory has been won only because the countries of the free world succeeded in combining their defense efforts and finding an appropriate response to the crises that punctuated the Cold War.

For forty years Western Europe lived in fear of a surprise attack by the Warsaw Pact launched from East Germany. The Atlantic Alliance matched this with NATO's joint military organization, a conventional and nuclear arsenal permitting a flexible response to the various possible contingencies and linking the European military apparatus to the American strategic forces. France made a unique contribution by stationing its First Army in Germany, while retaining control over its deterrent nuclear forces.

It is the firmness and cohesion of the Atlantic Alliance that has enabled the Cold War to be brought to an end. The Guadeloupe summit meeting in 1977, to which I invited President Jimmy Carter, Chancellor Helmut Schmidt and Prime Minister James Callaghan; NATO's "dual-track" decision in 1979; and the deployment of American Euro-missiles from 1983, showed the USSR that Europe would not surrender to military blackmail and that the insane arms race would ruin the Soviet economy first. It is to Mikhail Gorbachev's credit that he took note of this and adjusted the USSR's foreign and defense policies accordingly.

But while the threat has changed, not all the military risks have vanished. We have entered a period of uncertainty and confusion in Eastern Europe and in the USSR itself. Even after the disarmament agreements currently being negotiated, the USSR will continue to have an enormous nuclear potential and the largest and most powerful conventional army in the world.

Western Europe must therefore maintain a strong defense, capable of facing the risks of the twenty-first century, which will not all originate in Europe. I am thinking, for example, of the global implications of the demographic imbalances, of the centers of instability in the Mediterranean Basin and the Middle East, and of all the outbreaks of terrorism.

Faced with this new strategic landscape and all the uncertainties, we must define a number of clear principles.

First, the military alliance of the Western European countries and the United States is still needed. Above all, the United States' withdrawal would compromise Europe's security. And the withdrawal of unified Germany would bring the construction of the Europe of the Twelve to an end.

The second principle: As a sharp reduction in American troops is bound to follow the Red Army's withdrawal behind Soviet frontiers, the time has come for the Europeans to take prime responsibility for their own defense. This presupposes the transformation of the Alliance into a Euro-Atlantic pact. And this means that a country like France must assume its full responsibility in this renewed alliance and within an integrated general staff, which would then be under European control.

The third principle: The process of détente between the two blocs must continue, so as to consolidate and enhance the guarantees obtained in the negotiations on arms reductions and "confidence-building measures." The Conference on Security and Cooperation in Europe (CSCE) is a forum for contacts and negotiations that has proved its usefulness. While it cannot replace the alliances, there are only advantages to be gained from the member countries of the two alliances using it to extend their dialogue with a view to arriving at new security agreements.

Europe has sadly too few politicians who have agreed to study these fundamental problems. We owe a debt of gratitude to Karel De Gucht, a young and brilliant member of the Liberal Group in the European Parliament, for opening the debate in this deliberately innovative work. His analysis and proposals will become one of the major points of reference for current thinking on the future of European security.

Valéry Giscard d'Estaing

Preface

I came across Europe for the first time while lying in my bed. I had been ill and, to distract me, my mother had borrowed a map of Europe from my uncle. Although I could not yet read very well, I deciphered the names of the countries and cities, many of which I had heard of before. I was surprised to see how small some well-known countries were, especially my own. As soon as I saw it, I liked Europe, because of its shape and color. Its size was also very practical. . . . Clearly, Europe is looking, turning, and making its way toward the world.

> Ludvik Vaculik
> "Mon Europe"[1]

The upheavals in Eastern Europe and the Soviet Union in the closing months of the last decade and the early months of the new one obeyed a completely individual, revolutionary set of rules.

The revolutionary climate prevailing at this time was not simply an extension of what had gone before; it did not follow automatically and at that specific moment from the inconsistencies of the communist model of society. History could easily have waited for many more years, just as Marx expected revolution in industrialized England, although it eventually occurred in agrarian Russia.

In his book *Order out of Chaos*, Nobel Prize winner Ilya Prigogine describes the behavior of unstable structures in nature:

We have discussed the concepts that allow us to describe the formation of dissipative structures, such as the theory of bifurcation. It is remarkable that near-bifurcation systems present large fluctuations. Such systems seem to "hesitate" among various possible directions of evolution, and the famous law of the large numbers in its usual sense breaks down. A small fluctuation may start an entirely new evolution that will drastically change the whole behavior of the macroscopic system.[2]

However, this conclusion does not apply only to nature. "The analogy with social phenomena, even with history, is inescapable. Far from opposing 'change' and 'necessity,' we now see both aspects as essential in the description of non-linear systems far from equilibrium."[3]

The events that changed the face of Europe could not have been predicted, certainly not on a time axis. They were neither an accident nor a necessity. Sometimes there was a feeling that history was hesitating. Seemingly small steps had consequences that were incalculable and had not initially been intended by their protagonists. The revolution swept across the continent like a shock wave, but these revolutionary changes were possible, took their eventual course, and can be explained only because of the long-term developments that preceded them in East and West.

These long-term developments are important principally as building blocks for the future: Once the fever of revolution abated, history resumed its course. But the need to choose remains. European can again take control of its history and do as Vaculik says: "Clearly, Europe is looking, turning, and making its way toward the world"; or it can slide toward the sea like the canoe in "Melopee" by the famous Flemish dadaist poet Van Ostayen:

> Under the moon slides the long river
> Over the long river wearily slides the moon
> Under the moon on the long river slides the canoe towards the sea
>
> Beside the tall reeds
> Beside the low meadow
> slides the canoe towards the sea
> slides the canoe with the sliding moon towards the sea
> Companions all on their journey to the sea the canoe the moon and the
>   man
> Why are the moon and the man together sliding meekly towards the sea[4]

"L'histoire est libre," but time and tide wait for no man.

NOTES

1. Ludvik Vaculik, "Mon Europe," *Lettre Internationale*, Nr. 18, Fall 1988, p. 14.
2. Ilya Prigogine and Isabelle Stengers, *Order Out of Chaos: Man's New Dialogue with Nature* (London: Heinemann, 1984), p. 14.
3. Ibid.
4. Paul Van Ostayen, "Verzamelde Gedichten" (Amsterdam: Uitgeverij Bert Bakker, 1982), p. 463. Own translation.

Time and Tide
Wait for No Man

1

Reappraising the German Identity

After 1982/83 the Federal Republic of Germany attempted to shake off the legacy of the Second World War and claimed the right to behave like a "normal" state, a state that did not need to feel inhibited by its past any more than, say, the United Kingdom, France, or Belgium. This left the outside world feeling ill at ease, even disgruntled at times. Not only the military aspects of the Second World War but also the Holocaust it had unleashed still made it difficult to see the Federal Republic as a nation among nations. Reason and instinct competed with each other in our minds, our reason telling us that every nation has had less than distinguished periods in its history, our instincts making it hard for us to distance ourselves from the total dehumanization and the attempt at the systematic extermination of our kind, which typified the Third Reich as no other despotic regime before or since.

The Federal Republic irrevocably took the path to a different experience of being German, one that is no longer dominated by feelings of guilt. The West German public found the courage to be carefree "Germans" again. West Germany had accomplished a great deal in the last four decades, and its citizens wanted to be able to feel proud of their achievements, without having to temper their pride, without needing to feel diffident, tortured by the past, because that is what the world expects. National pride became respectable again.[1]

New ideals were being sought, new means of identification, and this led to a public debate on national consciousness, the fatherland, the nation. Thought was again being given to the country's past.[2] Ten years before such words as *Volk, Heimat,* and *Vaterland* had still been taboo. In the mid-1980s they sounded normal again.

In education, too, attitudes changed. Where once no effort had been spared to prevent the emergence of a feeling of national identity and children had been confronted primarily with the negative aspects of German history, they were now taught from an early age to take a far more positive view of Germany.

After 1983 this renewed quest for the Germany identity was also apparent from a flood of publications under such titles as "Germany's Position in the World," "The Anxiety of the Germans: Observations on the Nation's State of Awareness," "German Unity Is Bound to Come," "The Identity of the Germans," "What Is Becoming of the Germans? Questions and Answers," "German Identity Today," "Helpless Normality: The Germans in Search of Themselves," "Back to Nationhood? Legal and Historical Reflections," "Reflections on Germany," "No Progress without Germany: Authors on the State of the Nation."[3]

The media too were playing an important part in this changing perception of being German. In 1979 West German television confronted its viewers with the horrors of the country's Nazi past by showing the "Holocaust" series. In 1984 everyone watched *Heimat*, a film that focused on the life of the ordinary man, the simple German forced to experience all the political and military violence that goes on above his head. Radio and television transmissions again closed with the German national anthem. Ten years before most reactions to the singing of the national anthem had been negative. Now the members of the national football team sang *Deutschland über alles* at the tops of their voices before international matches.

The change of attitude toward the nation was also apparent in various aspects of daily life. Shopping centers organized "German weeks," publicity campaigns centered on values that referred to the nation, and the first thirty years of the *Bundeswehr*, the West German armed forces, were commemorated with the issue of a special postage stamp. The references to the Hitler period that had once been a common feature of daily newspapers and magazines were becoming a rarity.[4]

The rediscovered *Heimatliebe*, or love of the home country, was also reflected in the attitude of West German politicians. When Helmut Kohl came to power in 1982, he promised a *geistig-moralische Wende*, a spiritual about-turn. The rediscovery and reappraisal of the German identity was clearly one aspect Kohl had in mind. The economic patriotism that, under Chancellor Schmidt in particular, had been based on the country's economic performance and general prosperity had to be complemented, in Chancellor Kohl's view, by a new, all-embracing national feeling of self-respect, no longer based solely on economic achievements but also, and above all, on Germany's cultural individuality, on German-ness. There was to be an end, once and for all, to forty years of *Vergangenheitsbewältigung*, of coping with the past.[5] Kohl realized that this would be possible only if the people were helped to come to terms with the ever present memory of their Nazi past.[6]

There is something of a parallel with President Reagan here. The American president wanted to free the United States from its Vietnam complex, the federal chancellor his country from its Auschwitz complex.[7] Helmut Kohl's virtual insistence in 1985 that Reagan visit the military cemetery at Bitburg, where a few members of the Waffen-SS also lie buried, must be seen in this light. Chancellor Kohl wanted to show that the German dead can be honored like all the others who have lost their lives in so many wars on European soil.[8] Japan's Prime Minister Nakasone also tried to reconcile Japan with its past with the similarly symbolic act of visiting the Yasu kuni shrine.[9]

The plans to establish a museum of German history in West Berlin and a museum of the history of the Federal Republic of Germany in Bonn reflect the same concern to give the Federal Republic a historical backbone.[10] Indeed, the plans for these museums emerged during the *Historikerstreit*, the violent "war" that broke out among German historians in the middle of 1986. In publications on National Socialism a few historians attempted to show that the Germans had no reason to keep their heads bowed always and forever. A small minority tried to play down Nazi crimes by saying, as Ernst Nolte did, that Germany is by no means a special case and that the mass murders that occurred under the Nazis are no different from the crimes committed under other dictators in the course of history, comparisons being made with Stalin, the Khmer Rouge in Cambodia, and the Americans in Vietnam. Nolte saw "the technical procedure of gassing" as the only difference from these other crimes.

Other historians tried to place this period in a wider context by referring, for example, to the "heroic German defense against the advancing Red Army in 1945" (Hillgruber), Germany's fatal geographical position (Stürmer), or the positive economic and social features of National Socialism (Broszat), which prompted an incensed reaction from other historians and such figures as the philosopher Habermas.[11]

Some of the ideas put forward by the "revisionist" historians were conveyed to the general public, in a palatable form, by the Bavarian leader Strauss: "We are an ordinary, capable, efficient nation which has had the misfortune to be twice governed by bad politicians. We have experienced an age of barbarity. This barbarity sprang from Hitler's brutal policy, but its fascination then infected others." And so: "Let there be an end to our attempts to cope with the past as if we were eternal penitents."[12]

Kohl's aims are perhaps best revealed by the election slogan of the CDU (Christlich-Demokratische Union) in 1987: Above a picture of the chancellor stood the words "*Die Deutschen haben ein Recht zu lächeln*"—the Germans have a right to smile.[13]

While it had once been primarily politicians of the CDU and CSU (Christlich-Soziale Union) who emphasized the country's own identity and national consciousness, during the January 1987 election campaign it was the SPD (Sozialdemokratische Partei) that had the national anthem played when canvasing for support on radio and television, and such Social-Democratic politicians as Johannes Rau and Oskar Lafontaine appealed for national self-confidence in their speeches.[14]

President von Weizsäcker too saw the reappraisal of the German identity as an important task. However, he showed far more diffidence and tact than Kohl, who sometimes seemed to normalize or even trivialize Germany's difficult past. "Of course," the Federal president said in his address on the occasion of the fortieth anniversary of the end of the Second World War, "very few nations remain untarnished by culpable involvement in war and violence throughout their history. But the genocide perpetrated against the Jews has no parallel in history. . . . We need and we have the strength to face the truth as best we can, without suppressing the facts and without bias."[15] But, as he had emphasized when taking the oath in the *Bundestag* on 1 July 1984, Germany must stop believing it could do nothing right:

We have particular difficulty, of course, with our national consciousness. But we are not the only ones in the world to have a difficult fatherland. We must and we have every right in the Federal Republic of Germany to admit to our national feelings, our history, the outstanding German question, the fact that we can be a committed member of the Atlantic Alliance and the European Community even though our hearts go out to those who live beyond the Wall.[16]

The Plötzensee memorial in Berlin, which commemorates the German opposition to the Nazi regime and Germans like von Stauffenberg, who made the unsuccessful attempt on Hitler's life, is intended to show that, although the Germans as a nation may have been responsible, they do not bear any collective guilt.[17]

That reviewing the past was still a tricky balancing act was, however, abundantly clear from the indignant reactions of both the members of the *Bundestag* and the public to the address by *Bundestag* President Jenniger on the fiftieth anniversary of the *Kristallnacht*. Careless use of words and an overly rational attempt to explain anti-Semitism and the success of Nazism in the Germany of the 1930s forced Jenniger to resign. As Otto Schily, a Green member of the *Bundestag*, said: "Jenniger undoubtedly meant well, but the result was a disaster."[18]

The growth of German self-confidence from the early 1980s was bound to have implications for the Federal Republic's foreign policy. A country that again has the courage to look itself straight in the eye may also look other countries straight in the eye. And just as any "normal" state may determine its relations with other countries on the basis of its own interests, the Federal Republic may defend and pursue its "natural" interests without being restricted by its past.

One of the natural interests of any normal state is in the maintenance of satisfactory relations with all its neighbors. The normalization of relations with the other Germany therefore came to occupy an increasingly central place in the Federal Republic's foreign policy. What state, after all, can accept that it has so little contact with a country with which it has a common history, language, and culture?[19] A quarter of the West German population was born in former German territories in Eastern Europe, three million of them in the German Democratic Republic (GDR).[20] How could West Germany rediscover its own German identity without seeking closer links with that other, yet so near, Germany?

In itself, there is nothing new in the goal of achieving better relations between all parts of Germany as it once was. Immediately after the Second World War it had been taken for granted that, in time, a united *Deutschland* would again emerge from the four occupied zones. And since that time the subject has never been far from West German minds. What was new, however, was that this desire for closer contact between the two Germanys was no longer felt only by the SPD and FDP (Freie Democratische Partei), but also surfaced in the CDU/CSU.

In the early 1970s Willy Brandt's *Ostpolitik* marked the historical breakthrough in relations between the two Germanys. After Konrad Adenauer had worked hard to integrate the fledgling Federal Republic firmly into the western camp, successive governments led by the CDU/CSU had, after all, pursued a policy that excluded all contact with the GDR. They regarded the Federal Republic as the only legitimate successor of the former Germany. CDU/CSU politicians claimed that any contact with the "so-called GDR" would mean unacceptable recognition of the communist regime.[21] Preventing the diplomatic recognition of the GDR by the international community was also the goal of the "Hallstein doctrine," which implied that the Federal Government would consider it to be an unfriendly act for any country with which it had diplomatic relations to want to establish similar relations with the GDR.

While the Grand Coalition (CDU/CSU-SPD, 1966–1969) was in power, the Christian Democrats showed themselves to be somewhat more willing to make—cautious—contact with East Germany. In this they were prompted by pressure from their coalition partner and also by the growing realization that isolating the GDR did not help to meet the needs of the German people on the other side of the Wall, nor indeed was it what their own people wanted.[22] This did not, however, prevent the Christian Democrats, once in opposition, from turning against the *Ostpolitik* of Willy Brandt's Social-Democratic Cabinet and, in 1973, voting against the ratification of the *Grundlagenvertrag*, or Basic Treaty, with the GDR.[23]

By signing treaties with the USSR, the GDR, and other Eastern European countries, Brandt formally accepted the territorial status quo in Central Europe and, with it, the loss to Poland and Czechoslovakia of what had been German territory before the war. This and the recognition of the GDR as a separate sovereign state within the "German nation" was unacceptable to the CDU/CSU because it excluded the possibility of German reunification within the pre–1937 frontiers. The arrangement for West Berlin and the fact that West Germans and West Berliners could visit the GDR and ethnic Germans in the USSR and other Eastern European countries could emigrate to the Federal Republic did not, in the CDU/CSU's opinion, compensate for what they saw as the abandonment of the fundamental goal of reunification.

As the CDU/CSU opposition continued to stand by what the Soviet Union commonly referred to as "revanchist ideas," Chancellor Kohl's succession to power in October 1982 after a vote of no confidence in Chancellor Schmidt seemed likely to be followed by a cooling of the relationship between the two Germanys. This fear was indeed justified: Although the new Federal chancellor confirmed the validity of the treaties with the Eastern European countries, he said that commitment to reunification would be the central element of his policy on Germany, his *Deutschlandpolitik*. CDU/CSU ministers also had far less compunction than their predecessors about publicly staking the Federal Republic's claims to the whole of Germany. When in early 1983 three West Germans died while being interrogated by the East German frontier authorities, relations between the two Germanys reached a new low point.[24] The *Ostpolitik* seemed to be a thing of the past, and German-German détente lay in the distant future.

After the CDU/CSU's convincing victory in the general election in March 1983 there was an unexpected change. The two Germanys reached agreement on a DM 1 billion loan to the GDR. The involvement in the negotiations of Franz-Josef Strauss, always regarded as one of the fiercest opponents of closer links with the GDR, made the news of this loan even more surprising. A second gigantic loan followed in 1984. Trade between the two countries grew appreciably. East Berlin, once forbidden territory, was visited by more, and more important, West German politicians than ever before. Visits by private individuals increased. Negotiations on common environmental problems, science and technology, cultural exchange programs, and so forth were resumed or stepped up. Shortly afterward it became clear that Chancellor Kohl was favorably disposed to a visit by the East German party leader, Honecker, to the Federal Republic.[25] The new CDU-CSU/FDP coalition thus persisted with its predecessor's *Deutschlandpolitik* and was equally prepared to make financial concessions and to demonstrate the necessary pragmatism.[26]

Although this change in the CDU/CSU's attitude came as a surprise to many people, various factors show that it was not so illogical as it appeared. Of crucial importance was the role played by Genscher, who has held the post of foreign minister in every government since 1974. His party, the FDP, which has helped to form most governments since the Federal Republic was founded, has been an advocate of West Germany remaining firmly in the western camp since Adenauer's time, but it was also an active supporter of Chancellor Brandt's *Ostpolitik*. While the *Ostpolitik* was Brandt's grand idea, it was chiefly Genscher who looked after its discreet, day-to-day application when Schmidt headed the government.[27] When tensions within the SPD and the SPD/FDP coalition in 1982 led to a Christian-Democratic/Liberal coalition with Helmut Kohl as chancellor, it was clear that Genscher, who remained foreign minister, wanted to continue this policy. And as his loyalty to European integration and the Atlantic Alliance was beyond question, he largely succeeded in reconciling the views of the CDU/CSU, which attached more importance to a stronger western military alliance and a tougher attitude toward the communist bloc, with the *Ostpolitik*.

The change in the CDU/CSU's attitude also stemmed from the realization that not only SPD and FDP voters but also the vast majority of the public wanted steady progress in relations between the two Germanys. The outcome of the 1987 election was to remove any lingering doubts about this. The CDU/CSU paid the price for thinking that, for the election campaign, it should revert to the language it had used in the past. The FDP won votes by adhering to a policy of resolute conciliation with the GDR and an active policy of détente.

For a while the CDU/CSU had forgotten that the *Ostpolitik* and the period of détente in the 1970s had led to a change of attitude throughout German society, which meant that no West German politician could afford to be held responsible for a deterioration in inter-German relations and all that it would entail, for example, for West Berlin.[28]

By pursuing an active *Ostpolitik*, the Christian-Democratic/Liberal coalition also wanted to refute the opposition's claim that agreeing to the deployment of American medium-range missiles on West German soil would have an adverse effect on relations with East Germany.[29] Furthermore, the West German public had grown accustomed to economic relations with their eastern neighbor and the advantages they meant for the West German economy. Jeopardizing these relations and advantages would have been a political risk for the Christian Democrats, which they were not willing to take, despite their basic emotions. Nor, as already mentioned, did a tense relationship with the GDR accord with Kohl's goal of reappraising the German identity, shedding the burden of the war years, and, like any normal state, striving to establish good relations with his neighbors.

The Kohl government's unexpected adherence to the previous coalition's *Ostpolitik* revealed an important new facet of West German politics: The goals of West Germany's foreign policy were no longer dependent on the parties that happened to be in power at any given moment. This was coupled with another important factor: The Kohl-Genscher government's efforts to improve links with the GDR were made at a time of serious East-West tension. In November 1983 NATO had begun to deploy the first Cruise and Pershing II missiles in Western Europe, the arms control negotiations had been broken off by the Soviet Union, and relations between the United States and the USSR had reached a low point. President Mitterrand even compared this cold war situation to the Berlin crisis and the Cuba crisis in the early 1960s.[30] Despite the icy temperature of East-West relations, and despite the good relations between Chancellor Kohl and President Reagan and the similarity of their views, the West Germans succeeded in maintaining and even strengthening their links with the GDR.

This points to a second new facet of West Germany's foreign policy: The efforts to establish good relations with the GDR had for the first time become largely decoupled from the dominant East-West relationship, in contrast to earlier periods, when the closeness of relations between the two Germanys was almost entirely dictated by the relationship between the United States and the USSR, the curve of German-German relations thus running parallel to the curve of relations between the two superpowers. This tendency toward the greater autonomy of relations between the two Germanys had already been apparent when Chancellor Schmidt tried to shield relations between the Federal Republic and the GDR from the tension that arose after the Soviet invasion of Afghanistan and the crisis in Poland.[31] The difference was, however, that the relationship between Schmidt and the then American President, Carter, had been very poor. Some people saw this as one explanation for Schmidt's attitude. The relationship between Kohl and Reagan, on the other hand, was on the whole very good. Reagan's sudden profession of faith in the SDI (Strategic Defense Initiative) in March 1983, without the Western European allies being consulted, will, however, have strengthened the Federal Republic's resolve to look after its own interests.[32]

The emergence and development of renewed German dynamism would not have been possible, of course, without the cooperation of the other German state to the east of the line dividing Europe. The GDR did indeed adopt a more flexible attitude toward the Federal Republic. This meant East Berlin toning down the traditional *Feindbild*, the antagonistic image, of the CDU and even more so of Franz-Joseph Strauss's CSU. The CSU in particular had been accused of having revanchist ideas about the other part of Germany. The negotiations on the first billion-mark loan in 1983 and the decisive role played by the Bavarian leader must have made it clear to the GDR's leaders that the Kohl government would stand by its predecessor's *Deutschlandpolitik*. Cooperation with the much-feared CDU/CSU was thus possible and, as Michael Stürmer put it ironically, the GDR was therefore "so gracious as to accept two billion marks in loans at market conditions"[33] and was able to make a few concessions in return without risk to itself.

The two Germanys thus made a typical swap, in which each obtained what it most needed: the GDR financial assistance, the Federal Republic more human contacts. The concessions made by the GDR in the latter respect in 1984 consisted in the exemption of young West Germans from the compulsory payment when visiting the GDR and East Berlin, a reduction in the amount paid by West German pensioners, and an agreement to allow East German pensioners (i.e., nonproductive citizens of the socialist state) to visit relatives in the Federal Republic more often. Telephone and postal links between the two Germanys were extended and facilitated. And the East Germans also removed the automatic machine guns they had placed along the Berlin Wall, which was, however, made just as impenetrable by other means. All these improvements may seem extremely trivial now, but at the time they were considered remarkable.[34]

In 1983 and subsequent years, the East German party leader Honecker, who had been partly responsible for the construction of the Wall in 1961, had taken the lead in attempts to establish better relations with the West. The more flexible East German attitude was in fact more than a temporary tactical ploy with Deutsche marks as its goal. This was apparent, for example, from Honecker's relegation to the sidelines of any members of the party leadership who opposed rapprochement with West Germany.[35] It was also evident when East Berlin tried to steer inter-German relations safely through the cold war atmosphere revived by the deployment of INF (Intermediate-Range Nuclear Forces) missiles. In early September 1983 Erich Honecker sent a letter to Helmut Kohl in which he appealed for a "coalition of reason" between the two German states and called on Bonn to use its influence in Washington to prevent the deployment of the Euro-missiles. Again, in late November, after the first series of Euro-missiles had been deployed in the Federal Republic, with the approval of the *Bundestag*, the East German party leader declared that he still wanted to maintain relations with Bonn. In itself this was not so illogical, if only because East Berlin had just been granted a gigantic loan by Bonn and wanted to go on tapping this excellent source of funds in the future. Nonetheless, it was remarkable that Honecker should so openly act counter to the then chilly East-West atmosphere and, just as his Czech counterpart, was showing a conspicuous lack of enthusiasm about the Warsaw Pact's decision to retaliate by deploying SS-22 missiles aimed at the West on East German soil.[36]

Even when it became impossible to prevent relations from cooling after heavy internal and especially external (Soviet) pressure had forced Honecker to cancel his visit to West Germany in September 1984, the break in the romance between the two Germanys proved short-lived. From early 1986 in particular the process of rapprochement made rapid progress. After fifteen years of negotiation an inter-German cultural agreement was at last concluded. And the first visit by the president of the East German *Volkskammer* (parliament) to West Germany, where it caused some considerable controversy, was followed by a spectacular increase in the number of meetings between leading East and West German politicians. Economics Minister Bangemann, Bavarian Prime Minister Strauss, FDP politician Mischnick,

State Minister Schäuble, and the premiers of the *Länder* of Baden-Württemberg and Rhineland-Palatinate, Späth and Vogel, met party leader Honecker. Walther Leisler Kiep of the CDU had talks with the GDR's number two leader, Günter Mittag. And the mayor of Hamburg, von Dohnanyi, subsequently met the first party secretary of the district of Dresden, Hans Modrow, who was to become the prime minister of the "new" GDR, eager for reform, toward the end of 1989. Mittag, who fared less well and was arrested while Modrow was in power, also visited Bonn, where he met Chancellor Kohl and the leaders of the FDP, CSU, and SPD. These examples of inter-German meetings in the first few months of 1987 show that, in the final analysis, the numerous political contacts that, according to some, "suddenly" occurred after the fall of the Honecker regime were no more than an extension of the earlier close dialogue, the difference being, of course, that the dialogue in late 1989 held out greater prospects of producing real results.[37]

Although a visit by Honecker to the Federal Republic was not yet possible, this minor blemish on closer inter-German relations was easily offset by the fact that the visits that did take place were at a sufficiently high political level to make serious negotiations possible. Furthermore, unlike a possible visit by the GDR's leader to Bonn, these discussions were not held in the glare of the spotlights of the world's press. It was realized, after all, that the resulting discretion was to the advantage of both countries, since a meeting between Kohl and Honecker that did not take place in the right international atmosphere was more likely to be counterproductive. An example of the discreet and gradual way in which the Germans tried to improve their mutual relations was seen in April 1987, when the national and international press reported at length on the news that Honecker would not be going to West Berlin for the celebrations to commemorate the city's 750th anniversary. The report that the municipal authorities of West and East Berlin would be reestablishing contact and that the two mayors would be discussing mutual problems attracted little interest, on the other hand.[38] This cooperation and consultation subsequently increased. Thus, when the mayors of East and West Berlin greeted each other in early November 1989 as the Berlin Wall was breached, they did so not as total strangers but as colleagues who had been prepared for this event by their previous discussions.

The improvement in relations was also translated into more substantial concessions by the GDR where human contacts were concerned. Willy Brandt's *Ostpolitik* had enabled East German pensioners to visit their relatives on the other side of the Iron Curtain. Other East German citizens were permitted to visit the Federal Republic only for "urgent family reasons," a favor granted by the GDR authorities in only a limited number of cases. In 1986 the number of visas issued rose dramatically to over half a million, compared with a mere sixty-five thousand in 1985. East Berlin's sudden flexibility did not mean that traveling to the Federal Republic had become easy, since it was still impossible for whole families to leave the country. Nonetheless, developments in 1986 did much to boost East Germans' hopes of being able to go to the "other side" before they retired. There were also indications from East Berlin that as many as three million people might be allowed to visit the Federal Republic every year in the future, a prospect that could leave no West German politician unmoved, whatever his or her political party or persuasion. The desire to help make this hopeful picture of the future reality was therefore to have a major influence on their actions, wittingly or unwittingly.[39]

How can this more flexible East German attitude be explained? The East German leaders certainly had two short-term reasons for seeking closer relations with the Federal Republic and providing the necessary quid pro quos. Their most important motive was undoubtedly the steadily growing debt burden with which they had had to contend since 1980 and which now had to be tackled as a matter of the utmost urgency.[40] Closer relations with West Germany were clearly the easiest way to obtain more financial resources. West German statistics published in 1985 show annual payments by the Federal Republic to the GDR of some DM 1.4 billion in transit payments for Berlin, road taxes for travel in the GDR, the compulsory exchange of money at the border, payments for the postal service, the disposal of waste from West Berlin, and money spent on buying the freedom of political prisoners. Nor should the guaranteed loans and the DM 1 billion or so reaching the GDR in the form of private remittances from West Germans to East German citizens be overlooked. The special relationship with the Federal Republic also ensures higher revenues from exports to the West than would otherwise be the case: goods from the GDR, the *treizième membre clandestin de la CEE*, as Jacques Delors put it while still French economics minister, were not subject to import duties when they entered the West German and thus the Community market.[41]

Second, the GDR's leaders hoped that closer relations with West Germany would ease the internal pressure caused both by the travel restrictions and by the constancy with which the West German dream was presented by television programs from the other side of the Wall. This was one of the factors that prompted the East German authorities to grant exit visas to some forty thousand "nonintegratables" from 1984 to 1986 so that they might settle permanently in the Federal Republic, thus ridding the GDR of this burden. The internal pressure did not ease, however, and it was, moreover, mainly young people, intellectuals and skilled workers, who left the country under this arrangement, an unacceptable drain on the GDR. East Berlin therefore decided to reduce the number of exit visas again drastically and to opt instead for another safety valve in the shape of more permits for journeys to the West for "urgent family reasons."[42] In so doing, however, the East German leaders paved the way for the further erosion of their regime and legitimacy. More and more East Germans were now able to go and see for themselves the West German paradise with which they were familiar from their television screens and then to return home with this western spectacle fresh in their minds, aware that the nature of the East German regime made them just as nonintegratable. The pressure this created under the seemingly immovable lid of the GDR boiler was to lead to a violent explosion in the second half of 1989.

Important though they are, the two motives outlined above cannot be the only explanation for the change in the GDR's attitude toward its West German neighbor. It had, after all, faced financial difficulties and internal pressure before, and the rapprochement with West Germany was in some respects so far-reaching that it could not have happened unless there had been some fundamental development in the GDR itself to make the East German leaders change their minds and consider it possible and safe to adopt a more flexible attitude and establish a closer relationship with West Germany. East Germany's greater flexibility consequently reflected the increased self-confidence and self-assurance of its leaders in their relations with their own people, the Federal Republic, and the Soviet Union. The year 1989 was to show that this self-confidence was unfounded.

In the 1970s, after Chancellor Brandt's *Ostpolitik* had led to the agreements between the two Germanys and so paved the way for more contacts between the two countries, there was grave concern in the East German party ranks about the possible implications for internal stability.[43] The resulting defensive attitude, which found expression in increased ideological campaigns and a wait-and-see attitude toward the Federal Republic, was further exacerbated by the Final Act of the Conference on Security and Cooperation in Europe signed in Helsinki in 1975. It set out, after all, not only such "good" principles as the inviolability of frontiers and noninterference in the internal affairs of other countries, but also such "ideologically unsound" principles as freedom of speech, conscience, religion, and conviction.[44] A decade later this uncertainty had given way to self-assurance. The GDR's leaders had learned from the experience of the 1970s that the East German ideological and social system could survive a period of détente and increased contact with capitalist Germany without suffering too much harm.[45] The GDR was one of the most stable countries in the Eastern bloc, with a communist party (the SED, Sozialistische Einheitspartei Deutschlands) that had the people firmly in its grasp. A situation like that in Poland was simply inconceivable. Or that, at least, was what the GDR's leaders thought.

Their greater self-confidence gave the East German leaders the courage for the first time to rewrite the traditional account of the country's history and make it rather more factual. Like the Federal Republic, then, the GDR began to rethink its own past. The legitimacy of the East German state had always been based on the fact that, unlike the Federal Republic, it had broken with Germany's feudal, bourgeois, and fascist past. The East German leaders realized, however, that this was not enough to give the GDR its own national identity. They therefore began gathering together all the "good" periods of pre-Nazi history so that a feeling of continuity between Germany before Hitler and the East German state might be created. They referred, of course, to the "prerevolutionary movements" in past centuries and to the "revolutionary ideas of the two great sons of our people, Karl Marx and Friedrich Engels."[46] However, the self-assured East German leaders also ventured to rehabilitate such controversial figures in Germany's past as Frederick the Great, Luther, Clausewitz, and Bismarck. It had been discovered, for example, that Bismarck had once signed a security pact with Russia and for that he must be appropriately honored.[47]

The GDR's leaders had become more self-confident, not only with respect to their own regime and people but also in their dealings with the Federal Republic. Ironically, while the *Ostpolitik* had been unable to destabilize or change the East German regime, it had led to what was for the GDR a positive, profound change in the attitude of successive West German governments toward East Germany. The West German public was, after all, becoming accustomed to a more relaxed and flexible relationship with their eastern neighbor, and as Chancellor Schmidt said, "A policy of détente is possible only if the situation in both countries is stable." As far as possible, SPD/FDP governments therefore eschewed any action that the GDR (or the USSR) might construe as an attempt to undermine or change the East German political or social system.[48]

West German governments were even sympathetic when the East German leaders took exceptional measures in situations they saw as a threat. During the Polish crisis between 1980 and 1982, for example, the Schmidt government took an understanding view when East Berlin not only closed the East German-Polish border but also increased the compulsory tax on travelers in order to combat any destabilizing effects of developments connected with Solidarity. The GDR's leaders will also have noted with satisfaction the ruling socialist SPD's skepticism about the free trade union, which it saw as a destabilizing element in the détente that was its goal.[49] The relief must have been even greater in 1983, when it became apparent that the Kohl government would by and large stand by its predecessor's policy toward the GDR, despite the fierce and "fundamental" criticism it had always evoked from the CDU/CSU. This naturally strengthened the position of the East German party leaders in their relationship with Bonn, which made for a better balance of power between the two Germanys.

However, they underestimated the subversive force of one aspect of West Germany's policy toward the GDR, where Bonn refused to sympathize with the East German position: Bonn's refusal in principle to recognize GDR nationality and to put an end to a situation in which any inhabitant of East Germany is automatically recognized as a citizen of the Federal Republic on arrival in West Germany. This policy, which was also controversial in the Federal Republic and was seen by many as no more than symbolic, was to be one of the basic elements of the crisis faced by the East German regime in the second half of 1989. The many tens of thousands of GDR citizens who took advantage of this West German constitutional right at that time proved that the East German leaders' self-confidence had been highly inappropriate.

The third element in East Germany's greater self-assurance concerned its relationship with the Soviet Union. Its internal stability and strengthened position in relations with the Federal Republic showed that the GDR was a strong and reliable link in the Eastern bloc. Indeed, East Germany's leaders could justifiably and reasonably claim not only to have faithfully adopted the Soviet model but also to have substantially improved on it in practice and, by Eastern European standards, to have achieved outstanding economic results.[50] Through their growing self-confidence and self-assurance in dealings with the Soviets, the GDR's leaders also showed an increasing tendency no longer to regard the "indissoluble bond of brotherhood" with the Soviet Union as a restriction on their freedom of action but as the basis for somewhat freer and more flexible diplomacy. And Big Brother to the east was expected to allow the GDR more room for maneuvering so that it might do more to promote its own, specifically East German interests.[51]

The adoption of a more independent attitude toward the USSR was made easier in the first half of the 1980s by the power vacuum that had emerged in Moscow with Brezhnev's death and the uncertainty over his ultimate successor. There was a similar power vacuum at the economic level, where the Soviet Union found itself compelled to make drastic cuts in economic assistance and energy supplies to its satellites. As a result, the Eastern European countries were forced, and also had an excuse, to look more to the economically stronger West.[52]

Although East Germany now had more room to maneuver, it was still subject to serious restrictions. Above all, the bond of brotherhood with the Soviet Union meant that some 400,000 Soviet troops were stationed in East Germany, and the GDR was more important than any other Eastern European country both for defense against the West and in helping to ensure internal stability in the Eastern bloc. When, at the time of East-West tension in 1984, Honecker appealed rather too emphatically for "the limitation of the damage" and the continuation of the dialogue between medium-sized countries in Eastern and Western Europe, regardless of relations between the two superpowers, he was called to heel by Moscow and by conservative members of the East German party apparatus and forced to cancel his planned visit to Bonn.[53] An additional reason for this pressure on Honecker was that his ideas and the burgeoning relationship between East and West Germany were also beginning to assume a dangerous dimension through their contagious effect on certain other Eastern European countries. In 1984 the limits within which East Germany might manifest its growing self-confidence and within which inter-German relations might develop further were thus defined more accurately: The Soviet Union had to be convinced of East Germany's absolute loyalty to Moscow and to the indissoluble unity of the communist bloc. East Germany would continue to respect these limits, especially as they were, in the final analysis, in its own interests.

The second restriction on East Germany's room for maneuvering was the fact that, despite its leaders' increased self-assurance, Soviet troops and Soviet supremacy over Eastern Europe remained the ultimate guarantee of their internal power and of the political stability within the communist camp that was so essential to the East German regime. East Berlin assumed that the surrounding Eastern bloc countries were very much less stable than the GDR itself and that destabilizing influences could just as easily blow over from the East as from the West, and perhaps even more quickly. It was also well aware that the East German state was more dependent for its continued existence on the assurance of a strong communist regime in both East Germany and Eastern Europe than were the other Eastern European countries. The GDR therefore supported a strong Soviet role in Eastern Europe and the attendant Brezhnev doctrine with conviction.

At first, Gorbachev's accession to power in Moscow benefited East Germany and inter-German relations. As he himself pursued a policy of rapprochement with the West, it was more difficult to object to essentially the same policy being pursued by the GDR, at least as long as it remained within the limits that had clearly emerged in 1984. To pursue a successful policy of rapprochement with Western Europe, the Soviet Union also needed a gateway to the West, and the Federal Republic was obviously the most suitable country for this purpose. The rapprochement between the two Germanys was therefore important to the Soviet Union as a means of influencing the opinions and actions of West German (and thus Western European) politicians and convincing them of the good intentions of the new leaders in the Kremlin. The East German leaders were aware that Moscow did not want to lose this line of communication with Bonn, and so with the rest of Western Europe, and tried to take advantage of this factor in their efforts to achieve their own national objectives.[54]

East Berlin's problems began to grow, however, with the realization that the communist pope in the Kremlin was not only departing from orthodox doctrine with growing frequency but also becoming less and less reliable in his adherence to the communist creed. It was becoming increasingly difficult, after all, to believe in Moscow's absolute loyalty to the communist regimes that it had installed. Nor could Moscow even be relied upon to uphold that indissoluble unity of the communist bloc so vital to East Germany. Thus the third element of East Germany's increased self-confidence, its relationship with the Soviet Union, also proved to have been built on sand.

NOTES

1. Jonathan Dean, "How to Lose Germany," *Foreign Policy*, (55)1984, p. 59.

2. Walther Leisler Kiep, "The New Deutschlandpolitik," *Foreign Affairs*, 63(2)1984/85, p. 316.

3. Joyce Marie Mushaben, "From Collective Identity to Collective Security? Changing Perceptions of Alliance Issues among the West German Successor Generation," Paper for the 6th International Conference of Europeanists, Washington, D.C., 1987, pp. 23–24.

4. "Leben wir in einer anderen Republik?," *Der Spiegel*, 5 August 1985, p. 32.

5. André Gisselbrecht, "Le débat des historiens sur le nazisme: révision, historicisation ou déculpabilisation?" (Paris: *Allemagnes d'aujourd'hui*, no. 99–100, January–June 1987). Extract in François Guérard, "Le débat sur l'identité allemande," *Problèmes politiques et sociaux*, no. 578, 19 February 1988, p. 36.

6. "Wäre ich Deutscher, würde ich schreien," *Der Spiegel*, 5 January 1987, p. 29.

7. Micha Brumlik, quoted in Jean-Marc Gonin, "Bonn: l'antisémitisme, ça se discute," *Libération*, 28 February 1986, p. 23.

8. Gonin, "Bonn," p. 23.

9. "Japan zit vast aan alle kanten," *Knack*, 28 May 1986, p. 12.

10. "Im Märchenwald des deutschen Gemüts. Interview mit dem Historiker Arnulf Baring über die geplanten Museen für Geschichte," Der Spiegel, 5 January 1987, p. 31.

11. For an overview of this debate see: Gordon A. Craig, "The War of the German Historians," *The New York Review of Books*, no. 21–22, 15 January 1987, pp. 16–19; Guérard, "Le débat sur l'identité allemande," pp. 30–47; *"Historikerstreit"—Die Dokumentation der Kontroverse um Einzigartigkeit der nationalistischen Judenvernichtung* (Munich/Zurich: Piper, 1987).

12. "Wäre ich Deutscher, würde ich schreien," *Der Spiegel*, 5 January 1987, pp. 29–30.

13. Advertisement for the CDU in *Der Spiegel*, 5 January 1987, pp. 100–101.

14. Jochen Thies, "Die BRD nach den Wahlen vom 25. Januar '87. Aussenpolitische Kontinuität und leichte Akzentverschiebungen," *Europa-Archiv*, 42(8)1987, p. 233.

15. Richard von Weizsäcker, "Ansprache bei einer Gedenkstunde aus Anlass des 40. Jahrestages der Beendigung des Krieges in Europa und der nationalsozialistischen Gewaltherrschaft," Chamber of the German Bundestag, Bonn, 8 May 1985, *Europa-Archiv*, 40(10)1985, pp. D265, D267.

16. Idem., "Ansprache des Bundespräsidenten der BRD nach seiner Vereidigung am 1. Juli 1984," *Europa-Archiv*, 39(20)1984, p. D593.

17. *Berlin: le mémorial de Plötzensee* (Berlin: Ed. Colloquium, 1985), p. 25.

18. Rolf Falter, "Jenniger geraakte klem tussen moraal en historisch onderzoek," *De Standaard*, 14 November 1987, p. 4.

19. *Tatsachen über Deutschland: die BRD* (Gütersloh: Bertelsmann Lexikothon Verlag, 1984), p. 81.

20. Dean, "How to Lose Germany," pp. 58–60.

21. *Die BRD, 1955–1966, Information zur politischen Bildung*, no. 176, 1983, p. 2.

22. *Die BRD, 1966–1974, Information zur politischen Bildung*, no. 191, 1981, pp. 9–11.

23. Ernest D. Plock, *The Basic Treaty and the Evolution of East-West German Relations* (Boulder, Colo., and London: Westview Press, 1986), p. 67.

24. Ibid., p. 221.

25. Ibid., pp. 222–223, and Dean, "How to Lose Germany," p. 58.

26. Plock, *The Basic Treaty*, p. 223.

27. Carlos de Sarego, "L'Allemagne à la recherche de son Europe," *Libération*, 28 February 1986, p. 22.

28. A. James McAdams, "Inter-German Détente: A New Balance," *Foreign Affairs*, 65(1)1986, p. 142.

29. Stanley R. Sloan, "East-West Relations in Europe," *Headline Series*, no. 278, 1986, p. 28.

30. Stanley Hoffmann, "The U.S. and Western Europe: Wait and Worry," *Foreign Affairs*, 63(3)1985, p. 630.

31. McAdams, "Inter-German Détente," pp. 141–42.

32. Plock, *The Basic Treaty*, p. 225.

33. Michael Stürmer, "Realpolitik und Vision. Perspektiven der Deutschlandpolitik," in Hans-Dietrich Genscher, ed., *Nach vorn gedacht . . . : Perspektiven deutscher Aussenpolitik* (Stuttgart: Bonn Aktuell, 1987), p. 84.

34. Plock, *The Basic Treaty*, pp. 220–221.

35. Edouard van Velthem, "Fin de Congrès à Berlin-Est: Honecker garde un oeil sur Bonn," *Le Soir*, 21 April 1986.

36. Plock, *The Basic Treaty*, pp. 222, 231; Dean, "How to lose Germany," p. 64; Gerhard Wettig, "Osteuropa in den Ost-West-Beziehungen," *Aussenpolitik* 37(1)1986, p. 12.

37. Carl-Christian Kaiser, "Lots of toings and froings across the border," *Die Zeit*, 17 April 1987, in *The German Tribune*, 3 May 1987, p. 4; Marlies Menge, "DDR: Neue Kontakte zur Bundesrepublik," *Die Zeit*, 20 February 1987.

38. "A grin, even if not a smile," *Die Stuttgarter Zeitung*, 16 April 1987, in *The German Tribune*, 3 May 1987, p. 4.

39. Kaiser, "Lots of toings and froings."

40. Plock, *The Basic Treaty*, p. 221.

41. Luc Rosenzweig, "L'instrument politique des échanges économiques," *Le Monde*, 3 September 1987, p. 5; Jonathan Dean, "Directions in Inner-German Relationship," *Orbis*, 29 March 1985, p. 611.

42. Werner Kahl, "Départs moins nombreux," *La Tribune d'Allemagne*, 21 June 1987, p. 5.

43. McAdams, "Inter-German Détente," p. 141.

44. H. van der Velden and H. A. Visée, *Ontspanning in Europe: De Conferentie over Veiligheid en Samenwerking in Europa* (Baarn: Het Wereldvenster, 1976), pp. 219–311.

45. McAdams, "Inter-German Détente," p. 142.

46. Gerhard Kiersch, *Les héritiers de Goethe et d'Auschwitz* (Paris: Flammarion, 1986), pp. 194–95. Extract in: Guérard, "Le débat sur l'identité allemande," pp. 51–52; Jeffrey Boutwell, "The German Search for Security," in Stephen J. Flanagan and Fen Osler Hampson, eds., *Securing Europe's Future* (London: Croom Helm, 1986), p. 124.

47. McAdams, "Inter-German Détente," p. 143.

48. Plock, *The Basic Treaty*, pp. 178–80, 200–201.

49. Ronald D. Asmus, "Die Zweite Ostpolitik der SPD. Mit Perspektiven aus den USA," *Aussenpolitik*, 38(1)1987, pp. 51–52.

50. Luigi Barzini, quoted in *Europa van Morgen*, 22 July 1987, p. 405.

51. Bernard von Plate, "Spielraum und Interessen in der DDR-Aussenpolitik," *Aussenpolitik*, 37(2)1986, pp. 150, 156–57.

52. F. Stephen Larrabee, "For Eastern Europe, Soviet ties must be rethought," *International Herald Tribune*, 12 March 1986, p. 6.

53. Elizabeth Pond, "Federal Republic of Germany: Westpolitik, Ostpolitik, and Security," in Catherine M. Kelleher and Gale A. Mattox, eds., *Evolving European Defense Policies* (Lexington, Mass. and Toronto: Lexington Books, 1987), pp. 234–35; Richard Lowenthal, "The German Question Transformed," *Foreign Affairs*, 63(2)1984–85, p. 308.

54. McAdams, "Inter-German Détente," p. 149–150.

2

The Change in the West German Perception of Security

West Germany's growing self-confidence did not only lead to the "normalization" of the attitude of the West German people toward their own country and to a greater desire for closer contacts with the GDR. It also resulted in their becoming more self-confident about their geographical position and security situation and increasingly viewing their own security from a national angle, just as the French and British are accustomed to doing. Nor was this entirely due to greater self-assurance: The traditional NATO strategy also seemed less and less appropriate to the West German situation.

In his book *A Grand Strategy for the West*, former chancellor Schmidt paints a picture of the West Germans' perception of their security situation. His description indicates that there is really nothing odd about the difference in American and West German views on European security. Both Americans and Europeans do well to consider the situation facing the economically strongest country in Western Europe in the mid-1980s.

West Germany is a small country, about the size of an average American state, say, Oregon or Colorado. But in Oregon or Colorado there are two or three million people. In West Germany there are sixty million. On top of that dense population there are, of course, military forces. I have mentioned our own forces numbering 500,000 soldiers; I should also mention the American forces, about 200,000, and French forces, British forces, Dutch and Belgian forces, Canadian forces, and even a Danish general. All of these are under a foreign high command.

Think of Oregon or of Colorado with six non-American forces, under a foreign high command, on their soil, and think also of the foreign high commander having some 5,000 nuclear weapons within his command and not under the host nation's control. . . .

I live in Hamburg.... If I get in my car and drive eastward, it takes me about forty-five minutes to get to what is called the "Iron Curtain." If the Russians would let me pass, it would take me another thirty minutes to get to the barracks of the first Russian tank division. And, vice versa, it would take them a little more than an hour to get to my home. Think of the people in Oregon having seven different armies and 5,000 foreign nuclear weapons deployed on their soil, and the Russians that close! It takes the Soviet fighter bombers just five minutes to appear in the sky above Hamburg.[1]

Two factors are clearly reflected in Helmut Schmidt's words. First, there is the manifest proximity of the military threat, which for the West Germans is not just an abstract concept to which reference can be made in all manner of grandiloquent speeches: It was so much part of everyday life that it could be described in terms of "an hour's drive." The constant presence of NATO forces in West German daily life, in the shape of troop movements, maneuvers, and so forth, further increased this awareness of the threat. This brings us to the second factor, the feeling of enormous dependence on NATO forces, a feeling of dependence that, partly because of the fairly limited control that can be exercised over these troops, was sometimes close to changing into a feeling of still living in some kind of occupied country.

These two factors were not, of course, new. What was new, however, was that, while once accepted as a fact of life, they began to prompt a process of analyzing and rethinking the Federal Republic's security in the early 1980s.

In the balance between awareness of the threat and awareness of dependence, the former had always carried more weight, and incidental questions or critical remarks therefore tended to be inappropriate and even irrelevant. Given the USSR's overwhelming military potential, its offensive strategy, its dominance of Eastern Europe, and its ideology and social system, was it not obvious that the threat to West Germany and Western Europe lay to the east? And, given this threat, was it not clear that NATO and the American military presence in the Federal Republic had been successful? They had, after all, acted as a sufficient deterrent to Soviet and Warsaw Pact troops not only to prevent a possible military offensive from the East but also to enable the West to withstand the kind of pressure and blackmail that had occurred during the Berlin crisis from 1959 to 1961.

In so ominous a situation it was not illogical but to be welcomed that West Germany's security policy was in fact dictated by Washington. The more the United States and NATO saw the Federal Republic's defense as the core of their strategy, the stronger the Americans' guarantee of security became. Moreover, the alternative that would follow a possibly successful military campaign or blackmail by the Russian bear would completely eliminate the now slightly restricted freedom of action. Consequently, the West Germans did not ask too many questions about their army, unlike the other

NATO armed forces, still being under NATO rather than national command even in peacetime.[2]

In the late 1970s and early 1980s the balance gradually began to shift the other way as the West German view of both the threat and the protectors changed. The perception of the Soviet threat had slowly assumed a different form in Western Europe and West Germany in the 1970s.[3] The treaties with the East, the favorable results produced by West Germany's *Ostpolitik*, and the long period of détente strengthened the feeling that it was possible to live with the Soviet Union. While it was realized, of course, that its military power was still growing, and the nature of the Soviet regime itself was still criticized, it was no longer automatically inferred that the threat was also growing or that the Soviet Union had aggressive intentions. The USSR was increasingly seen as a normal superpower, an actor on the world stage that, like the other actors, wanted to increase its power and influence but was also aware of its limitations and would not go beyond what was rationally admissible. As the Soviet Union was seen to pose less of a threat, disadvantages both of the defense system the West had developed to meet this threat and of the relationship of dependence to which it had given rise were more clearly sensed. This feeling was encouraged by a number of other developments, such as the election of a fairly belligerent American president.

This about-turn in the attitude of some West Germans, and of other Western Europeans, toward security was clearly revealed by the heated public and political debate in the early 1980s on NATO's 1979 dual-track decision. When in 1977 Chancellor Schmidt began to point to the increased Soviet threat following the deployment of SS-20 missiles, and two years later NATO decided to deploy its own medium-range weapons, the result was not, to the surprise of many people, greater public awareness of the threat posed by the East but growing anxiety about the large number of nuclear weapons deployed on European soil, whether of Soviet or American origin, and increasing skepticism about the Western defense system. The anxiety and suspicion led to an unseen mobilization of the people and culminated in the massive peace demonstrations that were a feature of the first half of the 1980s.

The first negative aspect of the existing security system on which attention increasingly focused as a result of the Euro-missile debate is clearly reflected in the following quotation, which might stand for the many thousands of pamphlets disseminated by the peace movement in the early 1980s:

You cannot ask a people to stick with a military strategy and military posture which insures that in case of conflict they will not survive. That is the European situation. In the 1950s, in an act of supreme idiocy, we decided to base their defense on nuclear weapons. Since then, we have been adding more and more weapons, more and more sophisticated weapons, more and more powerful weapons. And suddenly, the Europeans have noticed that Europe is a nuclear battleground. . . . We must have a policy that offers the European nations a chance to survive a military conflict—if possible a chance to win but at the very least a chance to survive.[4]

These words were not, however, uttered by some idealistic organizer of peace demonstrations, peace vigils, or peace chains but by Irving Kristol, a leading American neoconservative and a strong advocate of the reform of NATO.

Almost as shocking as the conclusion that under the current strategy there would be little chance of survival in the event of a military conflict, was for many West Germans the lack of appreciation in the United States and the North Atlantic establishment of the fact that many people in West Germany certainly did not consider this situation reassuring and saw it as sufficient reason to protest against it. The protest, reflected in the rapid rise of the peace movement, was very easily brushed aside as naive, idealistic, neutralist, anti-American, and, in West Germany's case, downright dangerous. This black-and-white thinking led a section of the West German public to feel even less understood and even less "safe" within the Atlantic security system and so to take an increasingly critical view of it, making them, in American eyes, even more neutralist and dangerous. As a supporter of the then U.S. president, Ronald Reagan, rightly put it: "It is not that the Europeans are intrinsically selfish, cowardly, or lazy. Rather, Europe's growing uneasiness stems from a rather sensible calculation of the risks and dangers around them."[5]

Defending Western Europe had indeed resulted in an enormous accumulation of conventional and nuclear weapons in Central Europe, making the resulting balance of power between the two military blocs in fact primarily a balance of terror, a balance that in theory guarantees that there will be no conflict between East and West, but also guarantees that Central Europe will be transformed into one gigantic Hiroshima if for some almost inconceivable reason a conflict should erupt nonetheless. Making a sensible calculation of the risks and dangers around them, the West Germans therefore realized more clearly than before that their security situation was anything but ideal and that there would be better guarantees of their security if the threat no longer existed and the possibility of a conflict was ruled out or drastically reduced.

A second negative aspect was that NATO and the United States, the main protector, were unable to convince the West German public that they were making serious efforts to remove some of the terror from the balance. The results of the disarmament and arms control negotiations had been very meager. And although it was clear that the famous Russian "nyet" was mainly to blame for the lack of progress, the fact remained that the NATO policy had not succeeded in achieving the disarmament on both sides of the East-West divide that the Federal Republic wanted. In the 1970s only the two SALT (Strategic Arms Limitation Talks) agreements were signed, imposing limits on the number of American and Soviet strategic missiles and missile defense systems. These agreements did not, however, concern the nuclear weapons deployed in West Germany. Progress at the MBFR (Mutual and Balanced Force Reductions) talks on conventional forces in Europe was equally unspectacular. The NATO dual-track decision in 1979 in fact meant the deployment of even more nuclear weapons on West German soil if the Soviets failed to dismantle their SS-20s. The decision possibly to deploy new Cruise missiles and Pershing IIs in Western Europe, which appeared to increase the likelihood of the escalation of a conflict and of military confrontation in Central Europe, was therefore a turning point for many West Germans, since the threat posed by nuclear weapons was now considered greater than the threat posed by the USSR.[6] It was also a turning point because it was seen as the failure of the Atlantic Alliance to ensure western security in a way that was acceptable to West Germany.

The impression that NATO and the United States were not really interested in negotiating with the USSR grew further when in 1986 the new party leader in Moscow began to put forward various fairly radical disarmament proposals, to each of which the West at first reacted negatively. During this period the United States also took various decisions that seemed to conflict with Western European and West German interests and sensitivities. For instance, in less than one week in June 1986 Washington announced that it would no longer respect the SALT II agreement, let it be known that, after an interval of seventeen years, it would begin producing chemical weapons again and, at the human rights conference held in Berne as part of the Conference on Security and Cooperation in Europe (CSCE), vetoed the agreement on a (limited) improvement of the human rights situation in Eastern Europe, to which the Federal Republic attached considerable importance.[7]

The western leaders brushed aside the Soviet Union's and Warsaw Pact's disarmament proposals as typical communist propaganda and evidently even failed to take the trouble to establish whether or not the new Soviet leader was really serious. They thus missed an opportunity to show their own public and the political parties that were critical of NATO that NATO and the United States were indeed seeking a reduction in levels of armaments in East and West. They also missed an opportunity to unmask those Soviet disarmament proposals, which were primarily intended as propaganda, by responding to them constructively. This would have forced the Kremlin to retreat, which would have put the halos of peace over the heads of the Soviet leaders in rather better perspective. Given NATO's unenthusiastic reaction, it was not therefore surprising that certain views found growing support: NATO was not genuinely interested in the Federal Republic's security interests; the Warsaw Pact's conventional superiority was a carefully sustained myth rather than fact; the aim was to perpetuate the inferiority complex of NATO's conventional forces, whether justified or not, and so ensure and legitimise continued American protection of Western Europe.[8]

The Euro-missile debate also added to the impression that NATO and the United States were not very concerned about reducing levels of armaments in Central Europe but were in fact trying to confine any conflict to Europe or, better still, Central European or German territory as far as possible. Maintaining a credible nuclear deterrent required the presence of "deployable" and "usable" nuclear weapons. As a result, it seemed that the size of the target area for these weapons was being steadily reduced. The problem, however, was that what was a limited war for NATO could be a total war for West Germany.

The evolution toward a military strategy that could be implemented in a geographically limited area began after the massive retaliation strategy lost credibility in the late 1950s with the USSR's development of strategic nuclear weapons capable of reaching the United States. The western threat to respond with a massive nuclear attack on the Soviet Union if it launched a conventional attack on Western Europe clearly ceased to command any respect. In the 1960s the massive retaliation strategy gave way to the flexible response strategy, which included the option of the limited and controlled use of nuclear weapons in Europe if an attack by the Warsaw Pact could no longer be contained by conventional means. German territory would therefore be the first affected. The likelihood of this happening was further increased when another requirement of the new strategy was not satisfied: the strengthening of conventional forces. This was bound to mean the fairly early use of short-range weapons. When growing doubt also began to be cast on the credibility of the flexible response strategy, President Carter decided in 1977 to develop the neutron bomb, a weapon whose relatively limited explosive force would make it highly practicable and enable it to be used near the front line. As this weapon would also have the cynical property of killing people while leaving buildings and equipment largely intact, Carter's decision led to a wave of protest among the West German people, and the plan was eventually dropped.[9]

This was also a foretaste of the even larger protest movement that emerged after NATO had paved the way in December 1979 for the deployment of Cruise missiles and Pershing IIs in West Germany and four other Western European countries. The peace movement and the opposition claimed that, as their name indicated, these "Euro-missiles" similarly increased the possibility of a limited nuclear war being waged in Europe and confined to the European theater.[10] They thus gave no credence at all to one of the arguments for deploying these nuclear weapons, that they would strengthen the link between the European theater and American strategic nuclear weapons. The tendency to limit the potential target area of nuclear weapons as far as possible was also revealed to West Germans in 1988, when the negotiations between the two superpowers on nuclear weapons in Europe led to an agreement on the double-zero option, eliminating nuclear weapons with a range of 500 to 5,000 km. Shorter-range missiles, many of which could only hit the German population, were not, on the other hand, included in the agreement, even though West Germany had made it clear that it wanted to see these weapons removed first.

A fourth aspect of the western defense system that led to objections being raised in the Federal Republic during the security debate of the early 1980s was conventional defense. There was a fear of a growing disparity between the allies' interpretation of the word *defense* and the West Germans' concept, which centers on "forward defense." This primarily meant trying to repel an attack in the immediate vicinity of West Germany's eastern frontier.[11] Thirty percent of the Federal Republic's population and 25 percent of its industrial capacity was located less than 100 km from this border. For Bonn it was therefore unacceptable that ground should first be conceded so that a counterattack could be launched from a strengthened position. Although the principle of forward defense was politically and psychologically the only possible option for West Germany, it was a concept that would be virtually impossible to implement in practice, as indeed had been revealed by official American documents, which stated that in a crisis the United States would be prepared to sacrifice a third of West German territory.[12]

A second essential aspect of the West German defense concept, the adoption of a strictly defensive posture by the West and the limitation of military operations on the adversary's territory as far as possible,[13] also appeared to be suffering steady erosion. The adoption of a more offensive defense strategy, whereby action would, if necessary, be taken well within the territory of the Warsaw Pact countries, was highly controversial in the Federal Republic because it seemed incompatible with the attempts being made to achieve rapprochement with Eastern Europe and because the Germans beyond the Iron Curtain would be the victims. It was, however, the line being taken in the concepts developed in the United States for the use of new technologies in the conventional defense of NATO. The follow-on forces attack (FOFA) concept, officially adopted by NATO in 1985 as the long-term objective, meant that targets deep in the enemy's territory would be destroyed at an early stage of the conflict to prevent reinforcements from reaching the scene of the battle.[14] Like the even more radical air-land battle doctrine, however, the FOFA concept helped to reinforce the idea of an aggressive and offensive NATO to which a section of public and political opinion ascribed.

A fifth negative aspect, which caused a further loss of confidence in the western military system, was that the American ally seemed to have absolutely no understanding of West German sensitivities. When Ronald Reagan became U.S. president in 1981, he made it clear that he intended to conduct a crusade against the USSR, which he labeled the "empire of evil." Considered as equally disturbing was the rather nonchalant way in which he and his closest advisers tossed around such ideas as the restriction of a nuclear attack to European territory and the firing of a nuclear "demonstration shot" as a warning to the USSR to go no further. The West Germans did not rate such statements on limited nuclear wars very high, regarding them as even more of a threat than nuclear weapons themselves. This growing uneasiness about the strategy and the American ally's thinking perhaps found most pointed expression in a book with the eloquent title *Angst vor den Freunden* (Fear of our friends) by Oskar Lafontaine, one of the SPD's leading lights: "For a long time only the Eastern European countries, the Soviet Union's allies, were afraid of their leading power. . . . What is new is that in recent years the West has increasingly come to regard the USA as a danger."[15]

Not only the people but also the West German and other Western European governments found the American remarks no more than moderately acceptable. As a result of NATO's decision to deploy medium-range weapons on their territory they already had enough internal political problems, which such simplistic statements only served to exacerbate. That the liege in far-off Washington did not even take the trouble to consider their difficult domestic position was not appreciated at all. The debate on INF missiles therefore revealed that the problems connected with nuclear weapons were largely political and demonstrated the waning trust between the United States and the European allies at both popular and political levels. The debate on the "third zero" option in 1988 and the allies' lack of understanding for the West German position were to lead to a further decline in confidence and result in even the most conservative and pro-American of West German politicians losing some faith in the United States and NATO.

The growing skepticism about the Western European security system was not only due to the various imagined or genuine negative aspects of the way in which western defense is organized. It also stemmed from the fact that a link was increasingly seen between the existence of NATO and American presence in Europe on the one hand and the continuing division of Germany and Europe on the other. NATO's military position and the presence of American troops in Europe, after all, justified a high concentration of Soviet troops in the Eastern European countries and the consequent influence and control exercised by the Kremlin over these countries. And this was impeding the development of normal relations between Eastern and Western European countries.[16]

What various politicians, such as George Kennan, former U.S. ambassador to Moscow, had feared when NATO was created had indeed become reality: With the rearmament of the two Germanys within the two military blocs, the Atlantic Alliance helped to militarize the division of Europe and to perpetuate the postwar status quo.[17] As a result of their geographical location the two countries formed the cores of the two alliances, and the continued existence of the two blocs and the authority of the two superpowers over their respective spheres of influence depended on the Federal Republic and the GDR remaining firmly embedded in NATO and the Warsaw Pact (although it was obvious that the positions of the GDR and the Federal Republic were not directly comparable). With their increased self-confidence and the Soviet Union seen as less of a threat, many West Germans became less willing to act as the keystone of the postwar political system.

Some West Germans also felt not only that NATO and the American presence had helped to perpetuate the division that emerged after the Second World War, but also that the NATO and American leaders had made very little effort to eliminate the disadvantages of this division, under which the Germans in particular suffer. The hope cherished in the late 1960s and early 1970s that NATO would at last take this specifically West German desire to heart was to remain completely unfulfilled.

The Harmel report on "the future tasks of the Alliance," adopted by the NATO Council in late 1967, contained a few new elements that gave the Federal Republic some hope.[18] One of the important factors was the admission that "the possibility of a crisis cannot be excluded as long as the central political issues in Europe, first and foremost the German Question, remain unsolved." Besides ensuring sufficient military strength and political solidarity, the Alliance was therefore allotted a second function: "to pursue the search for progress toward a more stable relationship in which the underlying political issues can be solved." The report also stated that "the ultimate political purpose of the Alliance is to achieve a just and lasting peaceful order in Europe accompanied by appropriate security guarantees." Thus "détente" now joined defense as one of NATO's objectives.

Another promising element was NATO's positive reaction to the USSR's proposal for a European security conference. At the preparatory meetings and the Conference on Security and Cooperation in Europe that eventually began in 1973, the Western European countries, within the framework of the European Economic Community (EEC), for example, played a particularly active and constructive role. The attitude of the United States, on the other hand, was generally more passive and, as time passed, was even regarded as negative, given the pressure Washington brought to bear on the allies. However, for Bonn the negotiations in Helsinki were important because, together with the treaties that had been concluded with the USSR, Poland, and the GDR in 1970 and 1972, they might form the basis for the development of closer economic, humanitarian, cultural, and other contacts with the Eastern European countries.[19]

When the Final Act was signed in Helsinki in 1975, it was clear that it would not herald a fundamentally new phase in relations with the Eastern bloc. This was due, first, to the reticence of the smaller communist countries, fearful that growing instability would follow any further opening to the West. Another reason was the attitude taken by the Soviet Union, which blithely continued to add to its arsenal and to enlarge its sphere of influence outside Europe. And this, in turn, was connected with the third reason, the fact that détente had an extremely negative connotation for the United States in view of its concern about its own worldwide interests, and it began to see the period of détente, hailed with such enthusiasm in Europe, as a highly successful attempt by the Kremlin to pull the wool over the West's eyes while continuing to increase its own power and influence. When the Reagan era began, after the Soviet invasion of Afghanistan and the crisis in Poland, it became clear that the Americans and NATO had no more time for the détente aspect of the Harmel doctrine. Indeed, in the first half of the 1980s NATO and American circles considered the word *Harmel* and the ideas associated with it to be virtually taboo, not to be taken seriously and to be avoided.

There was therefore nothing unusual about the widening of the gap between the Americans and the West Germans, who had certainly benefited from the period of détente. The Federal Republic found it unacceptable that what it had slowly and painstakingly accomplished in fifteen years of détente and the practical and fundamental advantages this had produced for the German people should simply be cast aside because of the crises sparked off by Afghanistan, Poland, and medium-range missiles. Bonn therefore did its best to shield its relations, particularly with East Germany, from the adverse consequences of the resurgent cold war atmosphere. This in turn led to criticism in the United States and other NATO countries of West Germany's supposed "unreliability" and "tendency toward neutrality," which caused consternation in the Federal Republic, since it had surely given clear evidence of its loyalty to the western camp with its determination to deploy the new NATO nuclear weapons. This difference of opinion was reflected in a continuing series of embarrassing incidents, such as the wave of indignation in the Federal Republic after US Under-Secretary of Defense Iklé had said that, if the West Germans were having problems increasing their defense budget, they should reduce their subsidies to the GDR.[20]

Although there were understandable reasons for the U.S. attitude, the West Germans still found it difficult to accept that their most important ally was not only doing little to alleviate the division of Europe and Germany but even seemed to fail to appreciate that West Germany considered better relations with East Germany and Eastern Europe to be essential and compatible with its loyalty to the Alliance. The almost paranoid tendency of the United States and other western countries to interpret virtually anything West Germany did as a "choice" between East and West, and so to regard any of its actions or statements that were not overly critical of its eastern neighbors as "suspect," was indeed typical of the way in which the West treated and in fact humbled the Federal Republic for forty years. It was also an indication of the western political, military, and intellectual establishment's surprising lack of knowledge and understanding of the West German situation.

Given the many signs of transatlantic ignorance and the growing impression that NATO and the United States not only could not or would not eliminate but also actually helped to sustain the threat and the division of Europe, it was not so surprising that West Germany increasingly began to see itself as the misunderstood member of the transatlantic family, a misunderstood but also more self-confident member, who might therefore draw certain conclusions at a given moment.

NOTES

1. Helmut Schmidt, *A Grand Strategy for the West* (New Haven: Yale University Press, 1985), pp. 19–21.

2. Yves Boyer, "Défense allemande et stratégie de l'OTAN," in *Sécurité et défense de l'Europe—le dossier Allemand*, Les sept épées, no. 36, 1985, p. 69.

3. Gregory Flynn and Hans Rattinger, eds., *The Public and Atlantic Defense*, (Totowa, N.J.: Rowman and Allanheld, 1985), pp. 117, 369–71, 386.

4. Daniel Graham and Gregory A. Fossedal, *A Defense that Defends: Blocking Nuclear Attack* (Old Greenwich, Eng.: Devin-Adur Publ., 1983), p. 107.

5. Ibid., pp. 106–107.

6. Ibid., p. 346.

7. Scott Sullivan, "The Allies at Odds," *Newsweek*, 9 June 1986.

8. Helmut Schmidt, "Arm in Arm mit den Franzosen . . . ," *Die Zeit*, 29 May 1987, p. 34; Jane Sharp, "After Reykjavik: arms control and the allies," *International Affairs*, 36(2)1987, p. 352.

9. Stanley R. Sloan, *NATO's Future: Toward a New Transatlantic Bargain* (Washington D.C.: National Defense University, 1985), pp. 39–43, 80.

10. Anne-Marie LeGloannec, "West German Security: Less of a Consensus?," in Catherine M. Kelleher and Gale A. Mattox, eds., *Evolving European Defense Policies*, (Lexington, Mass. and Toronto: Lexington Books, 1987), p. 172.

11. Ibid., p. 170.

12. Alex A. Vardamis, "German-American Military Fissures," *Foreign Policy*, no. 34, Spring 1979, p. 87.

13. André Brigot, "La politique de sécurité de la RFA," in *Sécurité et défense de l'Europe—le dossier Allemand*, Les sept épées, no. 36, 1985, p. 39.

14. Bernard W. Rogers, "U.S. Military Strategy in the U.S. European Command Area, and Readiness of U.S. European Command Forces, Critical Deficiencies in Capabilities, Resource Program Priorities," Statement before the U.S. Senate Armed Services Committee, 25 March 1987, pp. 7–8.

15. Oskar Lafontaine, *Angst vor den Freunden: Die Atomwaffenstrategie der Supermächte zerstört die Bündnisse* (Hamburg: Spiegel-Verlag, 1983), pp. 85–86.

16. Sharp, "After Reykjavik," p. 341.

17. Catherine M. Kelleher, "Containment in Europe: The Critical Context," in Terry L. Deibel and John L. Gaddis, eds., *Containment: Concept and Policy* (Washington D.C.: National Defense University Press, 1986), p. 391.

18. Sloan, *NATO's Future*, pp. 219–22.

19. H. van der Velden and H. A. Visée, *Ontspanning in Europa: De Conferentie over Veiligheid en Samenwerking in Europa* (Baarn: Het Wereldvenster, 1976), pp. 91–92, 127–28.

20. Pierre Hassner, "L'Allemagne dans les relations Est-Ouest," *Revue Française de Science Politique*, June 1987, pp. 313–314.

3

Toward a Political Interpretation of the Change in the West German Perception of Security

Although a growing proportion of West Germans were changing their perception of the Federal Republic's security situation, the view that the disadvantages of its dependence outweighed the advantages of the protection afforded by NATO and the United States was endorsed to very different degrees. Of the political parties, the SPD had been most deeply penetrated by the changed perception of security and went furthest in proposing an alternative to the existing security system. The new security thinking gradually developed by the Social Democrats and included in the official party manifesto at their Nuremberg congress in August 1986 was referred to, inter alia, as the "second phase of the policy of détente" and the "second *Ostpolitik*."[1] It was indeed a continuation of the *Ostpolitik* established by Chancellor Brandt a good fifteen years earlier, but differed significantly from it in one respect. The Social Democrats realized that the *Ostpolitik* they had formulated under the Brandt government had not been equal to the task of ensuring long-term and fundamental rapprochement between the two parts of Europe.[2] They attributed this failing to the fact that they had taken no account of the military aspects in their *Ostpolitik*, continuing to entrust this facet of East-West relations to NATO. Nor, in view of the Federal Republic's position in relation to the allies at that time and the Brandt government's position at home, could it have been otherwise. In the late 1960s and early 1970s Bonn's *Ostpolitik* was, moreover, suitably complemented by the then NATO policy, which was geared to further détente in relations with the East, as the Harmel report and the approach to the MBFR (Mutual Balanced Force Reductions) negotiations and the Helsinki conference showed.

The détente aspect faded, however, as the 1980s approached, thereafter disappearing almost without trace. It was becoming clear at this time that a far-reaching policy of détente could not be pursued if it was accompanied by a security policy based on the possibility of military confrontation between the two military blocs. Such duality, the SPD believed, would of itself lead to the end of the idea of détente. The Reagan administration drew the same conclusion. But while Washington deduced that the détente concept could be completely written off because it was impracticable, many SPD members took the opposite view: As the security policy hitherto pursued by the West had proved to be impracticable, it must be thoroughly reformed. And the *Ostpolitik* must, of course, now include aspects of military strategy.[3]

The SPD therefore put forward proposals and took initiatives that it believed would eventually lead to the "demilitarization of the struggle for power between the systems of East and West," the ultimate objective being "the creation, on the basis of a security community embracing the existing alliances, of a European peaceful order which will overcome these blocs." Through disarmament and cooperation with Eastern Europe the existing Yalta system in Europe could therefore be gradually replaced with a system of collective European security.[4]

According to the Social Democrats, the two Germanys bore a joint responsibility in efforts to achieve this objective. They must both play a pioneering role and offer their mutual relationship as a model for the establishment of a security community, a "security partnership" between East and West. This concept was one of the basic elements of the security policy proposed by the SPD. Given the enormous stockpiles of weapons in Central Europe, the peoples in the two parts of Europe would "either survive together or perish together." As, therefore, the security of one side was guaranteed only if the other felt secure, a "joint guarantee of peace, not against but with one another" was needed.[5] The SPD saw Eastern and Western Europe as having in their need to "survive together" a common goal, which transcended all differences between them and so made the development of a security community possible. The Social Democrats explicitly said, however, that while the two Germanys must set an example, this must not be seen as a sign of Germany going it alone: "Until there is a peaceful order in Europe, the Federal Republic's peace policy needs a security policy which also has military backing and is linked to the western democracies through the Alliance." Hence the importance of "partnership within the western alliance" and the need for the Federal Republic to maintain its "political and military links with the European Community and NATO." They also made it clear that "the Western Europeans will need the link with the USA's military counterbalance as long as the Soviet Union remains a heavily armed superpower in Europe."—All respectable and conventional sentiments.

Why, then, was the SPD accused of having neutralist tendencies and an anti-American and anti-NATO image? The problem—and the Atlantic Alliance was not really used to this—was that, although the SPD confirmed that West German security could be guaranteed only with the western partners, it also emphasised that this meant that the Federal Republic must be able "to define, introduce, and gain acceptance for its own security interests within the alliance." And this was linked to the SPD's above-mentioned long-term objectives and associated proposals for the demilitarization of the East-West conflict.

What precisely did this demilitarization mean to the SPD? The basic idea was that the goal should be *strukturelle Nichtangriffsfähigkeit*, meaning the structural inability of either military bloc to launch an attack against the other. This implied so changing and reducing the military strategy, training, structure, size, and arms levels of their forces that they would no longer be able to carry out a broad offensive and, in a crisis, would not provoke a preventive or preemptive attack. The aim must be conventional stability at the lowest possible level, with the quality of defense so improved that "forward defense" in the literal sense of the term would become possible and credible. Where nuclear weapons were concerned, the SPD's objective was the progressive creation of a nuclear-free Europe. Above all, the NATO strategy should eschew the early or first use of nuclear weapons. To avoid a preventive attack, medium- and short-range missiles must be dismantled and, of particular importance for the Federal Republic, all nuclear battlefield weapons must be removed. All these measures would greatly increase the possibility of political crisis management and largely eliminate the crisis-escalating effect of existing military units and weapons systems.

Another reason why the West German Social Democrats came in for so much criticism and were labeled unreliable was that they not only gave expression to their already "unacceptable" ideas on a new security policy in a few fine-sounding sentences for consumption by the electorate, but also were already attempting to put them into effect by means of a "parallel foreign policy." After being forced into opposition in late 1982, they had discussions with various Eastern European communist parties, without the Federal government being involved, and in some cases agreements were reached. In this they were able to use the contacts they had developed in almost fifteen years of government. Remarkable rapprochement was achieved particularly with the East German communist party, the SED, as the many mutual visits and the sometimes very close personal relations revealed. Despite its outspoken criticism, the Federal government was later to take indirect advantage of these contacts and visits by itself establishing closer contacts with the GDR's leaders. Besides the SED, talks were held with the communist parties of Hungary, Czechoslovakia, and other countries on the possibility of economic, ecological, and cultural cooperation.[6]

A remarkable outcome of the many contacts between the SPD and the SED was the joint document drawn up by the two parties in mid-1987 after years of discussion. This document, entitled "The struggle between the ideologies and joint security,"[7] confirmed that there were fundamental differences between the political systems of the two Germanys. However, an attempt was made to "de-emotionalize" these differences and to define rules and common interests. Of importance for the SPD, and also fascinating in the light of the crisis in the East German political system in 1989, were the following passages: "We cannot hope that one system will abolish the other. We can, on the other hand, hope that both systems are capable of reform and that the rivalry between them will strengthen the will for reforms on both sides." And: "Open discussion of the rivalry between the systems, their successes and failures, their advantages and disadvantages, must be possible within each system," after which the importance of the freedom of information, travel, assembly, and so on is emphasized.

Barely two years before their fall the East German leaders were clearly still sufficiently sure of themselves, so much so in fact that they agreed that the whole document, which included a few other statements rarely heard in the GDR, should be reproduced in the party newspaper, *Neues Deutschland*. The SPD tried to use this joint document (with very moderate success) as the key to establishing contacts with the peace movements, ecologists, churches, and other unofficial groups in the GDR, which saw it as a useful new means of exerting pressure. At the time it was hardly conceivable that the rivalry between the systems would so soon turn to the West's advantage.[8]

What most offended the western allies, however, were the agreements that the West German Social Democrats reached with the Eastern Europeans on military relations between East and West. In mid-1985 they concluded a draft agreement with the East German SED on a chemical-weapons-free zone in Central Europe, which was followed in October 1986 by an agreement on a nuclear-free zone in Germany. Discussions were also held with other communist parties in the Eastern bloc (including the USSR) on security problems, which resulted, among other things, in a joint declaration with the Polish United Workers' Party on criteria and measures for the creation of confidence-building security structures in Europe. Such agreements tended, however, to be regarded in the western camp as suspicion building.[9]

Being in opposition, the SPD could, of course, afford to make fairly radical proposals and take initiatives without undue concern for current realities and military and political relations. It should be added that the party manifesto adopted in Nuremberg was the result of a compromise between the various tendencies within the SPD.[10] Certain factions had been critical of the existing security system, but still supported the "Atlantic" views of former chancellor Helmut Schmidt. At the other end of the opinion scale, however, such politicians as Oskar Lafontaine were demanding a nuclear-free Germany and the withdrawal of the Federal Republic from NATO's integrated military command. The highly radical statements on the latter aspect in particular were given a great deal of publicity both at home and abroad, although they were endorsed by only part of the SPD. By placing excessive emphasis on them for electoral reasons and describing them as typical of the SPD's alarming lack of seriousness and sense of responsibility, Chancellor Kohl and the ruling CDU/CSU, however, did what they blamed the SPD for doing, that is, strengthening the image of an unreliable Germany.

Despite the fierce criticism leveled at them, the Social Democrats were convinced they were playing the same role as in the late 1960s and early 1970s, when, with their *Ostpolitik*, they had charted a course that was to be followed by all Federal governments for the next two decades.[11] It would indeed slowly emerge that the various ideas put forward by the Social Democrats on such aspects as making it impossible for either side to launch an attack, a nuclear-free zone in Central Europe, the gradual elimination of the division of Europe, and the call for the abolition of the "image of the enemy" were not just haphazard, unrealistic, and isolated illusions.

First, the SPD's ideas on security had not been simply snatched out of thin, opposition air but were the outcome of a debate that had been under way since 1979, when the SPD still headed the government in Bonn. The difference of opinion on these ideas, which had emerged at that time between the members of the SPD government and a large section of the party rank and file, was indeed one of the factors that brought down the Schmidt government in September 1982. Second, the trend in their security thinking was to some extent also a reversion to the traditional ideas to which the Social Democrats under Schumacher had subscribed after the Second World War. It was only in 1959, after all, that they had been forced by the international situation—Khrushchev's heavy pressure on Berlin—to abandon their basic principles: opposition to membership of NATO and to the rearmament of the Federal Republic so that the door would be left open for the reunification of the two Germanys. Although they did not go so far in their demands, it was clear that the Social Democrats' ideas in the 1980s pointed back in this direction, even if the goal now was not reunification but normal relations between the two Germanys.[12] Third and most important, the main lines of the SPD's security thinking were also endorsed in one way or another by a large section of the public, as was apparent from the peace movement's ability to mobilize support, by other parts of the West German political spectrum, and, with the passage of time, even by the Federal government.

Foreign Minister Hans-Dietrich Genscher's policy in particular revealed at a very early stage that, like the SPD, he had a completely different European security system in mind. However, he took an entirely different and above all far more discreet and subtle line in pursuit of his objective. He thus succeeded in progressively gaining the support of the Federal government and, to some extent, the Atlantic Alliance for the various elements of the security concept he envisaged.

Officially, the Christian-Democratic/Liberal government, with Helmut Kohl of the CDU as chancellor, the Liberal Hans-Dietrich Genscher as foreign minister, and CSU chairman Franz-Josef Strauss, who, though not a member of the government, wielded a great deal of influence as prime minister of the *Land* of Bavaria, did not believe West Germany's security situation had changed essentially. Partly as a result of the peace movement, which included supporters of the ruling parties, there was growing concern that the Federal Republic was apparently becoming an increasingly explosive nuclear powder keg, its fuse held not by the Federal government but by an albeit friendly superpower, on whose sangfroid West Germany thus depended. Nonetheless, any change in the West German security situation was due to the Kremlin's military buildup and the deployment of the SS-20s. Chancellor Kohl thus agreed with his predecessor's analysis, and his government therefore called for the implementation of the twin-track decision taken by NATO in 1979. Moscow must be made to realize that Western Europe and West Germany would not be intimidated by such Soviet pressure.

For the Kohl government NATO therefore was and remained the core of West German security, and it had no intention of undermining this pillar by discussing the German security situation with the GDR, as the SPD was doing. This would reduce the allies' confidence in West Germany, which would eventually erode its security. Not only the "Atlanticists" but also those who, like Genscher, attached considerable importance to a further expansion of inter-German relations stressed this view. They believed growing contacts between the Federal Republic and the GDR to be possible only if each superpower was sure that "its" Germany remained a firm part of its own alliance. As one of Chancellor Kohl's advisers put it, "Bonn's *Deutschlandpolitik* will endure only as long as it has the West's confidence and support; once that is no longer the case, it will, like Icarus's flight, end in a fall."[13] For someone like Helmut Kohl, therefore, the West's attitude largely determined the form taken by the *Deutschlandpolitik* and security policy in general. For a wily politician like Genscher, on the other hand, the aim was progressively to gain the West's confidence in and support for new aspects of policy of importance to West Germany and so to widen the scope of Bonn's *Deutschlandpolitik* and security policy.

One problem the Federal government faced was that, if the dialogue between the two Germanys was to be maintained and intensified, not only must each show complete loyalty to its superpower and allies, but also Central Europe must be kept as free as possible from the cold war atmosphere that had prevailed in 1983 and 1984. To overcome this dilemma, the two German states tried to ignore the prevailing East-West tensions as far as possible and to create an autonomous field of inter-German contacts, separate from global East-West relations and the role they played or were required to play in them (such as the deployment of nuclear weapons aimed at each other).[14]

When the East German party leader, Honecker, pressed for a German "coalition of reason," he received a positive response from Helmut Kohl, who, along with the ruling parties and the SPD, took up the idea of an inter-German "community of responsibility." This idea clearly reflected both countries' greater self-confidence, but it also stemmed from joint awareness that they were in the same boat since: first, each belonged to a military alliance in which it was obliged, for the sake of global East-West relations, to adopt a given attitude, which was not, however, in keeping with what it considered desirable for their mutual relations; and second, as their vulnerable geographical position meant that they would both suffer the same fate in the event of a military conflict, they faced a common threat despite their contrasting social systems and so must try to avert it together. Thus, although it might fiercely criticize the SPD's ideas, the Federal government's attitude clearly reflected the idea of a German community of responsibility, which had been emphasized by the Social Democrats.[15]

The idea of a community of responsibility embracing the two Germanys would continue to have some influence for the next few years, despite the damper temporarily put on the inter-German dialogue in mid-1984 under pressure from the Soviet Union. At the Conference on Disarmament in Europe held in Stockholm, together with the neutral and nonaligned countries, Bonn and East Berlin were actively seeking a compromise between the two blocs and emphasized their particular responsibility for preserving peace on the continent of Europe. This conference on the extension of the confidence-building measures was to be successfully concluded in September 1986 and to achieve a breakthrough in East-West negotiations in that for the first time the Warsaw Pact accepted the principle of on-site inspection.[16] Bonn would also continue to play a pioneering role during subsequent negotiations on conventional disarmament. Initially, however, the degree to which Bonn included security questions in its discussions with East Berlin was principally geared to preventing the deployment of nuclear missiles from having any adverse effects on inter-German relations. The western security system was thus not really questioned, nor was there any suggestion of possible alternatives to the existing East-West order, as the Social Democrats had proposed.

At an early stage, however, various discreet initiatives taken by the Liberal foreign minister, Genscher, showed that he was actively seeking closer and more comprehensive contacts with the Eastern European countries, the long-term objective he had in mind being a fundamentally different European security order. One of the features of Genscher's approach was that he was often very quick to anticipate developments in the USSR, Eastern Europe, East-West relations, and West German public or political opinion, even before their significance had been generally appreciated. Very often the aims he defended in negotiations and discussions within the Federal government or the Atlantic Alliance therefore seemed at first sight unrealistic or impracticable, with the result that the outcome of the negotiations was very frequently seen as a defeat for him, since he usually achieved only part of what he wanted. However, as he set his sights high and so moved the frontiers of the discussion in the direction he wanted, a "defeat" also meant in most cases that, despite the success they assumed they had achieved, the views of his interlocutors had evolved as he had wanted. This in turn laid the foundations for the frontiers and aims to be moved back a little further. The discussions in 1988 and 1989 on short-range weapons and the "third zero" option were an excellent example of this.

Another feature of Genscher's approach was that, with a complex series of apparently isolated and even rather pointless initiatives relating to Eastern Europe, he helped to pave the way for future changes and prepared West Germany itself to respond as quickly and efficiently as possible when certain developments occurred and to steer them in a direction that was favorable for Bonn. At first sight, many of these initiatives and contacts appeared to produce little or nothing practical and to be yet another of Genscher's failures. Eventually, however, his usually discreet efforts to improve relations with Eastern Europe proved important in that they led to the creation of a network of formal and informal contacts between politicians and officials in East and West Germany. Indeed, as time passed, the FDP minister's attitude was adopted by other West German politicians. This made it possible to establish a relationship based on mutual trust, to support reformists, to send out the right signals at the right time, and to predict developments to some extent. Unlike other Western European countries, the Federal Republic thus avoided standing helplessly and passively by as the rapid changes occurred in the former Eastern bloc. This also explains why the Federal Republic differs markedly from its Western European partners in having such close relations with Eastern Europe. The importance the White House attached to good relations with Bonn in mid-1989, prompting it to replace Britain with the Federal Republic as its most important ally, showed that Washington realised that the knowledge and experience needed for a response to the developments in Eastern Europe were primarily to be found in West Germany.

One of the more striking examples of Genscher's usually more discreet and less radical initiatives was the proposal he made on a visit to Prague in February 1986.[17] He felt representatives of the Federal Republic, the GDR, and Czechoslovakia might begin discussions in Geneva to consider how they could together contribute to the disarmament process in Europe. He thus indicated that he regarded the two Eastern bloc countries as potential partners rather than potential aggressors. Genscher's proposal therefore closely resembled an attempt to put into practice what the Social Democrats termed a "security partnership."

During the campaign for the *Bundestag* elections in January 1987 Genscher and his liberal party began to be more explicit about their ideas on relations with Eastern Europe. They called for a policy that would lead to a "second phase of détente," an objective they were said to have "stolen" from the SPD.[18] Soon after the elections, which were seen as a sign of approval of Genscher's policy of seeking détente, it became clear, however, that his proposal regarding a second phase of détente had been more than a mere electioneering gimmick.

In a speech that caused something of a stir at the World Economic Forum in Davos in February 1987,[19] Genscher became the first important western politician in a government post to say he was prepared to take Gorbachev at his word when he spoke of a common European house. The gist of his speech was that mankind faced the choice of perishing as a whole or surviving as a whole. Survival, however, meant working together to create "cooperative security structures." The ultimate objective was a

European peaceful order in which nations with different social and political systems can develop in peaceful competition and without fear of each other. . . . No nation would derive more benefit from such a peaceful order, which would overcome the division of Europe, than the Germans. It is therefore one of the main tasks of the Federal Republic's foreign policy and *Deutschlandpolitik* to be the driving force, within and as an established part of the western alliance, in steering East-West relations toward such a peaceful order.

Among other things, however, this presupposed conventional stability in Europe, and to Genscher this meant that current Soviet superiority must give way to "a situation in which the armed forces of both sides are capable only of defending themselves and no longer have the capacity to launch an attack."

Where the ultimate objective was concerned, there was little difference between the West German foreign minister and the leading opposition party. Where nuclear weapons were concerned, Genscher never explicitly advocated, for example, a nuclear-free zone in Central Europe, as the SPD had done. It was remarkable, however, how little emphasis his statements placed on the role of nuclear weapons in western defense. He also said at a very early stage that an INF agreement must be followed by negotiations on a reduction in the number of short-range weapons, and it was clear that his eventual aim was their complete removal. In two respects—the importance they attached to human rights and to the Helsinki process—there was, however, a significant difference between the views of the liberal and social-democratic parties. The rapid reforms in Eastern Europe in 1989 were to prove that Genscher was right to believe both aspects are essential.

Human rights were, in Genscher's opinion, a basic component of East-West relations, and so they must always be included in discussions with the Eastern Europeans. When he said he agreed to Gorbachev's idea of a common European house, he immediately added that human rights must also be respected in this house. For the SPD, on the other hand, human rights were often a tiresome obstacle in their efforts to establish closer contacts with Eastern Europe, an obstacle they sometimes preferred to ignore if it suited them. It thus did the SPD's image no good at all that its chairman, Willy Brandt, should go to South Africa in 1984 to meet the leaders of the antiapartheid movement and yet, on his visit to Poland, refuse to meet Lech Walesa or to support Solidarity in any way since it was seen as a destabilizing factor in East-West relations.[20]

Both Genscher and the SPD regarded the Conference on Security and Cooperation in Europe (CSCE) as a suitable forum for efforts to achieve a peaceful order that overcame the division of Europe. Unlike the SPD, which tended to mention the Helsinki process no more than sporadically, Genscher saw the CSCE process as an essential aspect of his thinking on security. This forum could, after all, be used to maintain a link between three essential components in East-West relations: the military aspects, economic and cultural relations, and human rights. The Helsinki Final Act, which concerned all three aspects, therefore indicated, to Genscher's mind, the direction that efforts to achieve a European peaceful order should take.[21] As was later to become clear, it was also the right direction. The upheaval in East-West relations and in the Eastern bloc was, after all, to occur both at military and economic levels and in the field of human rights and associated freedoms, with changes or stagnation in one respect influencing, slowing, or prompting changes in the other.

At the CSCE follow-up conference that began in Vienna in November 1986, the West German delegation tried to achieve progress in all three "baskets" and to prevent all the attention from being focused on just one. Even when the discussions in the Austrian capital began to proceed at a painfully slow pace, Genscher continued, alone in the wilderness, to insist on the importance of the CSCE forum. Bonn realized that the Vienna discussions gave the Eastern European countries an opportunity of further increasing their room for maneuvering and independence from Moscow and widening their contacts with the West. If the follow-up conference produced a satisfactory final document containing far-reaching new commitments, the various communist countries would see it as proof of the legitimacy of their reformist position or, conversely, as new pressure to implement further reforms. No wonder, then, that the front runners in the process of Eastern European reform, Hungary and Poland, were also trailblazers and thus West Germany's allies in Vienna. The favorable result that was achieved in Vienna two years later, contrary to all expectations, showed that the pressure exerted and strategy pursued by the Federal Republic in particular had not been in vain.[22]

While FDP Minister Genscher gradually developed his ideas on a future European peaceful order, the other two coalition partners were still overcome by grave doubts and disagreement about the position the Federal Republic should adopt on Eastern Europe and the USSR. Although the Kohl government had stood by the *Ostpolitik* pursued by previous governments, Helmut Kohl and the CDU/CSU took a relatively tough line on the GDR and the other communist countries during the campaign that preceded the elections in January 1987. Remarkable utterances at this time were Kohl's likening of the GDR to a concentration camp and of Soviet leader Gorbachev to Hitler's propaganda chief, Goebbels. At the elections, however, the Christian Democrats suffered serious losses, which were interpreted as the electorate's rejection of the CDU/CSU's views on Eastern Europe, especially as Chancellor Kohl's leading opponent within the government, Genscher, and his liberal party, advocates of a policy of détente, had gained votes. Once the elections were over, Kohl therefore softened his tone.

Nonetheless, fresh problems soon arose during the debate on the "double-zero option." Views on this subject differed widely among the Christian-Democratic members of the government: Some even rejected the standard zero option (and wanted to keep the medium-range weapons that had already been deployed), while others were prepared to accept a triple-zero option (which in practice might lead to some form of nuclear-free zone in Central Europe). This confusion created the impression that the CDU was obstructing progress in the disarmament process, which helped to ensure fresh defeats in the regional elections in Rhineland-Palatinate and Hesse. One result of all this, at any event, was the growing influence in the CDU of such politicians as Geissler, Späth, and the then mayor of Berlin, Diepgen, who called, out of conviction or for electoral reasons, for a more moderate foreign policy and a more conciliatory *Deutschlandpolitik*, and urged the party to pursue the policy proposed by Genscher.[23] These "reformists" within Chancellor Kohl's party had strong support from the Christian-Democratic president, von Weizsäcker, who constantly emphasized the importance of better and more relations with the Eastern European countries. During his visit to Moscow in July 1987, where he and Genscher tried to make amends for Kohl's far from diplomatic comparison of Gorbachev with Goebbels, he expressed various ideas that frequently came very close to Genscher's and the SPD's:

What is important is balanced defense, with neither side capable of launching an attack, the exclusion of the possibility of surprise attacks, and a growing appreciation of mutual dependence where security is concerned. . . . Only arms reductions can lead to peace. Peaceful cooperation at all levels will pave the way for further arms reductions.[24]

And therefore, "As we approach the next millennium, we must stop thinking in terms of blocs and frontiers between blocs." It is perhaps no coincidence that these words were spoken by a man who, like Willy Brandt, had once been mayor of West Berlin.

After a badly needed summer holiday, when he had an opportunity to reflect on the differences within his party and on the *Land* elections in September, about which he had reason to feel some concern, Chancellor Kohl seemed to have decided to take the line proposed by his foreign minister and the moderate wing of the CDU. This was evident, for example, when in late August he at last agreed to the dismantling of the "German" Pershing Ia missiles under the INF agreement, thus removing one of the last major obstacles to the implementation of the double-zero option. What was certainly surprising about this decision, which had been influenced by both internal and external considerations, was that while it was endorsed by the Greens, the SPD, and the FDP, it had the support of only part of Chancellor Kohl's own CDU. It was not approved, for example, by the leader of the CDU in the *Bundestag*, Alfred Dregger, and was totally rejected by Franz-Josef Strauss and the Bavarian CSU, who let it be known through their secretary-general that they did not agree to the Pershing Ia missiles being "sacrificed on the altar of Soviet affability."[25]

The decision on the Pershing Ia missiles marked a turning point in the Federal Republic's attitude toward NATO. For most CDU/CSU politicians loyal to NATO it signified the crossing of a line, of which there had been warnings, but which had been ignored by the allies. Bonn had repeatedly given Washington to understand that the inclusion in the INF package of a second "zero" (meaning the removal of nuclear weapons with a range of 500 to 1,000 km) would lead to a huge increase in internal pressure for a third zero (nuclear weapons with a range of less than 500 km) and would also threaten NATO's Montebello agreement on the modernization of tactical nuclear weapons.[26] Since the missile debate in 1983 Bonn had been proposing that nuclear weapons with a range of less than 500 km should be removed or reduced in number because they would be used first in any conflict and, moreover, would be targeted chiefly on German territory. The United States and the USSR, however, elected to begin at the top and remove the weapons that posed the greatest threat to themselves.[27]

Thus the very nuclear weapons the West Germans wanted to be rid of first were retained, prompting a CDU politician like Volker Rühe to comment that "no other country in the western alliance has on its soil nuclear weapons which, if launched, will destroy its own territory." Bonn's prediction and warning had thus proved true: After the signing of the INF agreement even the most fervent NATO supporters, such as Alfred Dregger, called resolutely for negotiations on further reductions in the number of short-range weapons so that the Federal Republic might have "the same level of security" as the other NATO countries. They also urged NATO to amend the Montebello agreement in the light of the latest developments in the disarmament negotiations and possibly even to dismantle some of its nuclear artillery unilaterally.[28]

The change in the attitude of the conservative wing of the CDU was at least consistent with its philosophy that West Germany and its security interests must at last be taken seriously and that Bonn should stop capitulating whenever confronted with faits accomplis by the Alliance. Alfred Dregger and others found it very hard to accept that they of all people, having always been West Germany's strongest proponents of President Reagan's and Prime Minister Thatcher's position, should now be let down by them. This feeling grew when, into the bargain, Mrs. Thatcher and other western leaders used the strict implementation of the Montebello decision on the modernization of short-range weapons as a new test of West German loyalty to NATO, as if Bonn had not yet provided sufficient proof of this by taking the politically difficult decision to deploy INFs, by maintaining the largest military force in Western Europe, and by making its territory available to foreign armed forces. These "partners" showed no understanding at all for the Federal Republic's specific security position, for the idea of a carefully considered "global concept," or for the domestic political problems that the fear of the Federal Republic's "singularization" entailed. What was completely unacceptable was that the loudest demands should be voiced by the British prime minister of all people. She it was, after all, who, just before the British elections in May 1987 as chance would have it, had been the first major western leader to yield to American pressure and agree to the double-zero option, which would remove nuclear weapons that threatened her country.

It was undoubtedly true that the West Germans were also using the question of an overall concept, in which a real effort would be made to establish which and how many weapons systems were needed for Western European security, as a tactic to avoid taking a decision at that particular time. Nonetheless, this concept was also of fundamental importance to Bonn because it wanted to prevent modernization from being effected less as a means of improving Western European and West German security than for mere reasons of principle and quasi-bureaucracy, or as a way of putting West Germany's loyalty to the Alliance to the test yet again. The fear of Germany's "singularization" was certainly somewhat exaggerated, since the western armed forces in the Federal Republic would also suffer and a few other European countries could be hit (far less extensively) by the short-range weapons. Yet it could hardly be denied that German territory would be hit first, that, in theory at least, the INF agreement increased the possibility of restricting a military conflict to Central Europe, and that the threat to the Federal Republic was therefore greater than, say, to the United Kingdom and France.[29]

In early 1988 the INF agreement and the resulting change of attitude in the conservative wing of the CDU/CSU led to a virtual consensus in the Federal Republic on the position it should adopt on nuclear weapons. The SPD too had meanwhile refined its views somewhat and, through Egon Bahr, accepted, for example, that a limited number of short-range weapons would continue to be deployed for an interim period, until the conditions for their total destruction were satisfied.[30] The government's attitude was therefore applauded from both the government and the opposition benches in the *Bundestag*, and not for the last time. All the parties were well aware that only agreement across party lines could ensure greater respect in the Atlantic Alliance for the Federal Republic's views and its real security problems, and that only then could other allies be persuaded to support the West German position, if only because its neighbors were afraid of an isolated, but united West Germany.[31] The pressure from and lack of understanding in the western camp in fact helped to bring about this remarkable rapprochement among the various political groupings.

The positions of the various parties on the conventional disarmament negotiations had also become closer. The idea of the "structural inability to launch an attack," for example, was accepted by Helmut Kohl,[32] while the SPD suggested various criteria and subtle distinctions that this and other concepts it had proposed should satisfy.[33] Even the Bavarian CSU leader, Franz-Josef Strauss, always one of the fiercest opponents of the FDP's and SPD's views, said after his spectacular journey to Moscow in December 1987: "The way to peace, to the reduction of mutual fear, and to the development of sustained confidence can be cleared only when armaments have been cut back to such a degree that all that is left is the existing defense capability, not the ability to launch an attack."[34] Fine words for someone who had always been labeled a superhawk. At all events, the deeper significance of the disarmament negotiations had been generally appreciated in the Federal Republic in 1988, which resulted in an approach that differed from that of most allies. Volker Rühe put it as follows: "The negotiations on conventional stability in Europe will only superficially deal solely with weapon systems. Basically they entail the future overall political shape of Europe as a whole."[35] And this in itself was a sign that the West German attitude toward Eastern Europe was assuming a different dimension.

NOTES

1. "Unser Weg zu Abrüstung und Frieden," Resolution on the SPD's peace and security policy, Party Congress in Nuremberg, 25–29 August 1986, 8 pp. (The following quotations from and references to the SPD program are derived from this document unless otherwise stated.)

2. Ronald D. Asmus, "Die Zweite Ostpolitik der SPD. Mit Perspektiven aus den USA," *Aussenpolitik*, 38(1)1987, p. 46.

3. Ibid., p. 47.

4. Renate Fritsch-Bournazel, "Interrogations stratégiques et quête d'identité," in *Sécurité et défense de l'Europe—Le dossier allemand*, Les sept epées, no. 36, 1985, p. 125.

5. Carl-Christian Kaiser, "Wandel durch Wettbewerb?" *Die Zeit*, no. 11, p. 10.

6. Asmus, "Die Zweite Ostpolitik der SPD," p. 46.

7. Grundwertekommission der SPD and Akademie für Gesellschaftswissenschaften beim ZK der SED, "Der Streit der Ideologien und die gemeinsame Sicherheit," *Politik*, August 1987, no. 3, 7 pp.

8. Marion Gräfin Dönhoff, "Ob endlich die Zukunft beginnt?" *Die Zeit*, 11 September 1987, p. 5; "In die Büsche," *Der Spiegel*, 14 December 1987, pp. 38–39.

9. "Chemische Abrüstung. Modell für eine chemiewaffenfreie Zone in Europa. Ein von SPD and SED entwickelter Rahmen," *Politik*, no. 6, July 1985, 7 pp.; "Grundsätze für einen atomwaffenfreien Korridor in Mitteleuropa. Gemeinsame Erklärung der Arbeitsgruppe SPD-Bundestagsfraktion und SED," *Politik*, no. 19, November 1986, 8 pp.; press release ("Eine gemeinsame Arbeitsgruppe der KPdSU und der SPD. . . . "), *SPD Press Service*, 13 October 1987, 5 pp.; "Joint Declaration on Criteria and Measures for Establishing Confidence-Building Structures in Europe," SPD/PUWP Working Group, Warsaw, 10 February 1988, 8 pp.

10. Stephen Szabo, "The German Social Democrats and Defense after the 1987 Elections," *SAIS Review*, (2)1987, pp. 57–59.

11. Asmus, "Die Zweite Ostpolitik der SPD," p. 55.

12. Szabo, "The German Social Democrats," pp. 52, 54–56.

13. Michael Stürmer, "Realpolitik und Vision. Perspektiven der Deutschlandpolitik," in Hans-Dietrich Genscher, ed., *Nach vorn gedacht . . . : Perspektiven deutscher Aussenpolitik* (Stuttgart: Bonn Aktuell, 1987), p. 79.

14. Walther Leisler Kiep, "The New Deutschlandpolitik," *Foreign Affairs*, 63(2)1984–85, pp. 325–326.

15. Ernest D. Plock, *The Basic Treaty and the Evolution of East-West German Relations*, (Boulder, Colo., and London: Westview Press, 1986), pp. 219, 224–225; "Beschluss des Deutschen Bundestages zur Lage der Nation im geteilten Deutschland vom 9. Februar 1984" and "Erklärung des Bundeskanzlers der BRD, Helmut Kohl, vor dem Deutschen Bundestag am 15. März 1984 zur Lage der Nation im geteilten Deutschland," *Europa-Archiv*, 39(20)1984, pp. D588–91.

16. Carlos de Sarego, "L'Allemagne à la recherche de son Europe," *Libération*, 28 February 1986, p. 22.

17. Ibid.

18. Jochen Thies, "Die BRD nach den Wahlen vom 25. Januar 1987. Aussenpolitische Kontinuität und leichte Akzentverschiebungen," *Europa-Archiv*, 42(8)1987, p. 219.

19. Hans-Dietrich Genscher, "Chancen einer zukunftsfähigen Gestaltung der West-Ost-Beziehungen," *Bulletin*, 4 February 1987, pp. 93–97.

20. Asmus, "Die Zweite Ostpolitik der SPD," pp. 51–53.

21. Genscher, "Chancen," p. 96.

22. Heinrich Schneider, "Über Wien nach Gesamteuropa? Der KSZE-Prozess nach dem dritten Folgetreffen," *Integration*, 2(12)1989, p. 53; "CSCE, A Framework

for Europe's Future: Vienna Follow-Up Meeting," *U.S. Information Service*, 1989, 79 pp.

23. "Coalition at sixes and sevens on disarmament," *The German Tribune*, 7 June 1987, p. 3.

24. "Staatsbesuch des Bundespräsidenten in der Sowjetunion," *Bulletin*, 15 July 1987, pp. 627–29.

25. "Conditions laid down for axing Bonn's Pershings," *The German Tribune*, 6 September 1987, p. 1.

26. Jeffrey Record and David B. Rivkin, "Defending Post-INF Europe," *Foreign Affairs*, 66(4)1988, p. 739.

27. Herbert Kremp, "Varied response to Bonn's triple-zero option," *Die Welt*, 19 May 1987, in *The German Tribune*, 31 May 1987, p. 1.

28. Volker Rühe, "Perspektiven der Friedenssicherung," *Europa-Archiv*, 421(23)1987, pp. 677, 680–681.

29. Christoph Bertram, "Brandmauer darf es nicht geben. Der Westen streitet über Abrüstung und Umrüstung in Europa," *Die Zeit*, 12 February 1988, p. 1; Kaltefleiter, in R. Strauch, "Western security experts find a surprising unanimity," *Der Tagespiegel*, 22 November 1987, in *The German Tribune*, 16 December 1987, p. 2.

30. Egon Bahr, "Western Europe—Soviet Union," Presentation to students and staff of the NATO Defense College in Rome on 10 May 1988, p. 20.

31. Thomas Meyer, "Eternal-triangle touch to Bonn's foreign policy," *Kölner Stadtanzeiger*, 8 January 1988, in *The German Tribune*, 17 January 1988, p. 2.

32. Helmut Kohl, "Grundsätze und Kernprobleme der Sicherheit in Europa, Rede auf der 25. Internationalen Wehrkundetagung in München am 6. Februar 1988," *Bulletin*, 11 February 1988, p. 200.

33. Karsten V. Voigt, "Von der nuklearen zur konventionellen Abrüstung in Europa—Kriterien konventioneller Stabilität und Möglichkeiten der Rüstungskontrolle," *Europa-Archiv*, 42(14)1987, pp. 409–418.

34. Franz-Josef Strauss, "Die Bilanz einer Moskaureise," *Bayern Kurier*, 9 January 1988, p. 2.

35. Volker Rühe, "West must not be seen as mere arbiter of Gorbatchov proposal of the week," *Süddeutsche Zeitung*, 22 September 1988, in *The German Tribune*, 9 October 1988, p. 3.

4

Growing Doubts about the United States and Nuclear Deterrence

The evolution toward a West German consensus on security policy and, more specifically, the change in the CDU/CSU's attitude can be partly ascribed to the fear that one of the cornerstones of the foreign policy pursued since the time of Adenauer was crumbling: the military protection afforded by the United States and, associated with it, the American nuclear deterrent that was to have extended over Europe like a protective umbrella.

A large section of the public did not see the Federal Republic's dependence on the United States and NATO as a problem. They believed West Germany's security could be guaranteed only by the existing western security system, which happened to be based on American leadership and on the threat that nuclear weapons might be used. There was therefore absolutely no reason for major changes in the existing security relationship.

This view was held not only by a section of the West German public but also by many in the other Western European countries. Even in France this line of reasoning could and can count on a wide measure of support. It is realized only too well, after all, that the Western European countries' independence owes much to American (nuclear) involvement in the defense of West Germany and Western Europe. For this segment of West German and Western European public and political opinion, the reverse is therefore the problem. They fear a weakening of the security relationship between the United States on the one hand and the Federal Republic and Western Europe on the other.

Such fear is a normal phenomenon in any alliance. We have learned to live with the specter of a transatlantic divorce that emerges from time to time—only to disappear again later. It has therefore never really been thought necessary seriously to consider what the periodic appearance of this specter has meant for the security of the Federal Republic and Western Europe. However, on 11 and 12 October 1986, at the meeting between President Reagan and General Secretary Gorbachev in Reykjavik, its true significance was revealed to many people for the first time. During the discussions in the Hofdi House the American president not only seemed prepared to abandon what was regarded as the primary means of guaranteeing Western Europe's security, nuclear weapons, the Americans also seemed no longer so resolute in their desire and concern to ensure Europe's security. The previous ironic warnings in the press that the Hofdi House in Iceland was haunted all at once had a ring of truth about them.

The shock caused by the Reykjavik meeting throughout Europe resulted in the many transatlantic warning lights that had previously been ignored now being observed very closely. An analysis of the links between various events and developments in past years led many to conclude that the security situation in Western Europe was not so stable as they had imagined. The ghost of Reykjavik was abroad in West Germany and Western Europe.

One of the interesting phenomena was that those who defended NATO and its strategy were shocked by a summit meeting at which no agreement of any kind was reached and thus nothing that might endanger European security was decided. There was, after all, no decision to remove all medium-range weapons from Europe or (almost) totally to eliminate all strategic weapons or generally to ban nuclear testing. It was realized, however, that in Reykjavik the ingredients had been chosen for a dish that was to be served in the future, a dish that would mean completely rewriting the traditional NATO doctrine.[1] If the leaders of the two world powers had not stumbled over the SDI ingredient, they would have concluded a disarmament agreement in Reykjavik so radical as to be beyond the wildest dreams of even a highly idealistic demonstrator for peace. The proposals discussed in the Hofdi House amounted to a "profound questioning if not revision of postwar assumptions about the nature, feasibility, and virtue of nuclear deterrence, as the mechanism for keeping the peace between East and West."[2]

After Reykjavik the Western Europeans also realized that this time they could not describe President Reagan's positive attitude toward these far-reaching proposals as another gaffe. Nor could it be construed as one last hasty attempt on his part to go down in history as the "president of peace." Due reflection revealed that, on the contrary, the agenda that President Reagan helped to draw up in Iceland was consistent with other decisions taken during his term of office.

The proposed reduction in nuclear weapons not only enjoyed the support of people from various parts of the American political spectrum, but also reflected the evolution of the Pentagon's own nuclear doctrine. If we consider earlier proposals put forward by President Reagan, we see that the discussions in Iceland on major reductions in the two nuclear arsenals were partly based on an American proposal dating back to the time when President Reagan was still being branded a full-blooded hawk: In November 1981 he had proposed a drastic reduction in the number of strategic nuclear weapons.[3] Leaving aside any objections there may be to the concept, the Strategic Defense Initiative, which he launched in his address to the nation on 23 March 1983, follows the same line. According to Reagan, the aim of the SDI was to make ballistic nuclear weapons "powerless and out-of-date" and to overcome the "present dependence on the threat of nuclear retaliation."[4] The SDI was also accompanied by a gradual reinterpretation by the Americans of the ABM (Anti-Ballistic Missile) treaty concluded in 1972, which virtually prohibits the development of a system of defense against missile attacks.[5] Later, in their attitude toward the double-zero option, the Americans were again to show that they wanted to reduce the number of nuclear weapons as quickly as possible.

Once the first Cruise missiles and Pershing IIs had been deployed on European soil and the Soviet Union's subsequent response had also been resisted, these nuclear weapons had performed their most important task for the Americans: They had shown that the American security commitment to Western European remained intact and that, despite internal opposition, NATO was a strong bloc capable of taking and implementing difficult decisions and was not susceptible to political pressure and blackmail by the Soviet Union. Now that the medium-range weapons had been actually deployed, they did not seem wholly commensurate with the strategic concept developed by the Americans, and it would therefore be better for them to be removed again.

In other sections of the American political world too a debate began on the place of nuclear weapons in the United States' and NATO's military strategy. It gradually became clear that the startling article published by McGeorge Bundy, George Kennan, Robert McNamara, and Gerard Smith in 1982, in which they advocated the "no first use" of nuclear weapons, was not simply an isolated, odd idea of a few "remorseful" politicians.[6] On the contrary, it was the harbinger of a fairly general trend among American political leaders of all complexions toward the abandonment of a form of deterrence that is excessively dependent on the threat of the (first) use of nuclear weapons. Thus an (implicit) consensus gradually emerged, based on acceptance of "no early first use" at least, and the casting of conventional defense in a more important role.[7] This trend also had its roots in the development of the military's own strategic thinking. It was having growing difficulty deciding how to translate the flexible response strategy into feasible military action and how to keep nuclear escalation under control. Issuing commands, communicating, and keeping a check on nuclear weapons would, after all, be extremely hard in wartime. It became increasingly difficult to advance credible hypotheses in which the use of nuclear weapons would give a military edge without being accompanied by unacceptable devastation in Europe and the United States.[8]

The question is in fact whether it was ever the intention of the authors of the flexible response strategy to develop a plausible set of options. When NATO officially adopted this strategy in 1967, it had been primarily a political response to the change in the military-strategic context and particularly the evolution toward a nuclear balance between the United States and the USSR. It was only after de Gaulle had decided, for this among other reasons, to withdraw his country from NATO's integrated military command that the NATO countries succeeded (after almost five years of discord and European resistance to McNamara's proposal) in agreeing on what was to be known as the doctrine of flexible response. For the other member countries it was then more than clear that the alliance urgently needed to close ranks again in this period of serious internal crisis. This amounted to Britain, West Germany, and the other European member countries abandoning their opposition to the new American concept. The main concern was thus clearly to demonstrate NATO's unity and continuing relevance and less to formulate a new military strategy, a scenario that, moreover, frequently recurs within NATO. The political solution that the flexible response doctrine constituted was never translated into terms relevant to military strategy. Nor, indeed, could it be given more concrete shape since this would inevitably have exposed the different national interpretations hidden behind this compromise, which was certainly not the intention of the decision on the flexible response.

That it was just a question of giving symbolic expression to political unity rather than finding a genuine consensus on the substance of the matter was also apparent from the fact that in practice the existing situation was simply consolidated. The acceptance of the United States' modified nuclear strategy went some way toward mollifying its concern about (strategic) nuclear weapons being used too early. On the other hand, as conventional forces were not strengthened, as McNamara had proposed, the threat of and the need for the use of nuclear weapons at an early stage of a conflict remained, and so the linking of the United States to the "fate" of Western Europe, considered so important by the latter and especially by West Germany, seemed assured. The flexible response decision thus reflected the political and military-strategic reality of the time, but it was also to remain a useful political compromise for another two decades thanks to its vagueness and ambiguity.[9]

Despite this, the American military authorities increasingly questioned the validity of the existing hypotheses on the use of nuclear weapons on the battlefield. Greater emphasis was therefore placed on the importance of avoiding a strike of this kind. This was apparent, for example, from the Pentagon's willingness to raise stocks of munitions in Western Europe to the point "where we will never be obliged to allow escalation to rise to the level of short-range weapons." The increase in munitions was one of the elements pertinent to the American military's global objective of improving the preparedness and endurance of the conventional forces. The search for means of avoiding the use of nuclear weapons also led to the development of alternative strategies, such as Air-land Battle and the Follow-on Forces Attack (FOFA) strategy adopted by NATO in 1984, in which conventional weapons and modern technologies are the key elements. The development of new technologies would enable more and more of the military tasks once performed by nuclear weapons to be transferred to conventional weapons.[10]

A similar tendency was noticeable in the development of the Soviet Union's military strategy, although it had always placed considerable emphasis on conventional forces and the restriction of a possible military encounter to the conventional level. This tendency has accelerated since the nuclear disaster at Chernobyl (April 1986), which has had a major impact on the Soviet military. Even a nuclear encounter limited to Western Europe might have unacceptable consequences for the Soviets due to the resulting radioactive fallout.[11]

That the Europeans did not really become aware of the trend in American security thinking until after the shock of Reykjavik was due, first, to the fact that initially President Reagan and his advisers had always spoken of the possibility of waging *and* winning a limited nuclear war, and of the advantages that the use of nuclear weapons in the European theater might therefore have; and second, to American insistence at this stage on NATO's deployment of medium-range weapons. This created the impression that the Americans wanted to strengthen the nuclear deterrent. With Western Europe's political leaders trying to find all kinds of military arguments to convince the public (and themselves?) of the importance of NATO's dual-track decision, it was forgotten that the United States wanted to deploy nuclear weapons in Western Europe primarily for political and psychological reasons, just as President Reagan's statements on a limited nuclear war could be ascribed principally to the political and ideological war being waged against the USSR. NATO's dual-track decision thus acted as a smoke screen that concealed more fundamental developments.

With all the attention in Europe focused on the Euro-missiles, the impression also arose that the deployment of these weapons was the essential element of Western European security. One of the explanations for this trend, in which the Americans wanted to allot a larger role to defense at the expense of deterrence, was that they always felt morally uncomfortable about the existence of nuclear deterrence. The futuristic SDI project essentially reflected these ethical motives. Furthermore, the Americans realized only too well that, given its geographical position, the North American continent (unlike Western Europe) did not really need a deterrent and could easily be defended if the nuclear element disappeared.[12]

These two aspects were not, of course, new to American society. Since the United States unfurled its nuclear umbrella over Western Europe, they had, after all, been a standard part of the American consciousness. However, when President Reagan adopted a verbally very aggressive attitude toward the Soviet Union during his first term and propagated the image of the Soviet Union as an "empire of evil," this consciousness grew stronger—for some because they were afraid of President Reagan's "belligerent" attitude, for others because they now distrusted the leaders of the "malicious" Soviet empire even more, and for both because the existence of nuclear weapons only made the United States' security situation even more dangerous. No wonder, then, that the idyllic dream of a safer and perhaps even "unassailable" America revived.

Added to this, nuclear weapons cannot be translated directly into military and political power. This is not surprising, given the underlying rationality of producing nuclear weapons. In many cases they are, after all, developed, produced, and deployed principally because the adversary also has, or might have, the same capability or the same weapons system. When President Truman had to decide whether or not the H-bomb should be constructed, one of his questions was, "Can the Russians do it?" When his nuclear advisers answered "yes,"[13] Truman decided it should be made.

In the final analysis, nuclear weapons remain deterrent weapons whose main objective is to prevent the adversary from using similar weapons. Not even the improvement and modernization of nuclear weapons, or the addition of innovations (such as the ballistic missiles and MIRVs or multiple independently targetted re-entry vehicles), have been able to increase their "usefulness." The contrary in fact tends to be true since, as a former member of the American National Security Council has said, "Our national security has been much diminished by these innovations and nothing we can do by adding more or better weapons can itself recover that loss of security."[14]

The Americans also began to become increasingly aware that nuclear strength is not only very difficult to translate into genuine political and military power, as the Vietnam War and the taking of American hostages in Iran had shown: It even has a paralyzing effect on foreign policy. It was realized that nuclear weapons ultimately have just as much of a deterrent effect on those who possess them as on those at whom they are aimed. As a result the Americans feel reluctant to undertake certain activities.[15] Advocates of strategic defense described the situation as follows:

When you shine a bright flashlight in the eyes of a wild animal at night, the animal freezes. Just so, American foreign policy, hypnotized by the transfixing glare of nuclear holocaust, has behaved like a startled, petrified animal. Almost any policy initiative must be evaluated in terms of the horrifying possibility that anything we do might lead to "increased tensions." And increased tensions might lead to "escalation." And escalation might end in the "ultimate escalation."[16]

The comparison of American foreign policy with the attitude of an animal petrified by fear may be somewhat extreme, but it does refer to a real fear that is constantly present in the American security consciousness, the fear that the United States itself would have to suffer on its own soil the (nuclear) consequences of a war that had broken out in Europe. This rational exclusion of the possibility of a conflict in which the superpowers would be directly or indirectly involved is, on the other hand, the strongest argument that can be advanced for retaining nuclear weapons.

The Americans' objective can therefore be defined as follows: ensuring an efficient form of defense for Western Europe that also minimizes the risks to themselves. The American insistence on enlarging the role of the defense aspect and reducing that of nuclear deterrence is therefore just another American attempt to satisfy this dual requirement, although it is clear that any responsible American politician will, and must, give absolute priority to the second aspect of this dual requirement: the limitation of risks to U.S. security.

A first step of this kind was taken in the early 1960s, when the American doctrine of "massive retaliation" had lost its credibility. This doctrine had meant that, in the event of a Soviet attack on Western Europe, the Americans would retaliate on a massive scale by destroying cities in the Soviet Union. Although the Soviet Union already had nuclear weapons, it did not yet have the means to transport them across the ocean to strike at American targets.[17] The choice of this strategy had been prompted less by a desire to find a rational and appropriate response to the threat that the Soviet Union then posed than by the Eisenhower administration's austerity policy and the European allies' failure to strengthen conventional defense. In a period of reconstruction it is easy to understand why this "cheap" strategy was chosen, and at the time it was also credible in view of U.S. inviolability.

In 1957 the launching of Sputnik shattered the illusion of American inviolability. It became clear that the Soviets were capable of holding European and American cities hostage with nuclear weapons. The implementation of the doctrine of massive retaliation would consequently result in mutual assured destruction, aptly abbreviated MAD. Along with the illusion of American inviolability, the basic argument for retaining the NATO strategy disappeared. It can indeed be said that since this time the idea of Western Europe being defended by American nuclear weapons fired at Soviet territory (or the threat of such action) has been a myth. The idea of linking the United States to Europe by means of nuclear weapons has since been a sop rather than a real strategic option.

It might indeed be asked if the Americans and, more specifically, the American Congress would ever have agreed to the Atlantic Alliance if they had not been convinced of their inviolability and nuclear superiority in 1949. At Yalta Roosevelt had announced, partly to reassure Congress, that American troops would be withdrawn from Europe within two years. Congress and the American public did not agree to further U.S. involvement in the Old World, nor were they at all eager for a power struggle with the Soviet Union. The attitude adopted by Stalin and his supporters in the ensuing years and the personality of the new American president, Harry Truman, were, however, to result in a complete about-face in the American approach.

While the search for ways of adapting the strategy to the new situation went ahead in NATO without a great deal of conviction, the Americans provisionally deployed Thor and Jupiter missiles in Europe in 1959. These weapons were primarily intended to counterbalance the Soviet Union's SS4 and SS5 missiles and to increase the confidence of the European allies in the United States' nuclear guarantee.[18] The arguments used at this time were thus the same as those advanced during the debate on NATO's dual-track decision in 1979. In both cases the decision to deploy weapons was no more than a means of evading the fundamental problem that the nuclear strategy had been overtaken by the facts and could no longer serve as the operational basis of the Atlantic Alliance. As in the 1980s, the decision on deployment taken in the late 1950s was followed by a heated debate on the value of the nuclear strategy.

In 1962 U.S. Secretary of Defense Robert McNamara let it be known to the NATO allies that the time had come for the massive retaliation doctrine to be officially buried and that a new strategy, which made more limited and controlled nuclear attacks possible, was to be adopted. This became the flexible response, NATO's official doctrine.

Like the Americans, President de Gaulle fully appreciated that East-West relations had entered a new era and that the necessary conclusions must be drawn from the change. His conclusions, however, differed from the Americans'. In his *Mémoires et Espoir* he describes how he perceived relations at that time. This description matches the concern felt in Europe in the 1980s so closely that it is worth quoting de Gaulle at some length:

In 1958 I feel that the general situation has changed since the creation of NATO. It now seems rather unlikely that the Soviet Union will seek to conquer the West. ... There is therefore every reason to believe that the East will increasingly sense the need for and attraction of détente. In the West, on the other hand, the military aspects of security have changed significantly since. ... Now that the Soviets have the means to destroy America, just as America has the means to destroy them, is it possible to imagine the two rivals attacking one another, except as a last resort? But what is there to stop them targeting their missiles on countries between them, in Central and Western Europe? NATO has therefore ceased to guarantee the existence of the Europeans. If the effectiveness of the protection is in doubt, why entrust one's destiny to the protector?[19]

De Gaulle's decision was as follows:

My plan is therefore to remove France not from the Atlantic Alliance, which I intend to maintain as the ultimate precaution, but from the integration achieved by NATO under American command; to establish with each of the Eastern Bloc countries, beginning with Russia, relations designed to bring détente, then agreement and cooperation; . . . and finally, to give France a nuclear potential such that no one can attack us without risking dreadful injuries.[20]

When he outlined this picture of the future, the development of an independent French nuclear weapon had already reached an advanced stage. Two years later, in February 1960, the first French atom bomb was exploded in the Sahara.[21] France gradually reduced its participation in NATO's military activities, and it became clear that de Gaulle was isolated not only in NATO but also in Western Europe. In 1961 his efforts to give France equal status with Britain and the United States through trilateral negotiations failed. A year later the French proposals for a European Union and European military cooperation (the Fouchet plan) suffered the same fate. The 1963 Franco-German friendship treaty also proved to be a disappointment. And 1965 saw a split with the other partners in the European Community, resulting in the famous "empty-chair policy."

In addition, the other NATO countries agreed to the American proposal for nuclear consultations within the Nuclear Planning Group (NPG), a proposal that, given the dominant role the United States continued to play, conflicted with every French principle. Although the European allies are informed and, in theory, consulted by the Americans in the NPG, they have absolutely no guarantee that they will be able to participate in the decision making at times of crisis. It was precisely this monitoring of NATO's (the United States') decisions that was de Gaulle's objective.[22] In 1966, he announced his decision that France was leaving NATO's integrated military command and that NATO must withdraw its military headquarters, all military facilities, and its armed forces from France by 1 April 1967. On this date France could therefore be declared a NATO- and U.S.-free zone, because NATO also decided to withdraw its political headquarters from France.[23]

NATO, thus slimmed down, meanwhile placed its trust in the flexible response. The new strategy meant that NATO would have enough conventional forces, short-and medium-range nuclear weapons, and strategic nuclear weapons to give it a whole range of military options with which to respond appropriately to any kind of aggression, without the aggressor knowing in advance what his aggression would cost him, and confronting him with the risk of no longer having control over the escalation of the conflict.[24] NATO also retained the option of using nuclear weapons first, possibly even before its conventional forces were overrun by the Warsaw Pact.

The new doctrine did not really reconcile the different views on nuclear strategy. Nor did it provide a coherent and usable offensive concept. Instead, it was a classic political compromise, which meant in theory that Washington or Chicago would not be directly exposed to any risks during the initial phases of an armed conflict in Europe but, as a result of possible escalation, would ultimately suffer a fate similar to Hamburg, Brussels, or London.[25] How the link between the United States and Europe would be forged in practice and how the strategy would operate in a crisis situation never became absolutely clear. The contention that such vagueness left the adversary in even greater uncertainty and so further increased the deterrent effect made answers to tiresome questions about credibility and practical applicability superfluous.

The second aspect of Robert McNamara's flexible response concept, the strengthening of conventional forces, was never implemented. The Americans badly needed their financial resources for the war of attrition on the other side of the Eurasian continent. The Western Europeans had always been opposed to this second aspect, and to them and, more specifically, the West Germans the emerging *Ostpolitik* also seemed more attractive than pumping money into new military equipment. As a result, excessive emphasis was placed on nuclear, and especially short-range nuclear, weapons. They would have to be used at an early stage in a crisis. With conventional defense so weak, the choice would, after all, be between launching the short-range missiles and letting them fall into the hands of the advancing enemy. The possibility of a conflict escalating into a "limited" nuclear war in (Central) Europe, with the United States perhaps literally remaining out of range, thus increased.[26]

The questions about the value of the American nuclear guarantee grew with the doubts about America's military, political, and psychological strength that emerged after the Vietnam debacle and the Watergate scandal. This also contrasted starkly with the Soviet Union's position of power. Leonid Brezhnev's empire seemed to be steadily expanding, as was apparent, for example, from Soviet activities in various developing countries and from the deployment of SS20 missiles. The absence of a serious American response to the Soviet Union's activities and arms buildup caused Helmut Schmidt even more concern than the threat posed by these weapons. He expressed this concern publicly in October 1977 in his famous speech to the International Institute for Strategic Studies (IISS) in London. The problem he broached in this context was thus again primarily a political one.

This, then, was the background against which NATO's dual-track decision was eventually taken in 1979. For the Western Europeans the deployment of medium-range weapons in Central Europe was thus first and foremost a political symbol of the United States' reaffirmation of its nuclear commitment to Western European security and its willingness to accept the associated risks. Second, these new nuclear weapons, which could also hit Moscow and, at the insistence of the Europeans, were deployed not at sea but on land, were bound to increase NATO's nuclear options and so guarantee better deterrence. The basic argument was that, when planning an attack on Western Europe, the leaders in the Kremlin would have to bear in mind that the West would respond to such aggression with a nuclear attack on Soviet territory. The new nuclear weapons meant that the Soviets would face this eventuality sooner than they would have before, since they would be deployed fairly close to the potential "theater of war." Consequently, if the Red Army continued to advance into Western Europe, these weapons were almost bound to be fired at Moscow, Kiev, or another Soviet city—unless the American president opted not to launch them.[27] There was, after all, absolutely no guarantee that the Americans would use these weapons. Given their ability to strike at Soviet territory, these "Euro-missiles" were rightly seen by the Soviets simply as an extension of the United States' strategic potential. Every American president is therefore well aware that the launching of these weapons will immediately be followed by a Soviet nuclear attack on the United States and so may have disastrous consequences for the Americans.[28]

It may be wondered if the decision to deploy American medium-range weapons on European soil was not a departure from what had been a constant goal of the United States' (and the USSR's) policy since 1957: preventing a conflict in Europe or elsewhere from escalating into a nuclear conflict between the two superpowers. If so, was it not logical that the Americans should try to withdraw this decision as soon as it had served its political and symbolic purpose? Even though it could be said that these nuclear weapons deployed in Europe increased the risk to the adversary and could not be replaced in this role with other weapons systems,[29] if they also entailed an increased risk to the United States, their supposed deterrent effect had little value in practice.

The INF agreement shattered Europe's illusions and showed it where its responsibility lay. The Europeans had to stop expecting an "extended deterrence" from the Americans in the form of a guarantee that they would use (or threaten to use) nuclear weapons to defend Western Europe or through the physical presence of nuclear weapons on European soil. Or, as Kissinger said as early as 1979, two months before the deployment decision: "I would say what I might not say in office that our European Allies should not keep asking us to multiply strategic assurances that we cannot possibly mean."[30] Such a demand for a moral, contractual, or "physical" nuclear guarantee undermines the relationship between Washington and the Western European allies.

This reveals part of the dichotomy that characterizes the relationship between Western Europe and the United States. On the one hand, the Europeans are afraid that the American nuclear guarantee is no longer credible and so no longer deters the Soviet Union. On the other hand, they are afraid that the Americans will use nuclear weapons contrary to the will and interests of Western Europe.[31] The call for an American nuclear guarantee thus ensures constant Western European suspicion of the United States.

An important reason why an American nuclear guarantee is pointless is to be found in the reasoning of the Soviet Union. The Soviet Union would not, after all, be prevented from attacking Western Europe, assuming it ever wanted to, by a moral, contractual, or physical guarantee from the Americans that they would defend Western Europe with nuclear weapons. What would deter it from launching an attack is the awareness, first, that there would then be so much at stake for the United States that it might itself react with an extreme course of action and, second, that there would be absolutely no certainty that "circumstances" would not result in a military conflict in Western Europe escalating into a nuclear war, which would also have unacceptable consequences for the Soviet Union.[32] As the confusion and the lack of accurate information and safe lines of communication in such a crisis would make rational analysis and monitoring of the situation extremely difficult, there would be absolutely no guarantee that the conflict could be limited geographically and in terms of the weapons used.[33]

The shooting down of Korean Airlines Flight 007 by the Soviets, the explosion of the American spaceship *Challenger*, the accident at the Chernobyl nuclear power station, and the downing of an Iranian airliner over the Persian Gulf by the Americans will have made it even clearer to both superpowers that what Robert McNamara emphasized in his book, *Blundering into Disaster*, can come true: "Things can go wrong."[34]

It is precisely this persistent risk of unintentional escalation that determines the conduct of the two superpowers and prompts them to act with the utmost restraint. Since the Cuba crisis the USSR and the United States have treated each other, and each other's immediate allies, with extreme caution. Even at times of crisis and serious tension between them they have avoided risks in their mutual relationship, even in situations where nuclear weapons were not involved. Even the (rare) tough action taken by a belligerent Ronald Reagan entailed relatively little risk: the invasion of Grenada and the support given to various freedom fighters, where preventing the guerilla movements from being defeated and keeping their adversaries waiting were more important than ensuring that the resistance groups emerged as the victors. Even in the case of the—at first sight—more risky bombing of Gaddafi's headquarters in Libya, it emerged that the Soviet naval ships had "by chance" just left the Libyan ports. In contrast to their prenuclear behavior as regards their military strategies and armament policies, the two superpowers have largely adjusted their foreign policies and conflict management to the realities of the nuclear age. They now regard the classical cost-benefit analysis of their military activities and the classical quantitative comparison of each other's military strength as irrelevant to their foreign policies and to conflict management. Military options that were once taken are no longer considered today.[35]

The argument that the Soviet Union is deterred from taking military action against the United States principally by the total lack of certainty

that a military conflict would not escalate into a nuclear encounter undoubtedly applies to the situation in Europe. A Soviet attack on Western
Europe would, after all, mean four nuclear powers being involved. Given
the extreme caution that has hitherto characterized the behavior of the
superpowers in situations or places where they might both be involved, it
can also be said that the deterrent effect would exist even if no nuclear
weapons were deployed in Central Europe.[36]

In this scenario, with deterrence the outcome not of a nuclear guarantee
but of a lack of certainty that a limited conflict will not culminate in a
complete nuclear apocalypse, the French and British nuclear weapons are
clearly not so insignificant, especially now that both the French and the
British have greatly increased and extended their nuclear capability and (like
the Chinese) will be able not only to inflict nuclear pinpricks in the 1990s
but also to do unacceptable, wholesale damage well beyond the USSR's
borders.

Deterrence is thus related less to numerical or qualitative superiority or
balances, or what is customarily known as "escalation control," than to the
existence of a credible and relatively unassailable minimum nuclear arsenal,
provided at least that it is backed by sufficiently strong conventional defense,
so that the enemy realizes it cannot overrun the Western European territory
without a fight. Although the deterrent effect is enhanced by the presence
of American troops in Central Europe, it can nevertheless be said that, given
further European cooperation and integration in the political and conventional military spheres, deterrence would be assured even if American forces
were to be withdrawn from Europe. In themselves the increased British
and French nuclear capabilities would make for an unacceptable risk and
leave the aggressor feeling sufficiently uncertain.

Furthermore, the aggressor would always have to consider the possibility
of an American response, since even a more self-sufficient and independent
Western Europe will continue to be of crucial importance to the United
States, one reason why even a more independent Western Europe must
maintain the closest possible relations with the United States. What is more,
even if the United States did not react immediately, it would be an unacceptable risk for the USSR to become involved in a conflict in Europe and
perhaps suffer serious losses, while the United States (and China) stood by,
laughing up their sleeves.[37]

Clearly, it will be some time before the Western Europeans gauge the
value of their own capabilities and fend for themselves entirely. Until October 1986 they were not even inclined to question their view of their own
defense and the Americans' role in it. The Americans, on the other hand,
had clearly learned from the debate and events surrounding medium-range
weapons. In Reykjavik they obviously felt the time had come for them to
distance themselves from NATO's 1979 dual-track decision and thus from
the American medium-range weapons deployed in Europe. The American

uneasiness about the current situation thus found concrete expression in the Icelandic capital in the virtual acceptance of Gorbachev's proposals.

A significant section of the political establishment in Europe continued to believe in the theory of the nuclear guarantee and the link between Europe and the United States. The Western Europeans, having in 1981 turned sharply against the zero option put forward by the Americans as a negotiating proposal (but agreeing to it at the time "since the Russians would surely not accept it"), attacked it even more despairingly after Reykjavik. Not only had they not been consulted when the "zero option" was mooted once again, but they also felt that the actual acceptance of this proposal would conflict with two of the objectives of NATO's 1979 dual-track decision, closer links between American and Western European security and a guarantee of enough intermediate rungs on the ladder of escalation needed for the flexible response strategy. They had, however, led their own public and politicians to believe that the western deployment decision was needed to counterbalance the SS-20s. When it was certain that these weapons would be removed, the Western European leaders were therefore no longer able to block this disarmament process. Thus, on 8 December 1987 the seal was put on the double-zero option by President Reagan and General Secretary Gorbachev in the Washington Agreement. During a European Parliament hearing Pierre Lellouche, assistant director of the Paris-based Institut français des relations internationales (IFRI), described this agreement as follows:

The Americans and Soviets have decided . . . to remove from the European theater anything (except the F-111 bombers based in Britain) that might lead to a rapid escalation of a European conflict in an intercontinental nuclear war. [The double-zero treaty] does no more and no less than limit war in Europe itself to the level of conventional armaments or tactical battlefield weapons with a range of less than 500 km, which will still be allowed. In other words, the double-zero treaty amounts to a "mutual sanctuarization agreement" between the two superpowers or, if you prefer, a "pact of nuclear non-aggression" in the territory of the two superpowers.[38]

The last to abandon their opposition to the double-zero option (in late August 1987) were the West Germans, who did not feel at all comfortable with the agreement since the nuclear missiles deployed in Europe that were not covered by the agreement, that is, those with a range of less than 500 km, were the very ones that would be used first in the event of a crisis or hostilities. Most would be deployed in the territory of the two Germanys, and they would also be targeted on their soil. Although the fear of "singularization" was exaggerated, the concern and uneasiness felt by the West Germans was understandable. This uneasiness grew when, into the bargain, the Americans tried to force on the West Germans a post-INF modernization program about which they were equally unenthusiastic. This program focused, after all, on short-range weapons systems, the very weapons seen as the greatest threat by the West Germans.[39]

The INF agreement again placed greater emphasis on short-range weapons and also made it more likely that they would be used (sooner) at a time of crisis, even though their actual military usefulness remained highly questionable. The former reservations about the use of these weapons (given the possibility of escalation) would also diminish with the removal of the INFs. As has already been stressed, this may well increase the deterrent effect in theory, but in practice it could well lead to a rapid escalation of a crisis.

In such a confusing situation, in which a rational evaluation of the adversary's intentions and activities would be very difficult, the USSR might decide at an early stage to knock out these short-range or battlefield weapons (possibly with conventional weapons) to prevent the West from using them. And conversely, NATO might decide to use these weapons earlier than necessary, for fear that they would otherwise be destroyed by the enemy. In the debate on short-range or battlefield weapons it was also forgotten on occasion that their use would have just as destructive an effect on Central Europe as the use of nuclear weapons with a range greater than 500 km. Is it then surprising that, like the two superpowers, West Germany and other Western European countries should want a "mutual sanctuarization agreement" and a "nuclear nonaggression pact" that would also be applicable to their situation?

That the Western European leaders were somewhat bemused by the INF agreement was due not only to the actual removal of the medium-range weapons, which turned a number of traditional scenarios and premises upside down, but also to the disconcerting conclusion that in barely a year the two superpowers had succeeded in serving up a significant part of the Reykjavik menu. This was surely a speed record in the history of East-West negotiations and a rare example of mutual determination. Positive features, of course, but rather dangerous for those who were not involved but must endure the consequences. The Western Europeans had certainly not forgotten that the United States and the USSR had put together the Reykjavik menu without so much as a word to the European allies. What the leaders of the once so proud Old World similarly found difficult to stomach was that they also had very little say during the INF negotiations. They were consulted and informed by the American negotiators more than ever before, but they did not themselves sit at the negotiating table where the decisions were taken on the nuclear weapons deployed in and aimed at Europe. A frustrating situation, and a humiliating one.

The disquiet that emerged in Western Europe after the INF agreement over the "nuclear guarantee" and continued willingness of the United States to defend Europe tooth and nail (and with nuclear weapons) was further accentuated by the report of the Iklé-Wohlstetter advisory committee on "discriminate deterrence," which was published a month after the signing of the INF agreement.[40] This report by the Commission on Integrated Long

Term Strategy, which had been requested by the U.S. Department of Defense and the National Security Council, referred to the possibility that growing threats outside Europe "would force the United States to divert far more of its foreign policy resources and defense assets . . . leading to a reduced American role in NATO." Clear language, then. It went on to say that:

To help defend our allies we cannot rely on threats expected to provoke our own annihilation if carried out. The Alliance has not succeeded in matching Soviet conventional forces on the continent, and for many contingencies our threat to use nuclear weapons against them has become progressively less credible in light of the growth in Soviet nuclear forces.

While appearing to be a correct analysis, it conflicts with the existing NATO strategy. The Pentagon report also goes a step further in treading on sensitive European toes. Besides stressing the desirability of nuclear inviolability for the American people, it says:

There should be less ambiguity about the nature of this deterrence. The Alliance should threaten to use nuclear weapons not as a link to a wider and more devastating war, although the risk of further escalation would still be there, but mainly as an instrument for denying success to the invading Soviet forces.

This is diametrically opposed to the European philosophy that either no one or everyone (Europe and the United States) should die the nuclear death. This passage is thus too much of a reminder of the possibility of a war limited to Europe, an impression that is further strengthened by the fact that (at the time the Pentagon report was published) it had just been decided to destroy the medium-range weapons, and negotiations were also being held on halving the number of strategic nuclear weapons, and yet the Americans were pressing for the modernization of short-range weapons.

The report thus had enough in it to cause concerned and shocked reactions among the Europeans. And while the American government might protest that it was not an official report, the people who had worked on the document (including Henry Kissinger; Carter's National Security Adviser, Zbigniew Brzezinski; the former supreme commander of NATO in Europe, General Goodpaster; and, as one of the chairmen of the committee, the then under-secretary of Defense, Fred Iklé) were just too important and influential for the report simply to be disregarded. It therefore increased the feeling that "we are witnessing the end of a strategy and the death of one concept of the Alliance."[41]

NOTES

1. Ian Davidson, "Europe and the East-West Balance Post Reykjavik" (unpublished paper read to Working Group 4, Toward a European defense identity, of the

4th Annual Conference of the Center for Policy Studies (CEPS), Brussels, 19 June 1987), p. 12.

2. Ibid., p. 3.

3. Ibid.

4. "President Reagan's SDI," *U. S. Information Service*, January 1985, pp. 2–3.

5. "U.S.-Kongres vreest dat regering ABM-verdrag toch wil laten vallen," *De Standaard*, 7 September 1987, p. 4.

6. McGeorge Bundy, George F. Kennan, Robert S. McNamara, Gerard C. Smith, "Nuclear Weapons and the Atlantic Alliance," *Foreign Affairs*, 60(4)1982, pp. 753–68.

7. Stanley Hoffmann, "The U.S. & Western Europe: Wait and Worry," *Foreign Affairs*, 63(3)1985, p. 640.

8. Davidson, "Europe and the East-West Balance," p. 10.

9. John Baylis, "NATO Strategy: The Case for a New Strategic Concept," *International Affairs*, 64(1)1987/88, pp. 43–46.

10. P. M. de la Gorce, "Des euromissiles aux armes 'intelligentes'," *Le Monde Diplomatique*, July 1987, p. 11.

11. Davidson, "Europe and the East-West Balance," pp. 11, 37.

12. Hoffmann, "The U.S. & Western Europe," p. 639.

13. Michael Krepon, *Strategic Stalemate: Nuclear Weapons and Arms Control in American Politics* (London: Macmillan, 1984), p. 43.

14. Carl Kaysen, quoted in Krepon, *Strategic Stalemate*, p. 59.

15. Sir Michael Palisser, *La nature de la puissance des Etats-Unis et de l'influence européenne*, Brussels, Fond. P. H. Spaak, 1985, p. 9.

16. Daniel Graham and Gregory A. Fossedal, *A Defense that Defends: Blocking Nuclear Attack* (Old Greenwich, Eng.: Devin-Adur Publ., 1983), p. 105.

17. Stanley R. Sloan, *NATO's Future. Towards a New Transatlantic Bargain*, (Washington D.C.: National Defense University, 1985), p. 39.

18. Ibid., p. 40.

19. Charles de Gaulle, *Mémoires et Espoir, le renouveau 1958–1962* (Paris: Plan, 1970), pp. 212–13.

20. Ibid., p. 214.

21. Michael M. Harrison, *The Reluctant Ally. France and Atlantic Security* (London and Baltimore: Johns Hopkins University Press, 1981), pp. 120–21.

22. Ibid., pp. 140–42.

23. Ibid., pp. 144–45.

24. *NAVO Zakboekje*, (Brussels: NAVO Voorlichtingsdienst, 1982), pp. 24–25.

25. Sloan, *NATO's Future*, p. 42.

26. Ibid., p. 43.

27. Ibid., p. 68.

28. Ibid., p. 73.

29. Christoph Bertram, "Europe's Security Dilemma," *Foreign Affairs*, 65(5)1987, pp. 952–53.

30. Jane Sharp, "After Reykjavik: Arms Control and the Allies," *International Affairs*, 63(2)1987, p. 341.

31. Zbigniew Brzezinski, *Game Plan: How to Conduct the U.S.-Soviet Contest* (Boston and New York: The Atlantic Monthly Press, 1986), pp. 22–23.

32. Godfried Benthem van den Berg, "European Security from a Common Deterrence Perspective," unpublished paper, 1988, pp. 17–18.

33. Baylis, "NATO strategy," p. 45.

34. Robert S. McNamara, *Blundering into Disaster: Surviving the First Century of the Nuclear Age* (New York: Pantheon Books, 1986), p. 141.

35. See, for example, Benthem van den Berg, "European Security," pp. 3–4, 11–13.

36. C.-G. Fricaud-Chagnaud, "Comment réarticuler sécurité européenne et puissance américaine," *Le Monde Diplomatique*, February 1988, p. 18.

37. Ibid.

38. Pierre Lellouche, "Pour une Europe de la Défense," European Parliament, Political Affairs Committee, Public hearing on the new elements of European security policy, Brussels, 30 November 1987, p. 12.

39. Christoph Bertram, "Brandmauer darf es nicht geben. Der Westen streitet über Abrüstung und Ausrüstung in Europa," *Die Zeit*, 12 February 1988.

40. *Discriminate Deterrence*, Report of the Commission on Integrated Long Term Strategy, Washington, D.C., January 1988, 69 pp.

41. C.-G. Fricaud-Chagnaud, "Comment réarticuler sécurité," p. 18.

5

"La mort d'une certaine conception de l'alliance"

The feeling that a strategy was coming to an end was accompanied by the realization that this also meant the end of a certain concept of the Atlantic Alliance as we have known it for the past four decades. With nuclear weapons dominating the NATO strategy, it was logical that the owner of these weapons (the United States) should occupy a dominant position in the Alliance and be regarded as chiefly responsible for ensuring Western European security. As the United States was found to be limiting and changing the nuclear factor in its (and thus NATO's) strategy, however, the Atlantic Alliance as the "American nuclear protectorate for Europe" seemed to be coming to an end, with the U.S. role in NATO slowly but surely changing from dominant protector to supportive ally.[1]

This change must be seen as part of the United States' painful and laborious process of growing awareness that it was no longer the superior superpower it considered itself to be. When Ronald Reagan took up residence in the White House in 1981, he became the leader of a disillusioned and morally and militarily weakened superpower, which had evidently still to come to terms with the sledgehammer blow it had been dealt in Vietnam, and which had hung half-stunned on the ropes of the world boxing ring for a decade, while its opponent had continued to skip round, scoring points in Vietnam, Cambodia, Laos, Ethiopia, South Yemen, Angola and Mozambique. Its Soviet opponent also took advantage of this period for a major expansion of its military apparatus. In the early 1970s the United States had also had to relinquish its economic and monetary supremacy. Under Carter the United States' uncertainty and doubt about its own abilities continued to grow. While the Americans were being shamefully humiliated in Iran, where their embassy staff was taken hostage, Brezhnev ordered the Red

Army to invade Afghanistan. To the new president, Reagan, it was only too clear that this apparent decline of American power and influence was due to a lack of national willpower.[2]

His remedy was therefore to reaffirm discipline, willpower, patriotism, and other traditional values, to place extreme emphasis on the dangers and immorality emanating from the Soviet empire, and above all to increase American military strength (which Carter had already set in motion). This led, among other things, to the invasion of Grenada, primarily important from a psychological viewpoint; active support for all manner of freedom fighters; and the bombing of the headquarters of the Libyan archenemy, Gaddafi.

During Ronald Reagan's second term of office, however, it became clear that his efforts had not really produced the results hoped for. Despite the show of military strength, the intervention in Lebanon, for example, was a failure. This serious loss of face was made worse by the Irangate affair. This in turn had an adverse effect on Reagan's struggle against the communist threat in Central America, where the situation was again not developing as he had hoped.

It also became clear that Reagan's attempts to restore America's international status by increasing the defense budget had helped to weaken the American economy and were one reason for the serious budget, balance-of-trade, and balance-of-payments deficits. They had had precisely the opposite effect of what had been hoped: The United States became (financially and economically) more dependent on the outside world than before.[3] Above all, the fairly sudden realization that the United States had become a "prisoner of foreign capital" increasingly gave rise to serious concern, apprehension, and even indignation. The foreigners were, moreover, so strong economically only "because we look after their defense." There was thus some panic over this "loss of national sovereignty" and hurt national pride too, when, for example, the whole of CBS's record division was taken over by the Japanese.[4] President Reagan's policy caused serious budgetary and financial problems without achieving the main objective, the unequivocal reaffirmation of American power.

The Americans could therefore no longer avoid the conclusion that their relative loss of power was due less to a lack of will than to two other basic facts: The United States no longer had the means to play its superpower role as before, and relations among the various countries and regions of the world had changed so much that this was no longer possible.

Despite obvious psychological resistance, it is evident that from late 1985 the United States slowly began to attune its policy to the fewer opportunities open to it. In 1985 the American Congress passed a very radical law entitled, significantly, the Balanced Budget and Emergency Deficit Control Act. This Gramm-Rudman-Hollings Act (after the names of its initiators) was intended to eliminate the budget deficit by the end of 1991. This was to be achieved with a mechanism that would automatically come into operation whenever the government saved too little and the deficit exceeded an amount set for each year. The decision that half of the imposed economies were to be made in the defense budget flatly contradicted the objectives originally adopted by the president and his defence secretary, Caspar Weinberger. The Reagan revolution in military spending triggered a counter-revolution in Congress (supported by Democrats and Republicans), which might never have occurred if the military authorities had been rather more moderate with their orders and plans in 1981 and 1982.[5] Independent of the Gramm-Rudman-Hollings Act, internal Pentagon reports in late 1987 warned that even with a rising defense budget (*quod non*) the United States would be unable to finance the military buildup planned by Weinberger.[6]

The intended savings were only to make a real impact after 1988 and thus after President Reagan had left the White House. The onus thus fell on the Bush administration to achieve the planned economies. It also had to decide by how much each section of the defense budget was to be reduced. Savings in certain budget items would be difficult, however, since they related to long-term projects which could not simply be abandoned. As a specific amount had to be saved each year, the inclination was to concentrate on expenditure where cuts would produce very early results. One item where savings could easily be achieved was the maintenance of the armed forces and keeping them operational and in readiness. It soon became clear that the troops stationed in Europe would not escape this surgery.[7]

While Reagan was still president, Weinberger's successor, Frank Carlucci, had said:

As I look at the budget figures that are being debated, it is becoming very clear to me that we may well be talking about a different kind of military force, at least a different size military force. . . . I would rather have a smaller force that is effective and that has the necessary equipment, the necessary ammunition, the necessary personnel, than to have a larger structure that is not effective.

And he added the following warning: "I think we have to look at everything. I don't think anything can be sacrosanct."[8] It ought to have been clear even then that the American troops in Europe would not escape the cuts.

Besides the effect of the American budget deficit, another development was slowly permeating the American way of thinking and acting and would also have a growing influence on the structure of the Atlantic Alliance. As it was now realized that, despite the injection of huge resources, the United States' attempts to regain its old supremacy had failed, there was a growing awareness that the balance of power in the world had changed so much that the United States could no longer play its old role of leading superpower and, indeed, that no single country or region could assume so dominant a role again, even if it were relatively stronger than the others. After all, the

United States managed to attain its former status only because its present rivals or opponents (Western Europe, Japan, the Soviet Union) were still using all their strength to rise again from the rubble of war, and its future rivals (China, South-East Asia, etc.) were still underdeveloped.

The United States joined in the postwar race for world power with a seemingly unassailable lead and so imagined that its superiority was part of the natural scheme of things. At this time the United States also entered into its various foreign (military) commitments, which were, first, considered necessary in view of the threat emanating from the Soviet Union since the Korean War (a threat to which it often overreacted, however, and which resulted in its entering into excessive and overly protracted commitments) and were, second, made possible by American global supremacy. By the early 1970s the United States consequently had over a million soldiers stationed in thirty countries, it was the pivot of five military alliances throughout the world, it had signed mutual assistance treaties with forty-two countries, it belonged to fifty-three international organizations (of which it was again not the least important member), and it was providing economic and military support for almost one hundred countries.[9]

The American power monopoly turned into a duel for power between the United States and the USSR, and from the early 1970s gradually gave way to a more pluralistic distribution of resources and power throughout the world. This inevitably reduced the opportunities open to the United States to influence and control events unilaterally. Nonetheless, the United States stood by many of its foreign commitments. The current problems and tensions were consequently unavoidable and logical.

Paradoxically, however, these problems are due not to the failure of the United States' postwar foreign policy but to its success in creating a world that largely resembles the United States itself. The American policy (based in Europe on the Marshall Plan) of transforming various parts of the world into democratic, prosperous, and peaceful regions was, after all, bound to reduce the United States' own power in relative terms, although no one surely anticipated that Japan, in the 1950s still one of the developing countries and attending the first meeting of Third World countries in Bandung (1955), would now be seen as the greatest economic threat to the United States.[10] After successfully achieving its objectives, however, the United States failed to take the next logical step of delegating responsibility to those regions which had largely adopted American values and goals.[11]

As the United States gradually began to put its budgetary house in order, it slowly adjusted its foreign policy in the latter half of the 1980s to reflect the limits imposed on it by the change in the world situation. The Americans' growing awareness that they must adjust their involvement in world events was evident, for example, from the enormous response to the book *The Rise and Fall of the Great Powers* (1988),[12] in which the historian Paul Kennedy describes the current position of the United States in the world and compares it with the fate suffered by the various superpowers in the past. The Hapsburgs, the seafaring Dutch, Napoleon's France, the British Empire, Czarist Russia, the Germany of Bismarck and of Hitler—all developed an impressive military apparatus and an extensive, powerful empire, only to see it shrivel in time because it was not based on a productive economic structure and because these powers entered into more obligations than they could meet and waited too long to adjust their worldwide interests and commitments to the available resources. This "overstretching" was bound to end in failure.

Henry Kissinger and Cyrus Vance, secretaries of state under Nixon, Ford, and Carter, gave the future president the following advice in 1988:

He must focus American resources and energies on areas where precisely defined U.S. national interests are at stake. He must not be reluctant to admit that there are important issues, even conflicts, in which the United States has no special role to play because our vital interests are not engaged. But he must not shrink from defending our interests. It is true that this is a more restrictive approach to the defense of American objectives than that in the immediate postwar period. We believe, however, that America's international standing and national security need not be diminished because we adopt more selective and collaborative international strategies based on new realities. Our position can be strengthened by taking into account the growing strength of other regions.[13]

The failure of the Alliance to adjust promptly to the change in the relationship between the United States and Europe resulted in the tension within NATO increasingly coming to the fore. The United States found it very difficult to accept Western Europe as both a formidable economic rival and an ally in need of protection and one that, the Americans felt, expected to be protected by the United States without itself seeming prepared to join with the United States in the worldwide defense of the values for which the Alliance stood. This was evident, in American eyes, from the Europeans' reservations about or rejection of the suggestion after the Soviet invasion of Afghanistan and the crisis in Poland that they should boycott the Olympic Games, impose a grain embargo, and reduce trade with Eastern Europe (especially in such highly technological products as the gas pipeline), all because they were afraid of undermining the few positive achievements during the period of détente. This alleged Eurocentric attitude came to a peak in 1985/86, when the Western European allies really specialized in criticizing anything Washington did in its struggle with the West's adversaries, like the interception of the hijackers of the *Achille Lauro* and the fight against communist Nicaragua. And to make matters worse, all (except Mrs. Thatcher's conscientious Britain) refused to support the United States in the action it took against the incarnation of all that conflicted with western democratic values, Gaddafi's Libya. Indeed, they not only refused their support but even went so far as to hinder the American action, as when

France refused to allow American aircraft to fly through its airspace. Not surprising, then, that an embittered American should write the following letter to the editor of the *New York Times*: "Many thanks to the French for giving us Americans permission to enter their country in 1944." Or as the *Washington Times* put it: "We spend U.S. $120 billion a year, we sacrificed American lives during World War Two, and what are we now getting in return?"[14]

The Europeans also have the annoying trait of suffering simultaneously from a superiority complex and an inferiority complex. On the one hand, it is clear from all they say that they regard the Americans as uncultured, partial, naive, and incapable of grasping the complexity of the modern world. On the other hand, they constantly feel shortchanged by the United States, powerless in their dealings with Washington, which allows them too little say. But when the so-intelligent and sensitive Western Europeans are consulted, all that is heard is a cacophony of opinions, and the "European desire to be involved" becomes, ironically, a practical impossibility. Being asked to consult the allies before action is taken therefore equates with passivity, inertia, and an inability to act.[15]

Just as irksome is the dichotomy of European political thinking on the United States. Whatever the Americans do or say, the Europeans are immediately opposed, and if the United States then changes to the direction advocated by the Europeans, they even manage to condemn the change and to defend the position they once so obstinately condemned.[16] This dichotomy finds clearest expression in the constant debate on the coupling or decoupling of the United States and Western Europe in the security sphere. The Western Europeans are afraid that the United States will decouple itself from European security and defense and are therefore trying to involve the Americans more deeply in the defence of Western Europe. This, however, gives them the feeling of being colonized where their security is concerned. If the United States seeks to make Europe less dependent, the debate starts again from the beginning. This European shuttling between two extremes was very apparent during the debate on the deployment and withdrawal of the Cruise and Pershing II missiles. Reagan's adviser on arms control, Kenneth Adelman, gave an apt description of the situation in early 1987 when asked for his views on European fears about the withdrawal of American nuclear weapons from Europe:

Extraordinary, utterly extraordinary, because the Europeans are now at last saying that they love the bomb and that it has served as a deterrent for 40 years. Before they were besieging my office, urging us to come to an agreement, any agreement, with the Soviets. Now they are putting the brakes on. It's fantastic.[17]

This also reveals another aspect of the dichotomy in the European attitude toward the most important of the NATO allies. They feel uncomfortable and threatened whenever the relationship between Washington and Moscow is hostile and try to get them talking again. The Europeans feel better when the dialogue between the White House and the Kremlin is resumed. They begin to worry again when the relationship between the two superpowers becomes rather too friendly, with the prospect of an agreement that might decide the fate of the Europeans without their being consulted.[18]

This dichotomy is a constant feature in the history of the Alliance and always makes for tension. A clear example is to be found during the Cuba crisis in 1962. Asked about the European reaction to the American response to the deployment of Soviet missiles in Cuba, Secretary of State Dean Rusk replied that, if the United States did nothing the allies would be unhappy on the grounds that if the senior partner in the alliance would not act firmly so close to home, it could not be depended on to defend people thousands of miles away; and that if the American response was a firm one, the Europeans would be unhappy at the prospect of being dragged into war over an issue that had nothing to do with them.[19]

Given this attitude, with a lack of European leadership, unanimity, and initiative, it is logical that the dominance, arrogance, and unilateralism of the United States should grow. Until the structure of the Alliance is fundamentally altered, this schizophrenia cannot be expected to disappear. Not only the Americans but also the Western Europeans should logically feel uneasy about the lack of adjustment to the structure of the Atlantic Alliance, because in the final analysis the United States is the only NATO country to discuss Europe's fate with the Soviet Union. The European partners may well be informed and consulted by the United States, but as the former French Foreign Minister Raymond said: "When George Shultz starts asking for your advice, you know he's probably already made up his mind."[20]

Furthermore, at times of crisis the American president has the ultimate say on NATO's nuclear arsenal and thus on Europe's survival, even though we have no say at all in the choice of this president. And, as was stressed after the Libyan crisis, why should the French (and other Western Europeans) always be prepared to accept unilateral American decisions and activities when they do not agree with them?[21] President Mitterrand therefore gave a correct description of the Western European feeling of uneasiness in an interview with the *International Herald Tribune*: "It is sometimes forgotten that we are a sovereign state. We are loyal and strong supporters of the alliance. Our interests . . . are however not necessarily identical with those of the USA. We have our own methods and ideas."[22]

Indeed, why should the Europeans support the Americans when they have so often seen them make rather symbolic aims the core of their foreign policy and a test of the European allies' loyalty: the bombing of Gaddafi's headquarters (overlooking the fact that France, for example, was taking at least as effective action against the Libyan leader by supporting Sudan), opposing Iran's mine-laying operations (forgetting that the United States itself supplied weapons to Iran and that most of the tankers were being damaged by Iraq), and so on. And as the United States, unlike Western Europe, wants to be a global superpower, is it not then more than logical that the United States should itself defend interests typical of this global superpower status? Can the United States really expect its allies to support these rather symbolic acts, which are primarily designed to reaffirm its superpower status?

The problems that plagued the Atlantic Alliance in early 1986 were therefore no more than the logical expression of the structural imbalances within the Alliance, imbalances that, moreover, became even less acceptable to the Europeans as a result of changing East-West relations and, more specifically, the Soviet Union's changing attitude. Or as Arbatov, advisor of the Soviet leaders, said: "We are going to put you at a serious disadvantage: we are going to take away your image of the enemy."[23]

The Alliance was established in the late 1940s in response to what everyone clearly saw as the military threat from the Soviet Union. It was only logical, then, that the United States, the only country able to provide an adequate military counterbalance, should be very much the dominant member of the Alliance. Now that many felt the raison d'être of the Atlantic Alliance was beginning to fade and the East-West duel was gradually shifting from the military to the political and economic spheres, the Europeans found both the dominance of the Alliance and the United States' traditional dominance within the Alliance less easy to accept.

In the case of the United States this was because its view of possible political, economic, and human relations with the East differed significantly from the Western European view. If only because of its geographical position, the United States obviously has less interest in closer relations with Eastern Europe. This difference of view is certainly not new, but it used not to pose any problems since the opportunities for closer political, economic, and human contacts were fairly limited. In the case of the Atlantic Alliance it is because, as a military organization, it is unsuitable for and incapable of negotiation with its eastern neighbors on political and economic issues.

This dichotomy periodically brought the problem of burden sharing and withdrawal to the fore. In the early 1970s Senator Mansfield made it an annual habit to propose a reduction in the number of American troops abroad. Sometimes only fierce lobbying by the White House thwarted these proposals. The year 1981 saw the launching of a new series of proposals from congressmen, calling primarily for an increase in European defense efforts and for a decision whether or not to withdraw some American forces from Europe to be made conditional on the result. Most alarming of all was the 1984 Nunn Amendment, which would have meant the United States reducing its troops in Europe by ninety thousand men unless the European allies increased their conventional efforts and, among other things, raised their defense spending by 3 percent a year. The difference between the Nunn Amendment and the proposals put forward during the Mansfield era was that it was supported by congressmen of all political complexions and was, moreover, aimed specifically at Europe. President Reagan had great difficulty warding off the proposal.[24]

After 1984 no amendments of this kind were proposed, perhaps because it was realized that this tactic would accomplish nothing with the Europeans, or because it was feared that the new proposals would be approved by Congress, which was certainly not what senators like Sam Nunn really intended. Such figures as Henry Kissinger actively pleaded for the withdrawal of American units from Europe. In the aftermath of the American bombing of Libya, Secretary of Defense Richard Perle let it be known that the United States should consider such a step, clearly because of the criticism from Europe. The same tactic was also used, for example, in early 1988 to force the West Germans to drop their demand for direct negotiations on short-range weapons and to agree to the modernization of NATO's nuclear weapons in Europe.[25]

In 1987 and 1988, burden sharing and troop withdrawal were still high on NATO's agenda. However, a different approach to the two problems was now adopted. While the debate had once tended to be emotional and often followed quite specific transatlantic incidents, it was now far more objective. Furthermore, the atmosphere was no longer so anti-European as it had once been. Japan was now the main economic bogeyman. Opinion polls also indicated that the American public and political elite were very much in favor of defending Europe and of NATO. Not even a shift, feared by many, from the Atlantic to the Pacific could be deduced from these polls.[26] The withdrawal proposals that were formulated were far closer to what Jimmy Carter's National Security Adviser, Zbigniew Brzezinski, had suggested a few years earlier in an article entitled "The Future of Yalta":

America should, therefore, initiate a longer-term process to alter the nature of its military presence in Europe gradually, while making it clear to the Europeans that the change is not an act of anger or a threat (à la the Mansfield resolution) but rather the product of a deliberate strategy.... But, in any case, it should be accompanied by appropriate European efforts to assume greater responsibility for the defense of Europe not only on a purely national basis but through enhanced European defense coordination. The United States should particularly encourage efforts at increased Franco-German military cooperation and eventual integration.[27]

The former implicit "punitive measure" label was increasingly giving way to "positive withdrawal." In "Bipartisan Objectives for American Foreign Policy," Kissinger and Vance also referred to the logic, benefits and necessity of greater Western European independence in defense and security and associated this with the fresh vigor of the process of European integration:

Europe will inevitably play a greater part and have a larger voice in the defense of its own territory. This reflects the reality of Europe's strength. . . . Growing intra-European defense cooperation, possibly in the form of a European defense community, should be endorsed. With the European Community moving toward virtual economic integration by 1992, it is especially important that a revised structure for the defense of Western Europe also be in place by then.[28]

The American government and diplomatic service, once highly suspicious of closer Western European cooperation outside NATO, began to play a far more positive role. Richard Burt, U.S. ambassador to Bonn, was still intimating to the Western European allies in 1986, in connection with the SDI project, that they should not consult each other with a view to adopting a joint position.[29] When speaking of Western European cooperation two years later, his tone was completely different:

While we should oppose de-Americanization, further Europeanization of the Alliance makes sound strategic and political sense. The United States wholeheartedly supports the strengthening of the European pillar. We welcome the revitalization of the WEU and intensification of the Franco-German security relationship, as well as discussions within the framework of European Political Cooperation.[30]

From late 1987 President Reagan was also to be heard repeatedly emphasizing that "we in America welcome multilateral and bilateral defense cooperation among our European partners, of the sort that the Western European Union, and the Germans, and the French, and other governments have demonstrated within the overall framework of the Alliance."[31]

Traditionally, however, it was added that this cooperation must take place within the framework of the Alliance. Despite this, in January 1988, just after Franco-German cooperation had been formally stepped up, U.S. Secretary of Defense Carlucci described the Franco-German dialogue as a highly desirable means of strengthening the Alliance,[32] even though it did not form part of the Alliance framework (as the Americans were to discover when they, unlike Eastern European military observers, were not permitted to attend the Franco-German maneuvers). On a visit to Europe in February 1988 a number of leading U.S. senators in the field of foreign and defense policy similarly praised Franco-German military cooperation. When asked in Paris what they thought of Mrs. Thatcher's unfavorable attitude toward this cooperation, Senators Byrd and Nunn replied:

We told our British friends that our reaction was positive to the German and French brigade and to the Joint Commission. . . . We'd like to see the cooperation expanded between France and Great Britain. We were assured today that this development in no way competes with NATO. . . . We think this is a very, very positive development in terms of holding Europe together.[33]

Embarrassingly, the British thus again found themselves lagging behind developments. Franco-British contacts on closer nuclear cooperation had, after all, foundered on British stubbornness.

The more positive and constructive attitude in the debate on the withdrawal problem was also to be detected in the debate on burden sharing. Previously, the approach to this problem was almost entirely quantitative, with the United States enumerating a number of major differences between American and European defense efforts to show how scandalously little the European allies were doing for their own defense. In 1986 and 1987 the burden-sharing problem and the consequent threat of the withdrawal of some U.S. troops again sprang into prominence, and it was no coincidence that this came at a time of serious tension between the European Community and the United States over the subsidization of agriculture and the Airbus.[34] The American presidential election campaign in 1988 was seen by members of Congress like Pat Schroeder as the right moment too to draw attention to Europe's inadequate defense contribution.[35]

As a result of the continuing flow of disarmament proposals from the USSR, the general atmosphere of détente and the fact that American defense spending was also declining, the burden-sharing problem disappeared from the agenda. In the light of developments in the East the Western European members of NATO were unlikely, after all, to be persuaded to release more financial resources for defense. Official European, NATO, and even American reports had also pointed out that the European contribution to western defense was not so insignificant. European defense spending from 1970 to 1987 rose, for example, by 34 percent, the United States' by 15 percent. The Europeans account for 85 percent of expenditure on NATO defence; they provide 90 percent of the troops, 90 percent of the artillery, 80 percent of the tanks and combat aircraft and 65 percent of the most important naval ships. Unlike the United States, almost all the Western European countries also have conscription, which imposes a heavy social, economic, and political burden. A country like West Germany also has had to put up with more than 400,000 foreign troops, and with over 5,000 military exercises and 100,000 low-level flights by the various air forces on or over its territory each year.[36]

Washington thus appeared to be gradually coming to regard the European allies more as equal partners. The United States of America was slowly transferring part of its role in western defense to Europe. Indeed, this was true not only of defense but also increasingly of other areas, where this tendency has been under way longer. Thus Japan and Western Europe (and primarily West Germany) were expected to give the international economic and monetary system stronger support and so take some of the load off American shoulders. The allies were also expected to do more to ease the developing countries' debt problems. That this can take amusing and unexpected turns was evident, for example, from an article indicating how the United States could be relieved of its economic problems:

Our allies should finance most of the new capital requirements of the principal third world debtors through major contributions to the capital of the World Bank. This could significantly improve our trade balance by enabling these countries to import U.S.-made goods in much larger quantities.[37]

The growing awareness within the Alliance that the Europeans must play a larger role in ensuring their own security and defense was also apparent from a document drawn up by an hoc committee of the North Atlantic Assembly in April 1988.[38] The Ad Hoc Committee on NATO in the 1990s consisted of fourteen representatives from the various NATO countries and was chaired by U.S. Senator Roth. The United States was also represented by Sam Nunn, chairman of the U.S. Senate Defense Committee. The ad hoc committee proposed major changes to allow the Alliance to adjust to the fundamental shifts in the international environment and in relations among the allies. It advocated, for example, various practical measures to enable the European members of the Alliance to cooperate more closely in their defense. The Western European allies should draw up an annual "European security report," a proposal with which the ad hoc committee also officially recognized the value of a separate European analysis; the chiefs of staff of the Western European NATO countries should meet at regular intervals; closer cooperation between the French and Spanish armed forces (neither integrated into the military command) and the forces of the other member countries should be encouraged and facilitated, as should the sharing of tasks among the member countries; and efforts to create a Europe-wide defense market should be stepped up.

Even more important was the proposal for the establishment of a "European division": "Building on the concept of the Franco-German brigade now being organized, other European countries should be invited to contribute military units to such a division. Creating a European division could enhance the potential for more extensive joint European forces in the future."

On the question of multilateral cooperation, the report says that the Western European Union

is not the exclusive arena in which European defence cooperation can be promoted. The studies, collaboration, and consultation within the framework of the European Economic Community, the Independent European Programme Group (IEPG), and the Eurogroup in NATO also make important contributions. . . . The European allies should initiate a study of institutional changes that the establishment of a real European pillar in the Alliance would imply, and especially the place and role that the Western European Union and the European Economic Community would have in building this pillar. The creation of a European pillar eventually requires rationalizing the efforts and location of the numerous European institutions.

It is noticeable, in other words, that while the European Parliament had to fight tooth and nail before being allowed to discuss security and defense aspects within the framework of the European Community (and still meets with resistance from the Council and national governments), an Alliance institution has made proposals "for the short term" that go further than what many Europeans consider possible even in the long term.

The North Atlantic Assembly's report also contained a number of fascinating proposals in the chapter on NATO's strategic concept. Although it reiterated and confirmed most of the classical elements of the NATO strategy, it also included a few elements that were relatively new to the Alliance and partly originated from West Germany and initially even from the SPD. The report proposes "no early first use" as the guideline for NATO's nuclear strategy and indicates that ultimately, when the Soviet Union's ability to attack Western Europe has been substantially reduced, it might be possible to consider a security system in Europe that is far less dependent on nuclear weapons, as part of a less-threatening "common security relationship between NATO and the Warsaw Pact countries." The report says that the various ideas put forward by "alternative" or "defensive defense" experts in Western Europe should be closely studied. The Ad Hoc Committee on NATO in the 1990s concludes with the view that the Alliance position on Eastern Europe could in principle be modeled on the Federal Republic's *Deutschlandpolitik*.

In 1987 and 1988 there were various signs that the United States would be withdrawing some of its troops from Europe in the future and that the Western Europeans would be allotted a larger role in ensuring their own defense, in exchange for which the United States was prepared to support the process of European integration and to accept a greater degree of European independence. The Western Europeans were therefore able to prepare for these tendencies and take them as a basis in the development of a European security system. When, however, the forty-five-year-old European geostrategic landscape completely collapsed in late 1989 and early 1990, it became clear how difficult it was in the final analysis to draw all the logical conclusions from these tendencies.

Despite the developments that indicated a gradual change of approach to NATO, it would prove very difficult to accept fundamental changes in the western security system. After forty-five years of NATO the Alliance was considered a natural phenomenon, a normal feature that is simply part of Europe. This is to forget that the Alliance did not just arrive out of the blue: It came into being only a few years after the Second World War, when the Soviet threat was felt to be extremely serious. What is also forgotten in this context is that President Truman had great difficulty overcoming

the resistance of part of his own administration and of the U.S. Congress
to the Atlantic Alliance and to its transformation into a military organization, and that he succeeded only by taking one step at a time and presenting
the conflict situations in Greece, Czechoslovakia, Berlin, and Korea as possible forerunners of an all-out Soviet attack on Western Europe. What is
overlooked is that George Kennan, regarded as the architect of the American
containment policy, had above all emphasized the nonmilitary aspects of
the communist threat and had therefore opposed the concept of the Atlantic
Alliance and NATO. He felt that after the war the United States should
also have applied the principle underlying the Marshall Plan to Western
European defense. He called for a "dumbbell" concept, with separate Western European and North American entities: The Western Europeans would
establish their own defense organization in which the Americans would not
participate, but which would be given a unilateral political and military
guarantee by the Americans and, if necessary, might also receive American
military support.[39]

Over forty years later Kennan's concept of European security and transatlantic relations seems to have a chance of being implemented. But the
labor pains will be severe.

NOTES

1. David P. Calleo, *Beyond American Hegemony: The Future of the Western Alliance*
(New York: Basic Books, 1987), pp. 3, 11.

2. Ronald Brownstein, "Losing Its Grip," *National Journal*, 2 June 1988, p. 308.

3. Ibid., p. 311.

4. Felix Rohatyn, "Restoring American Independence," *The New York Review
of Books*, 18 February 1988, pp. 8–9.

5. Charles William Maynes, "Lost Opportunities," *Foreign Affairs*, 64(3)1986,
p. 418.

6. Molly Moore, "Carlucci Inherits a Pentagon Facing Bleakest Months of the
Reagan Era," *Washington Post*, 6 November 1987, p. A14.

7. Ibid.; François Heisbourg, "Europe/Etats-Unis: le couplage stratégique menacé," *Politique Etrangère*, 52(1)1987, pp. 113–16.

8. John H. Cushman, "Carlucci Hints Budget Plan Portends Shrinking Military," *New York Times*, 13 November 1987, p. A16.

9. Paul Kennedy, "Le déclin (relatif) de l'Amérique," *Politique Etrangère*,
52(4)1987, p. 865.

10. Jan Bohets, "Veertig jaar na het Marshall-Plan. Amerikaans leiderschap, toen
en nu," *De Standaard*, 17 November 1987.

11. Calleo, *Beyond American Hegemony*, pp. 11, 216–18.

12. Paul Kennedy, *The Rise and Fall of the Great Powers, Economic Change and
Military Conflict from 1500–2000* (London: Unwin Hyman, 1988).

13. Henry Kissinger and Cyrus Vance, "Bipartisan objectives for American Foreign Policy," *Foreign Affairs*, 66(5)1988, p. 920.

14. Yves Laudy, "A quoi servent les alliés?" *Libre Belgique*, 18 April 1988; "Allies Divided by Terror," *International Herald Tribune*, 18 April 1986.

15. Charles Krauthammer, "U.S. Allies' Passivity Underscores NATO Rift," *International Herald Tribune*, 29 April 1986.

16. G. T. Allison and A. Carnasale, "Europeans: Contrary Today, Contrary Tomorrow," *International Herald Tribune*, 27 February 1986.

17. E. Marcuse, "Adelman aux Européens: à vous de jouer, sinon . . . ," *Le Vif/ L'Express*, 13–19 February 1987, p. 88.

18. See, for example, Jane Sharp, "After Reykjavik: Arms Control and the Allies," *International Affairs*, 63(2)1987, pp. 340–43.

19. Michael Mandelbaum, "The Luck of the President," *Foreign Affairs*, 64(3)1986, p. 405.

20. Joseph Fitchett, "Europe sees lesson in INF diplomacy," *International Herald Tribune*, 5 February 1988.

21. P. Geyelin, "The French had cause to demur," *International Herald Tribune*, 12 April 1986.

22. A. Krause, "An interview with Mitterrand, Executive Powers in Reserve," *International Herald Tribune*, 28 May 1986.

23. P. Bocev, "Une autre diplomatie . . . ," *Le Figaro*, 30 June 1988.

24. Phil Williams, "The Nunn Amendment, Burden-Sharing and US Troops in Europe," *Survival*, January-February 1985, pp. 2–6.

25. K. Feldmeyer, "Vor Abkopplung ist zu warnen," *Frankfurter Allgemeine Zeitung*, 2 June 1986.

26. John E. Rielly, "America's State of Mind," *Foreign Policy*, no. 66, Spring 1987, pp. 45–50.

27. Zbigniew Brzezinski, "The Future of Yalta," *Foreign Affairs*, 63(2)1984/85, p. 299.

28. Kissinger and Vance, "Bipartisan objectives," pp. 908–9.

29. C.-G. Fricaud-Chagnaud, "Comment réarticuler sécurité européenne et puissance américaine," *Le Monde Diplomatique*, February 1988, p. 18.

30. Richard R. Burt, "Nuclear deterrence has served us well for 40 years," *USIS Official Text*, 14 April 1988, p. 5.

31. "U.S., NATO destiny remain linked, Reagan says," *USIS Official Text*, 23 February 1988, p. 4.

32. "Le sécretaire américaine à la défense a interrogé M. Mitterrand sur ses idées en matière de dissuasion nucléaire," *Le Monde*, 13 January 1988.

33. "Byrd says INF treaty will strengthen Alliance," Byrd news conference on 10 February 1988, *USIS Official Facts*, 12 February 1988, pp. 2–3.

34. Heisbourg, "Europe/Etats-Unis: le couplage stratégique menaée," pp. 112–13.

35. Pat Schroeder, "The allies are freeloading," *International Herald Tribune*, 3 May 1988.

36. Bernard W. Rogers, *U.S. Military Strategy in the U.S. European Command Area, and Readiness of U.S. European Command Forces, Critical Deficiencies in Capabilities, Resource Program Priorities*, U.S. Senate Armed Services Committee, 25 March 1987, pp. 13–15; *Enhancing Alliance Collective Security: Shared Roles, Risks, and Responsibilities in the Alliance. A Report by NATO's Defence Planning Committee*, December 1988, 79 pp.; *Threat Assessment: Report submitted on behalf of the Committee*

on *Defence Questions and Armaments* by Mr. Stokes, Rapporteur, Assembly of Western European Union, 33d Ordinary Session, 2 November 1987, Doc. 1115, p. 47.

37. Rohatyn, "Restoring American Independence," pp. 9–10.

38. *NATO in the 1990s*, North Atlantic Alliance, Committee on NATO in the 1990s, April 1988.

39. David P. Calleo, "Early American Views of NATO: Then and Now," in Lawrence Freedman, ed., *The Troubled Alliance: Atlantic Relations in the 1980's* (London: Heinemann, 1983), pp. 7–12; Stephen Ambrose, *Rise to Globalism* (London: Penguin Books, 1989), pp. 78–131; George Kennan, *Memoirs 1925–1950* (New York: Pantheon Books, 1967), pp. 406–7.

6

French Independence in Doubt

The changes that occurred in West German thinking on security, in NATO's military-strategic options, and in the American attitude toward the security of Europe forced the French to abandon some of their illusions about their security situation and gradually to adjust their policy. While the national consensus on total French independence in the military sphere had been overpowering in the 1970s and had seemed incompatible with military cooperation with and support for other Western European countries, it was increasingly realized in the first half of the 1980s that France must make a greater commitment to the defense of Europe and especially West Germany—without, of course, French independence being affected. This naturally raised the question of how to reconcile the two elements, French independence and practical Western European military solidarity and cooperation.

This development in French thinking on security during the 1980s occurred in two stages, two periods of gradual change that largely coincided with the process of coming to terms with the consequences, first, of NATO's 1979 dual-track decision to deploy INF weapons in Europe and, second, of the decision taken in 1986/87 to withdraw these weapons. Paradoxically, the developments surrounding the dual-track decision taken by NATO in 1979 gave rise to a very profound change in the French attitude toward Western European security, even though France, not being integrated into NATO's military structure, was not officially party to this decision, and the then French president, Giscard d'Estaing, had said at the time that "the dual-track decision is no concern of France."[1] A few years later, however, it was found that this official neutrality ("neither approval nor disapproval"), which was in keeping with the principles outlined by Charles de Gaulle, could not be maintained.

When in March 1966 de Gaulle decided to leave NATO's integrated military structure, he felt that only an independent France with its own nuclear weapons could ensure national security. As a result of the change in the nuclear-strategic relationship between the United States and the USSR, and especially the Soviet Union's ability to threaten the United States with nuclear weapons, the American security commitment was, in de Gaulle's opinion, no longer adequate. An American president would not, after all, risk American cities to protect Western European cities. Furthermore, the interests of the United States and Western Europe (and especially France) were not identical, as the crises in Algeria, Suez, Berlin, and Cuba had shown. The decisive factor perhaps was that France had never been treated as an equal partner by the United States and Britain, as de Gaulle was to experience at his first official meeting with the American NATO general Norstad after his return to power in 1958. When General de Gaulle asked Norstad how many American nuclear warheads there were on French soil and where they were located, Norstad replied that he was regrettably not allowed to answer the question, to which de Gaulle retorted: "Well, Mon Général, that is the last time, and mark it well, that a French leader will ever hear such an answer."[2]

The French leader did not, however, see the regained *indépendance nationale* as in any way changing France's obligations under the NATO Treaty. He made it absolutely clear that, like the other signatories of the NATO Treaty, France would assist West Germany in the event of an attack from the East. This would certainly be true of West Berlin, where France was one of the four governing powers. In 1966 the French also decided to keep their troops in West Germany, though close to the French border. France's independent position implied, however, that in a crisis the French president would himself decide where, how, and when the French would help to defend West Germany, which also meant that, bearing French national interests in mind, he could decide both to withdraw French troops from West Germany and to order them to take unilateral military action on West German soil to check an advancing enemy. This unpredictable attitude certainly did not make things easy for the NATO commanders.[3]

The French decision to leave NATO's integrated military structure had the disadvantage for NATO that the troops of the first French army no longer appeared in the operational plans of the Alliance and that the NATO tactical nuclear weapons in the hands of the French forces were now replaced with weapons from France's own nuclear arsenal. France's withdrawal from the NATO structure also obliged NATO to withdraw from France. Not only did all the foreign troops stationed in France and at NATO's headquarters in Paris have to find a new location, but also in the logistical sphere NATO was no longer able to use the airfields, ports, and supply depots in

France.[4] The strategic depth that NATO would need in the defense of West Germany (and Western Europe) was partly lost, although (secret) agreements were reached by France, West Germany, and NATO permitting some facilities to be used in certain circumstances, provided that the French political authorities gave their approval when the time came.

The implementation of de Gaulle's decision in 1967 was accompanied by the signing of the Ailleret-Lemnitzer Accord concerning continued cooperation between France and NATO. This accord was later supplemented and refined by other, more comprehensive agreements, such as the Valentin-Ferber Accord of 1974. These agreements govern the manner and circumstances in which NATO and French armed forces may be placed under the "operational control" (not, therefore, the "operational command") of NATO's commanders for specific missions and for a specific period. Since 1967 France has also been represented in all NATO's major military bodies through bilateral liaison missions. It is similarly involved in a few of NATO's specialized bodies, and above all extremely close cooperation has developed between the air forces of France and the other NATO countries.[5]

Ironically, France's decision also had implications that conflicted with its own interests: The Alliance became more dependent on American leadership than ever; the Federal Republic's status in the Alliance grew appreciably; the political and structural obstacles to the development of closer European defense cooperation assumed unprecedented proportions; and French influence not only on developments in the western military camp but also on East-West relations became even weaker.[6]

President de Gaulle was, however, able to adopt this position because France had its own national nuclear capability, it was favorably located geographically, and, moreover, the basic external requirements for an independent French security policy were satisfied: the American military presence in Europe and especially West Germany; the Federal Republic's political, economic, and military integration into the western camp through the European Community and NATO; and the impossibility of German reunification.[7] To its considerable relief, France was thus able to withdraw to the role of indirectly involved, outside observer of the German theater, where it was left to the Germans, other Western Europeans, and the Americans to prepare for a possible performance. As Raymond Aron put it, "For the first time in many years we are in the second rather than the front line."[8] Having been involved in a destructive military confrontation with their eastern neighbor in 1870, 1914, and 1940, the French must indeed have seen this new situation as a great relief and comfort.

Under Presidents de Gaulle, Pompidou, and Giscard d'Estaing France succeeded without much difficulty in combining its quasi-independent security policy and its commitment to help West Germany with its defense only at a time of crisis *and* if it so decided. Even President Giscard d'Estaing, who had very close and friendly relations with Federal Chancellor Schmidt, with whom he formed the driving force for the further economic and monetary development of the European Community, kept largely to the line adopted by his predecessors where security was concerned. During his seven years in office Giscard d'Estaing discreetly ensured that the military relationship with France's allies was strengthened and that the plans for French forces to fight alongside the allies were further elaborated. The decision to increase conventional forces and various (not very specific) statements by the French president also indicated greater willingness to help defend West German territory from the beginning of a crisis. President Giscard d'Estaing even referred to a possible change from a "national sanctuary" protected by nuclear weapons to an "enlarged sanctuary," which would also encompass other European territory, and his prime minister, Jacques Chirac, took the same line.[9] This tendency was, however, counteracted by the 1977–1982 program law, which provided for a reduction in the number of French troops in West Germany and for the redeployment of troops in France, away from the border with Germany. Nor was there any increase in military cooperation projects or agreements.[10]

At the beginning of his presidency François Mitterrand did not see European integration and Franco-German cooperation at either political and economic or military levels as having any real priority.[11] The effects of NATO's 1979 dual-track decision, however, were soon to force him to play an active part in the security debate. A few of the basic requirements for French military autonomy seemed, after all, threatened by developments connected with the INF debate. The heated debate in West Germany in the early 1980s on the deployment of American medium-range weapons led to French fears that "neutralist" tendencies might gain the upper hand in the Federal Republic. Many West Germans were seen to have almost "Gaullist" doubts about American military protection and, just as France had done fifteen years earlier, to be advocating an alternative security policy more appropriate to their own national interests.

It was also noted that the Federal Republic was increasingly putting its national interests first in the European Community. With the persistent crises in the Community, West German disappointment in the process of European integration had grown significantly. If this led to a passive or negative attitude toward European integration, the consequences might be very unfavorable for the Community and thus for France. France's security, status, and influence do not depend, after all, only on its military power; France is equally dependent on the political and economic power that it largely derives from a Community in which West Germany is actively involved. It therefore seemed necessary to do something to counteract the growing West German doubts about the purpose and advantage of pouring yet more energy and especially money into European integration and the Community.

Further West German alienation from the process of European integration would lend even more strength to the proposals for an alternative security policy, one aim of which, as the French with their nationalist tradition and their idolization of *la nation* understood only too well, would be the establishment of better relations with East Germany. The traditional fear of German reunification, of West Germany going a separate way, of a new Rapallo, in short of *les incertitudes allemandes*, had resurfaced in France. The rise of the West German peace movement was, moreover, seen as a sign of weakness in the face of Soviet threats and blackmail, of which the French were very well aware. They therefore regarded West German pacifism as a *mouvement de peur*, which was undermining West Germany's integration into the western camp. This attitude also seemed to be taking a hold on the Federal government, as had become clear not only under Chancellor Schmidt, who had, for example, taken a very lethargic view of the Polish crisis in 1982, but also under Chancellor Kohl, who actually managed, at a time of icy East-West relations, to speak of a community of responsibility consisting of the two Germanys. As Raymond Aron remarked, it seemed that for the first time the French were afraid not of German strength but of German weakness.[12]

Nor did the French complain, as they had in the past, about excessive West German dependence on the United States, and in fact they viewed with grave suspicion the anti-American slogans used by sections of the West German peace movement, the Greens, and some Social Democrats. In French minds, after all, they cast doubt not only on the Federal Republic's place in the western camp and the impossibility of German reunification, but also on the third basic external requirement for French military independence: American presence in the Federal Republic.

The threat to the three basic external requirements for the French military strategy was not the only factor to force France to take greater account of its Western European neighbors and particularly West Germany. The French became increasingly aware that their semi-independent position was threatened by the rapid advance of technology. If an independent military apparatus is to remain credible, new high-tech weapons systems need to be constantly developed. The development of such new weapons systems as the emerging technologies (ET) and intelligent weapons, of antisatellite weapons (ASAT), and space systems and weapons as a result of American and Soviet research efforts, and of other sophisticated defense systems (ABMs, etc.) was, however, beyond French means. Nor was France itself capable of developing the space program that Paris considered necessary. Its inability to keep pace with technological developments on its own was evident from its general dependence on the intelligence obtained by the American AWACS (Airborne Warning and Control Systems) and satellites for military information on the adversary's potential and activities. It did not, for example, have the resources for the immediate detection of the launching of an enemy missile.[13]

It was also feared that future technological developments would give the Soviet Union and United States new defense capabilities to which France would have no adequate response and which might neutralize the deterrent capabilities of the smaller nuclear powers, like France and Britain. Furthermore, technological advances were already changing the strategy of both East and West, with growing emphasis being placed on conventional and space aspects (at the expense of the nuclear component). These were, however, the two components in which France was weakest and that it was virtually incapable of developing solely with national resources.[14]

This brings us to another and also the most basic factor that led Paris to conclude that it had to stop regarding the European security debate as none of its concern. The growing doubts about the United States' security commitment to the defense of West Germany and Western Europe (and thus of France), the technological advances and the evolution in the military strategies of East and West, also revealed the limitations and inherent inconsistencies of the French military strategy.

The possibility of deciding independently whether or not to take part in an armed conflict in Europe in which they are not initially involved is, according to the French, assured by the *force de frappe*, France's national nuclear capability, which may be used only to defend French territory or the "national sanctuary." Just as Paris felt that the United States' nuclear capability could not be used to defend Western Europe (from which Paris therefore drew its own conclusions), French nuclear weapons could not be placed at the service of other Western European countries. The French president's power to take decisions independently might mean that he would in fact decide to assist the western allies directly. French conventional forces were, however, primarily intended for an intense conflict of limited scale and short duration, as the beginning of the *manoeuvre nationale de dissuasion*.

The heavy emphasis thus placed on nuclear deterrence and the *idée de la non-guerre* mean that only limited resources are available to France's conventional forces to help defend West Germany and the other Western European countries efficiently or to act as an effective reserve force. French conventional forces are not structurally suited or well enough equipped to perform a global task of this kind for a protracted period. They cannot be deployed very quickly, and their range is not very extensive. In practice, France would therefore have difficulty in exercising the option of assisting its allies.[15]

The possibility of an independent French decision also means, however, that France has the option of not engaging in a war (*l'option de non-belligérence*). France's own nuclear deterrent would enable its president to keep his country out of the hostilities and possibly to intervene only if the enemy's forces seemed likely to break through NATO's defenses and so pose a direct threat to French territory. The French foresee, in other words, the possibility of *une première bataille* or *bataille à l'avant* (a first battle or battle at the front) fought in West Germany and other Central European countries by NATO, with the French involved only marginally or not at all, and, in the event of the allies failing, a *deuxième bataille* or *bataille de France* (a second battle or battle of France).

Even then, however, the French strategy does not predict a global, long-term conflict. Nor, given the dominance of the nuclear component in French strategic thinking, are French conventional forces prepared for such a conflict. The French strategy is based, after all, not on defense against an attack, but on deterrence and thus the prevention of an attack. Or as former Defense Minister Hernu put it succinctly: "There should be no battle because our defense posture is based on deterrence." In a conventional conflict the enormous superiority of the East would in any case force France to surrender. Consequently, Paris gears the whole of the country's defense to nuclear deterrence. A large conventional force is therefore unnecessary, undesirable, and, moreover, far too expensive. The French *manoeuvre nationale de dissuasion* entails the brief and massive use of conventional forces and the launching of tactical nuclear weapons as a final warning to the enemy. This warning, limited in duration and geographical area, must inflict major losses on the enemy to leave no doubt that France is serious and that further threats or an invasion of French territory will automatically result in the launching of French strategic weapons, which are capable of destroying population centers in the USSR itself.

However, France says that, even though it is not part of NATO's integrated military structure and retains the option of taking an autonomous decision, it feels duty-bound to meet its NATO and Western European Union (WEU) obligations to give military assistance to the other member countries and certainly West Germany if they are attacked. The French president thus retains the option of helping the allies from the very beginning of a conflict. Under bilateral agreements with NATO the necessary arrangements have been made to put this option into effect. As the French nuclear strategy requires that the decision on the use of the armed forces remain a completely autonomous French decision, French solidarity with the western allies is, however, restricted in two ways. First, it cannot be assumed that France will automatically become involved in the event of a crisis. Second, France cannot participate in forward defense on the German-German border since Paris must have its limited conventional forces available in case it wants to carry out a *manoeuvre nationale de dissuasion*, as described above.

Paris has never been able to explain how France would reconcile the *option de non-belligérence* and solidarity with the allies in practice. It has, however, sought refuge in the argument that this uncertainty heightens the deterrent effect (although it also creates options for adversaries since they can speculate on the lack of immediate solidarity among the western allies). Nor was Paris compelled to answer this question since the required western solidarity was already assured by the other NATO partners and above all by the United States' nuclear and conventional involvement.[16]

The uncertainty over future American involvement in the defense of West Germany, the diminishing role of nuclear weapons, and the growing importance of the conventional aspect in NATO's and the Warsaw Pact's strategies (and, therefore, of the Warsaw Pact's conventional superiority) revealed the inconsistencies and limitations of the French strategy more clearly than ever and also made them increasingly unacceptable.

The French strategy was such that the French armed forces were least likely to be deployed in support of the Western European allies at a time when such intervention would be most essential, at the beginning of an attack from the East or when such additional support is needed to overcome an unfavorable situation on the battlefield. The French strategy thus increased the chance of NATO being defeated and the forward defense failing. This would also bring forward the time when, and also make it more likely that, the French would have to resort to their *manoeuvre nationale de dissuasion*, and the French strategy and national deterrence would thus be put to the practical test.[17]

In 1980 François Mitterrand, then leader of the opposition, remarked: "Can you imagine a large country like the Soviet Union . . . engaging in a conflict only to withdraw in confusion forty-eight hours later?" This thought was intended as a criticism of NATO's flexible response strategy, but it applied equally to France's own strategy and its threat to use tactical nuclear weapons as a warning. The use of strategic weapons would simply rule out any possibility of survival. The launching of the French strategic weapons might, after all, lead to the death of around fifty million people in the Soviet Union, or about a sixth of its population.[18] However, the Soviets can do the same to France, the difference being that the whole of the French population would then cease to exist. The question is therefore whether at that moment self-deterrence would not be greater than deterrence of the enemy.[19]

Doubts about a decision by the French president to use nuclear weapons grew further when technological advances gave the potential enemy more and more options for attacking France with conventional weapons of all types and strengths. Many of these options would, however, in no way justify a decision by the French president to launch a nuclear counterattack, although he would not always have appropriate conventional options in such a situation.[20]

The French also became increasingly aware that, despite all the professions of faith in the *sanctuaire national* and the independent nuclear deterrent, the distance between the Federal Republic's eastern frontier and France is less than three hundred kilometers and, given the present military–technological possibilities, the concept of *bataille successive* is therefore more an illusion than a genuine option. This gave rise to serious doubts about what Pierre

Lellouche described as the quasi-mystical clichés used by the French leaders to express their faith in nuclear weapons. President Mitterrand's statement during the television program *L'Heure de la Vérité* in November 1983 was just one example of this: "The kingpin of the strategy of deterrence in France is the head of state, me: everything depends on what he decides. Everything else is immaterial." The above-mentioned expression of former minister Hernu's belief in the infallibility of the nuclear deterrent can also be counted among these clichés. It did not therefore seem inappropriate for Pierre Lellouche to ask: "Are we talking about strategy or religion?"[21] After all, even if the French *dissuasion nationale* did succeed in stopping a Warsaw Pact invasion on France's eastern border, what would be left of French national sovereignty and grandeur in a hostile environment?[22]

NOTES

1. Bruno Racine, "La France et les FNI," *Politique Etrangère*, 53(1)1988, p. 75.

2. Jim Hoagland, "De Gaulle: Americans too, should reassess him," *International Herald Tribune*, 22 September 1988.

3. Michael M. Harrison, *The Reluctant Ally: France and Atlantic Security* (London: Johns Hopkins University Press, 1981), pp. 156–58.

4. D. Middleton, "Why NATO, its fingers crossed, counts on the French," *International Herald Tribune*, 13 June 1986.

5. Siegfried Thielbeer, "Paris, die NATO und die Vorneverteidigung," *Frankfurter Allgemeine Zeitung*, 29 December 1987, p. 5.

6. Stanley R. Sloan, *NATO's Future: Toward a New Transatlantic Bargain* (Washington, D.C.: National Defense University, 1985), p. 38.

7. Ingo Kolboom, "La politique de sécurité de la France: un point de vue allemand," in Karl Kaiser and Pierre Lellouche, eds., *Le couple franco-allemand et la défense de l'Europe* (Paris: IFRI, 1986), p. 71.

8. Quoted in Kolboom, "La politique de sécurité de la France," p. 71.

9. Nicole Gnesotto, "Le dialogue franco-allemand depuis 1954: patience et longueur de temps . . . ," in Kaiser and Lellouche, eds., *Le couple franco-allemand*, pp. 22–23.

10. Harrison, *The Reluctant Ally*, pp. 183–84, 193–200.

11. A. W. de Porte, "France's New Opportunism," *Foreign Affairs*, 63(1)1984, pp. 153–55; Kolboom, "La politique de sécurité de la France," p. 77.

12. Kolbloom, "La politique de sécurité de la France," pp. 76–80.

13. David S. Yost, "France's Deterrent Posture and Security in Europe. Part 2: Strategy & Arms Control Implications," *Adelphi Papers*, no. 195, 1984/85, pp. 32–33; Raymond Tourrain, *De la défense de la France à la défense de l'Europe* (Besançon: Cripes, 1987), pp. 111–13, 212.

14. Jolyon Howorth, "Resources and Strategic Choices: French Defence Policy at the Crossroads," *The World Today*, 42(5)1986, p. 79.

15. Franz-Joseph Schulze, "La nécessité d'une réaction de défense immédiate et commune," in Kaiser and Lellouche, eds., *Le couple franco-allemand*, p. 164; Pierre Lellouche, *L'avenir de la guerre* (Paris: Mazarine, 1985), p. 277; David S. Yost,

"France's Deterrent Posture and Security in Europe. Part 1: Capabilities and Doctrines," *Adelphi Papers*, no. 194, 1984/85, pp. 12–14; Yost, "France's Deterrent Posture and Security in Europe. Part 2," pp. 26–27.

16. Yost, "France's Deterrent Posture and Security in Europe. Part I," pp. 6–7, 10–12, 51–53, 59–60; and "Part 2," pp. 11—12, 21; Lellouche, *L'avenir de la guerre*, pp. 256, 265–70; Thierry de Montbrial, "Sur la politique de sécurité de la France," *Commentaire*, 40(10)1987/88, p. 647.

17. Yost, "France's Deterrent Posture and Security in Europe. Part 2," pp. 11–12, 21.

18. *Mémento Défense-Désarmement 1988* (Brussels: GRIP, 1988), p. 94.

19. Yost, "France's Deterrent Posture and Security in Europe. Part 2," pp. 22–24.

20. Lellouche, *L'avenir de la guerre*, pp. 258–59.

21. Ibid.

22. Yost, "France's Deterrent Posture and Security in Europe. Part 2," pp. 24–25.

7

Together, yet Alone

The doubts about the three basic external requirements for French defense, the problems raised by technological development, and the weaknesses of the French military strategy they revealed prompted France to begin making adjustments to certain aspects of its security policy, which indicated a move toward greater solidarity with the western allies. Paris began to realize that both defending France and maintaining its sovereignty and military independence meant taking greater account of the defense and security interests of, above all, West Germany and also cooperating more closely with the Western European partners. This led to unilateral military measures designed to increase the possibility of French help in the defense of the allies, political steps in support of the Atlantic Alliance, and more bilateral cooperation with West Germany and multilateral cooperation with the various Western European countries.

The reorganization of the French army in 1983 resulted in the transfer of the Third Army Corps to Lille near France's northern border with Belgium. Given the weakness of the Belgian and Dutch army corps in the northern part of the Federal Republic, the vulnerability of the north-south line of communication in the Benelux countries and West Germany, and the consequent need for reserves for NATO's NORTHAG (Northern Army Group), this was seen as a remarkable move, principally because France had previously only deployed its troops in readiness for a possible military intervention in the southern part of the Federal Republic.

The reorganization of the army also led to the creation of a rapid deployment force, the *Force d'Action Rapide* (FAR). This special conventional unit is required to be capable of reacting very quickly in a conflict on French soil, elsewhere in Europe, and in the rest of the world. The establishment of the FAR would enable France to fight alongside the allies sooner and further inside West German territory. The FAR was also seen as a practical response to changes in the Soviet strategy, in which growing emphasis was being placed on "operational maneuver groups."

A third important decision was to regroup the French tactical Pluton nuclear weapons (tactical weapons that were renamed prestrategic weapons) under a single command, separate from the French conventional forces. This would make it easier for the conventional forces to be used in West Germany if they were needed. The former direct link between conventional forces and tactical weapons had been a serious obstacle to possible French intervention in a conflict in the Federal Republic. It was also decided to increase the range of the Hadès missiles (tactical nuclear weapons intended to replace the Plutons in 1992) to more than 350 km. To the French this appeared at first sight to have the political advantage that, unlike the Plutons, their tactical nuclear weapons would no longer be targeted on West Germany but on Eastern Europe.[1]

The fear of a possible *dérive allemande* and of a further crumbling of transatlantic cohesion, both of which were further to expose the weaknesses of the French security policy, similarly prompted François Mitterrand to begin actively supporting NATO's 1979 deployment decision, which meant France abandoning its position of uncommitted observer. After making several favorable references to NATO's dual-track decision in 1981, he became involved in the West German missile debate in January 1983. In a speech to the *Bundestag* two months before the West German elections, he put in a very strong plea for the deployment of the American medium-range weapons and warned of the dangers of decoupling the European and American continents.[2] The "least Atlantic-oriented" member of the Alliance could hardly have done more to support and justify what was, in the final analysis, a truly Atlantic decision. For Chancellor Kohl Mitterrand's address was therefore a more than necessary electoral boost (for elections that he was indeed to win).

To François Mitterrand's West German political counterparts, the Social Democrats, who had made opposition to the deployment of INF weapons their key issue, this speech seemed, on the other hand, like a stab in the back. They also had difficulty in coming to terms with a French socialist president who advocated that West Germany be kept firmly under American hegemonic protection, when the French themselves always refused to submit to American domination and, moreover, constantly accused the West Germans of taking too Atlantic or too pro–American a line.[3] They clearly could not appreciate that their French political colleagues should want to perpetuate West German dependence so that they could preserve their own independence.

François Mitterrand saw his speech in West Germany and his active support for the deployment particularly of the Pershing II missiles (which could

reach the Soviet Union itself) as absolutely essential in view of his apprehension at the decline of *l'esprit de résistance* in Western Europe.[4] According
to the French, the Soviet Union, already superior to Europe in nuclear
terms, had in the SS-20 a military instrument intended primarily to achieve
a political goal: the decoupling of the two sides of the Atlantic Ocean. A
bold reaction in the shape of the implementation of the NATO dual-track
decision was needed, similarly for political reasons, to reaffirm the cohesion
of the Alliance and, after a period of vacillating American participation in
European defense, to involve the United States more deeply, symbolically
at least, in Europe once again. For France itself the SS-20 missiles, and the
resulting endorsement of the importance of its own nuclear capability, had
helped to ensure that for the first time there was a virtual consensus in
France, the exception being the communist party, on its deterrent capability,
the socialists having abandoned their opposition in the late 1970s.[5]

Besides the support for the NATO dual-track decision, another symbolically significant event revealed the importance that France attached to
underpinning the crumbling Atlantic foundations: In 1983 the North Atlantic Council held its first meeting in Paris since France's withdrawal from
the integrated military structure of the Alliance. François Mitterrand also
tried to curb the West German drift to the East and the decline in western
cohesion by strengthening Western European military relations through the
Western European Union and especially through the bilateral military relations between Paris and Bonn. It was logical for France to turn first to
Bonn since the Federal Republic, financially and economically the strongest
country in Western Europe, could also provide a solution for the military,
space, and other high-tech projects that were becoming too expensive for
France. Only by sharing the cost and effort involved in the research on and
development and production of new systems and projects with other countries could France avoid structural disarmament.[6]

By showing Bonn that it attached more importance to West German
security and wanted to step up cooperation, Paris also tried to counteract
the decline in West German enthusiasm for the process of Western European
integration as a whole. In this way it wanted to demonstrate that it would
be useful for West Germany to improve its relations with its western
neighbor.

In February 1982 François Mitterrand and Helmut Schmidt decided that,
as well as intensifying their bilateral consultations on foreign policy, the
two countries should have an "in-depth exchange of views" on security
problems. In October 1982, barely three days after becoming Federal chancellor, Helmut Kohl went to Paris for further discussions on this declaration
of intent. Three months later the growing Franco-German dialogue was
institutionalized with the reaffirmation of the 1963 Franco-German Elysée
Treaty. The French and German foreign and defense ministers would hence-
forth have discussions before each Franco-German summit meeting; the

Franco-German Commission established in October and comprising military and civil officials of the four ministries would meet four times a year; and the commission would set up three working groups for military cooperation, politico-strategic issues, and joint armament projects.[7] In the last of these areas rapid progress seemed to be made from the end of 1982 at the bilateral and multilateral negotiations on the joint development of various weapons and space systems. Negotiations began on such new projects as a Franco-German helicopter, a European combat aircraft, antitank systems, an observation satellite, and the Hermes space shuttle.[8]

The bilateral Elysée Treaty had emerged twenty years earlier, after France had itself scrapped most of its European defense projects, and specifically the 1950 Pleven plan for the establishment of a European defense community and the 1961 Fouchet proposal. The treaty, which might have formed a sound basis for Franco-German military rapprochement and cooperation, was, however, assigned to the already full wastepaper basket only a few months later. After de Gaulle had implicitly forced the West Germans to choose between European-French defense and transatlantic-American defense, the German *Bundestag* made it clear, by adding a preamble favorable to NATO and the United States, that Bonn refused to give its French partner priority. In the eyes of President de Gaulle this preamble made the Elysée Treaty worthless. Instead of greater rapprochement, then, the Franco-German cooperation agreement led to a fundamental split between the options that Bonn and Paris had taken for their security policies. What de Gaulle had sought to prevent, an overly strong American-German link, was reaffirmed and strengthened. The gap between the two capitals was to widen further after October 1963, when Ludwig Erhard, an outspoken champion of the Atlantic Alliance, took over the reins from Adenauer.[9]

In the early 1980s President Mitterrand avoided making the same mistake as his illustrious predecessor. His aim was not a European Europe as opposed to an Atlantic Europe, but a European Europe within an Atlantic Europe. By strengthening the Franco-German military link, he attempted to strengthen and complement the threatened German-Atlantic link. This was also evident from the French initiative to reactivate WEU.

Western European Union was established in 1954 after the plan for a European Defense Community (EDC) had been thwarted by the French Assembly. The EDC had originally been the brainchild of French Prime Minister René Pleven, who saw it as a European solution to the problem of German rearmament. The Americans had insisted on the rearmament of West Germany, agreeing to increase the number of American troops in and military support for Western Europe after the outbreak of war in Korea only if the Europeans significantly stepped up their defense efforts. By establishing a European Defense Community, the French wanted to prevent German rearmament within the framework of the Atlantic Alliance. Within the Alliance Paris would be able to exercise less influence on the further development of West Germany's status. It was also afraid of the United States' far too tolerant attitude toward the Federal Republic. Washington's priority, after all, was to curb not the West German but the Soviet threat. Furthermore, the EDC would prevent the reestablishment of a "German" army.

The Pleven plan called for the integration of the member countries' troops to form a European army under the overall command of a European defense minister. He would be a member of a European defense council and accountable to a European assembly. Just as a check was kept on the West German coal and steel industry through the ECSC (European Coal and Steel Community), the French wanted to keep dreaded German rearmament under control through the EDC. According to Pleven, the EDC would give Europe a unique opportunity to achieve military equality with the United States and the Soviet Union, a claim that was intended to make the EDC project reasonably acceptable to the section of French public and political opinion that was reluctant to see the French armed forces absorbed into a supranational entity, especially as the British forces would remain national, the United Kingdom having refused to join the European supranational organization, just as it had rejected membership in the ECSC.

The plan was fiercely criticized by the United Kingdom and the United States, and could not in any case have been implemented in the short term. The other Western European countries also had greater confidence in a sound relationship with a strong America than in a relatively weak France, which did not have so much to offer in the military sphere. France itself also began to have growing doubts that an EDC without Britain would be strong enough to act as a counterbalance to the West Germans.

As the negotiations on the EDC proceeded, the project increasingly became Atlantic rather than European, which was not what the French had originally intended. The EDC treaty that was signed on 27 May 1952, but still had to be ratified by the national parliaments, stipulated that the EDC troops would be placed under the command of the (American) NATO supreme commander for Europe if one of the member countries was attacked, thus forging a military link between the EDC and the Atlantic Alliance. The French saw that the Pleven plan was losing its supranational European character, realized that its original objectives could not be achieved and now, unlike the Americans, took a far more skeptical view of the EDC. Paris was, however, in a weak position since it felt American troops were needed in Europe to prevent any future German militarism and to counteract the Soviet threat, of which there was considerable fear throughout Europe in the early 1950s. As the French also needed American support in their struggle in Indochina, they were forced to accept what were for them unfavorable developments in connection with the European Defense Community.

Stalin's death, the end of the war in Korea, and the generally more relaxed international climate led to a sharp reduction in the fear of a Soviet invasion of Western Europe toward the end of 1953. The French withdrawal from Indochina a year later also largely eliminated the second reason for France's dependent relationship with the United States. The arguments of the *anti-cédistes*, the opponents of the EDC, therefore began to make a greater impact, which ultimately led to the French Assembly's refusal on 30 August 1954 to consider the ratification of the EDC treaty.[10]

The French Assembly's decision made it clear that the solution to the German problem would be not European but Atlantic. However, this was due primarily to the balance of power at the time and thus less to inconsistent action by the French. The French decision meant above all that, whatever form it might take, the Atlantic solution would not be dressed up in European clothes. Nonetheless, it signified the loss of an organization that might well have assumed a genuine European dimension in the future. The road to a future European dimension in the security sphere was obstructed not only by the failure to establish the EDC but also by the fact that this failure created a gap that would increasingly divide Bonn and Paris, the gap between the idea of an *Europe européenne* and that of an "Atlantic Europe."[11]

As a result of the French decision there was still no solution to the problem of German rearmament and the continuing presence of American troops in Germany. Paris was therefore forced to accept an alternative solution. The Paris agreement (October 1954) establishing WEU modified the Brussels Treaty (March 1948) and admitted West Germany and Italy to the military assistance treaty that had been signed by France, the United Kingdom, and the Benelux countries. Unlike the North Atlantic Treaty, the Paris Treaty required the member countries to assist each other by military means if one of them were attacked. The treaty was, however, deprived of its potential power and options by the transfer to NATO of authority relating to military matters under Article 4 and a resolution adopted in September 1950. West Germany was thus integrated militarily into U.S.-led NATO through the back door of WEU. This also cleared the way for the establishment of a West German army, which would, however, be placed entirely under NATO command.

What France had sought to prevent thus became fact. Given their experience with the EDC project, however, the French had come to realize that, as this was bound to happen one way or another, it was better that it should be by the clear-cut WEU method: West Germany's rearmament was limited and controlled to some extent (it may not, for example, have any nuclear weapons of its own); Britain as well as the United States would continue to station troops in West Germany, though with no great enthusiasm; the French national army remained intact; and, above all, French national pride was not hurt since membership in the Western European Union did not entail the relinquishment of any sovereignty.[12]

On its establishment in 1954 the Western European Union had immediately performed the task for which it was created: It provided an acceptable method for West Germany's military integration into the western camp and, more specifically, the Atlantic Alliance. In the ensuing thirty years WEU's activities and impact were therefore extremely limited, a fact to which it owe its nickname of "Sleeping Beauty." On the few occasions when WEU seemed to grow in importance, it was because it was considered to be the right instrument at the time for solving a temporary problem. Once the problem had been overcome, it was left to return to its slumbers. WEU's reserve and support function became apparent, for example, during the settlement of the Saar problem and the crisis over Britain's accession to the European Community, when WEU formed a temporary link between the "Six" and Britain.[13]

Waking this Sleeping Beauty was seen by François Mitterrand in 1984 as a suitable means of reconciling France's traditionally independent defense policy with the desire to anchor West Germany and the other Western European countries rather more firmly in the western military camp at that difficult period of "neutralist" and "pacifist" turmoil. It was also a response to the criticism from surrounding countries that they were being disregarded as a result of the intensification of Franco-German relations.

The French memorandum of January 1984 proposing an exchange of views on Europe's security problems within WEU's Council was welcomed by the Belgians, Italians, and West Germans, who evidently shared the view that there was something to be gained from reawakening WEU. They also saw it as an excellent means of showing the Americans that they were really prepared to increase their efforts for their own defense. The Netherlands and especially the United Kingdom were very skeptical, but as the British did not want to run the risk this time of letting the French and Germans go their own way, they too were prepared to shake WEU out of its sleep. The result was that in June 1984 the Council of WEU met at ministerial level for the first time in ten years. At the following meeting in October, Western European Union's revival was confirmed by the Rome declaration.[14]

After emphasizing the Seven's attachment to the Atlantic Alliance, the Rome declaration stated that they would seek through the council to harmonize their views on defense questions, arms control and disarmament, the effects of developments in East-West relations on the security of Europe, Europe's contribution to the strengthening of the Atlantic Alliance, and the stimulation of European cooperation in the development and production of weapons systems. The institutional provisions of the declaration were primarily geared to reactivating the Council and placed considerable emphasis on the public relations function of the Assembly of the Western European Union, which was to be able to make clear to the public the contribution that Europe makes to the security debate.

Soon after the WEU summit meeting in Rome, however, the French in particular began to lose interest in this organization. And in 1985 it became abundantly clear that its revival had been no more than a transient phenomenon. The "invitation" issued by the Americans to the European allies in March 1985 to decide "within sixty days" whether or not they wanted to participate in the SDI project challenged the WEU member countries to translate their recent professions of faith in WEU into deeds. For WEU it was even more of a challenge since it was clear that Washington had a strong preference for separate SDI cooperation agreements with individual European countries. In Europe, France in particular and some West German leaders feared that this approach would prevent the Western Europeans from participating in the research project as equal partners and so reduce their role to that of subcontractors, while the SDI project would, moreover, give the Americans an even greater technological lead. They were also anxious that SDI would prove too attractive to Western European researchers, industrialists, and financiers and so weaken their own research potential. The French therefore proposed the establishment of a European Research Coordination Agency (EUREKA). At the meeting of WEU's Council in April it was decided to strengthen Europe's own technological capacities and so to establish a technological community. A common position on the American proposal was not, however, adopted, something that France in particular had wanted. Britain had already prevented this item from being placed on the agenda for the WEU meeting and had also let it be known that it was opposed to a common WEU position.[15]

In short, the WEU institutions did not display the hoped-for dynamism, and there was just as little sign of the harmonization of views through WEU. Having once again briefly performed her reserve and support function, Sleeping Beauty had now gone back to sleep. In the difficult year of 1984 the Alliance had happened to need a European institution to shore up the Atlantic structure, and as the position of Ireland, Greece, and Denmark meant that European Political Cooperation (EPC) could not be used as a forum for the discussion of security matters, WEU stepped into the breach. This function of helping out the Atlantic Alliance had already been apparent in the Rome declaration of October 1984, from which it was clear that WEU's revival was meant first and foremost to benefit the Alliance, just as its establishment had been.

Nor, indeed, given its institutional features, is the Western European Union capable of acting as the driving force of growing European integration and cooperation in security and defense, despite its outward European appearance and the emphasis placed on its Europeanness in all manner of declarations. Unlike membership in the European Community, WEU membership, after all, commits its members to nothing. It is not therefore surprising that they respect a given agreement or declaration only as long as it seems useful to them.

At the end of 1984 and in 1985 the vitality seemed to disappear not only from WEU but also, by and large, from Franco-German cooperation. Barely three years after the revival of the Bonn–Paris axis and despite continuing favorable official statements, the various committees appeared to be marking time. A number of specific cooperation programs came to a standstill or were even abandoned. France withdrew from the work on the development of a European combat aircraft; fresh difficulties arose over the battlefield helicopter program; certain aspects of the Hermes space shuttle project were opposed by the West Germans; and the French proposal for the development of a joint communications satellite was even denied all West German support. The two governments lacked the political will to overcome the problems that commonly arise in international cooperation projects, as when the commercial interests and traditions of national industries and budgetary and political priorities differ.[16]

Like the revival of WEU, the American invitation to decide "within sixty days" whether or not to participate in the SDI project had problematic implications for Franco-German rapprochement. The Elysée had immediately rejected the American proposal and countered it in April with the European proposal for the EUREKA project. Both Washington and Paris expected West German cooperation, exclusive by preference. Although the Federal Republic did not want to hurt either's feelings and the West German government included some fervent supporters of the European project, Foreign Minister Genscher among them, the French believed the West Germans favored the Americans. This led to French resentment at the West German attitude, although they were themselves partly to blame since they had made the old mistake in the early stages of the EUREKA–SDI debate of forcing Bonn to choose between the Franco-European and the American-Atlantic project. It was certainly due in part to the tension between Bonn and Paris over the American SDI initiative that the above-mentioned cooperation projects failed or came to a standstill. It also showed once again that the relationship between Paris and Bonn is not in practice bilateral but tripartite, with Washington always in attendance as the third party.[17]

Nor, from late 1984, was there sufficient political will to achieve concrete results in the exchange of views on a possible approximation of the two countries' security policies and on more practical French involvement in the defense of the Federal Republic. On each side of the Rhine the disappointment and doubt about the other country's attitude and sincerity grew.[18] Paris felt that it had done most in the process of rapprochement and that Bonn had done little in return and was, moreover, still too Atlantic in its outlook. In the Federal Republic it was thought that the French were still too nationalistic in their ideas on defense and had not really tried to accommodate West German security requirements. Now that the first of the Pershing IIs had been deployed in West Germany and the peace movement was beginning to wane in strength, France apparently saw the danger as less acute, and the most important motive for rapprochement with West Germany had thus vanished.

It seemed that the French had simply taken a line they had taken earlier: If the basic requirements for the independent French position are threatened, simply create the impression for a while that rapprochement with the allies in the security sphere is being sought and a European alternative is to be proposed and then, once the danger has passed, revert to the old familiar position. This had also happened in the early 1970s, when Willy Brandt's *Ostpolitik* reigned supreme, when the credibility of the American security commitments was weakened by the Mansfield proposals, Vietnam, and Watergate, and when there was rapprochement between the two super-powers (leading to SALT I and the ABM treaty). The French leaders briefly emphasized the importance of the American link with European defense and attempted to revive the Western European Union, only to lose interest in both aspects again shortly afterward.[19]

The situation in the first half of the 1980s did not seem any different. The change in the attitude of the "ever-present third party" toward the Soviet Union, the outcome of the summit meeting in Reykjavik in October 1986, and the acceptance of the double-zero option, which led to the Washington Treaty of December 1987, would, however, ensure that the French could not return to their accustomed position and indeed forced them to take more radical steps.

NOTES

1. David S. Yost, "France's Deterrent Posture and Security in Europe. Part 1: Capabilities and Doctrines," *Adelphi Papers*, no. 194, 1984/85, pp. 60–64.

2. François Mitterrand, "20e anniversaire du Traité de coopération franco-allemande. Discours devant le Bundestag," in Karl Kaiser and Pierre Lellouche, eds., *Le couple franco-allemand et la défense de l'Europe* (Paris: IFRI, 1986), pp. 336–37.

3. David P. Calleo, *Beyond American Hegemony: The Future of the Western Alliance* (New York, Basic Books, 1987), pp. 181–88.

4. François Mitterrand, *Réflexions sur la politique extérieure de la France* (Paris: Fayard, 1986), p. 44.

5. Bruno Racine, "La France et les FNI," *Politique Etrangère*, 53(1)1988, pp. 80–81.

6. J. Lacaze, "L'avenir de la défense française," *Défense Nationale*, July 1985, pp. 30–31.

7. Nicole Gnesotto, "Le dialogue franco-allemand depuis 1954: patience et longueur de temps . . . ," in Kaiser and Lellouche, eds., *Le couple franco-allemand*, pp. 24–25.

8. François Heisbourg, "Coopération en matière d'armements: rien n'est jamais acquis . . . ," in Kaiser and Lellouche, eds., *Le couple franco-allemand*, pp. 118–23.

9. Gnesotto, "Le dialogue franco-allemand," pp. 16–17.

10. Stanley R. Sloan, *NATO's Future: Toward a New Transatlantic Bargain* (Washington, D.C.: National Defense University, 1985), pp. 9–31; Michael M. Harrison, *The Reluctant Ally: France and Atlantic Security* (London: Johns Hopkins University Press, 1981), pp. 27–30.

11. Gnesotto, "Le dialogue franco-allemand," p. 13.

12. Ibid., pp. 13–15.

13. Peter Schmidt, "The WEU—A Union Without Perspective?" *Aussenpolitik*, 37(4)1986, pp. 386–89.

14. *Assembly of Western European Union, Western European Union: Information Report*, 1986, pp. 16–19, 50–57.

15. Bernard Brigouleix, "L'UEO et la 'Guerre des Etoiles'. Les Sept en quête d'une réponse commune à l'initiative du président Reagan," *Le Monde*, 23 April 1985, p. 4; Henri de Bresson, "La réunion de l'UEO. M. Dumas: Le défi pour l'Europe est d'abord technologique," *Le Monde*, 25 April 1985, p. 2.

16. Heisbourg, "Coopération en matière d'armements," pp. 119–23; Gnesotto, "Le dialogue franco-allemand," pp. 28–29.

17. Pierre Lellouche, "La France, la SDI et la sécurité de l'Europe," in Kaiser and Lellouche, eds., *Le couple franco-allemand*, pp. 268–69; Gnesotto, "Le dialogue franco-allemand," pp. 28–29.

18. Karl Kaiser and Pierre Lellouche, "Le couple franco-allemand et la défense de l'Europe: synthèses et recommandations," in Kaiser and Lellouche, eds., *Le couple franco-allemand*, pp. 312–14.

19. Haig Simonian, *The Privileged Partnership: Franco-German Relations in the EC, 1969–1984* (Oxford, Eng.: Clarendon Press, 1985), pp. 170–72, 183–84; Ingo Kolboom, "La politique de sécurité de la France: un point de vue allemand," in Kaiser and Lellouche, eds., *Le couple franco-allemand*, pp. 75–76, 82.

8

The Shock of Reykjavik

The rashness with which President Reagan had almost agreed in Reykjavik
to proposals that might have drastically changed the strategic landscape in
Europe and East-West relations, the United States' failure to consult its
allies, just as it had failed to consult them on the SDI project, the change
in Reagan's attitude toward the INFs, the way in which Washington urged
the zero option and later the double-zero option on the reluctant Western
European allies, and the eventual signing of the Washington Treaty in
December 1987 made the French even less sure about the United States'
security commitments to Western Europe. This time U.S. involvement in
the defense of Europe seemed threatened by the attitude not only of the
West Germans but also of the Americans themselves. Paris thus faced a
fundamentally different situation. The lack of single-mindedness, which the
French saw as so characteristic of their West German partner but which had
always been held in check by the Americans, had now even affected Washington itself. There was clearly no relying on Washington anymore. The
French also feared this was just the beginning of a further erosion of American involvement. Indeed, various leading figures in America, NATO's
Supreme Commander Rogers among them, had warned that the removal
of American medium-range weapons from Europe would be followed by
a reduction in the number of American troops.[1] The budgetary difficulties
with which Washington was having to contend could only accelerate this
trend.

This change in American thinking was clearly possible only because a
new generation of leaders had come to power in the Kremlin and was
pursuing a policy that differed radically from that of its predecessors. This
development in the Soviet Union, and subsequently in Eastern Europe, was

a new factor that might further affect the other two basic external requirements for the French security policy: a West Germany firmly entrenched
in the western camp and the impossibility of German reunification. While
developments in the communist bloc were considered in the United States
to be relevant primarily to its military strategy, they were also seen, particularly in West Germany, as relevant to political, economic, cultural, and
personal East-West relations. In Paris it was gradually realized that this
might lead to a fundamental change in West Germany's position. Whereas
some West Germans had seemed in the past to cling to "neutralist" ideas
out of a sense of fear, without in practice having any realistic options for
sweeping changes in relations with the Eastern European countries because
of the ossified situation there, such options were now multiplying. In other
words, the German drift to the East out of a sense of fear was gradually
giving way to a drift to the East out of a sense of reality and conviction.

The Washington Treaty showed that disarmament agreements with the
Soviet Union are possible if the Atlantic Alliance at least demonstrates the
necessary political will and the necessary dynamism. After forty years a
drastic reduction of the military confrontation in Central Europe and some
weakening of the division between Eastern and Western Europe at last
seemed possible. The firm place in the western camp that the Soviet Union's
attitude had led West Germany to consider necessary and obvious for forty
years was no longer the only possible option.

The INF agreement of December 1987 did not only affect the basic external requirements for France's security policy; it also further exposed the
ambiguity and shortcomings of France's military strategy and resources,
and this at a time when the French defense budget was coming under even
greater pressure because of technical advances and other factors.[2] The Washington agreement, under which medium-range weapons were dismantled,
resulted in greater attention being focused on tactical nuclear weapons and,
above all, the importance of conventional defense.

France feared a growth of pressure particularly from West Germany for
a reduction in the number of nuclear weapons with a range of less than 500
km or for their removal altogether. This would also increase the pressure
on Paris to allow French tactical or prestrategic nuclear weapons to be
included in the disarmament process, since the INF agreement made the
West Germans more sensitive than ever to the impact of the remaining
short-range weapons, which would be targeted on their territory. They
included the French Plutons, in whose use Bonn would, moreover, have
no say at all, as they had in the case of NATO's tactical nuclear weapons.
The planned deployment of the Hadès, the Pluton's successor, also met
with mounting criticism. With their range of 350 km, these new weapons
systems would not hit West German soil, but "German" soil nonetheless,
which, in view of the improvement in relations between East and West
Germany, was just as unacceptable. Furthermore, there was a growing

feeling that the deployment of new nuclear weapons of this kind was in no way in keeping with the general disarmament process and that this would undermine the prospect of basic changes in Eastern Europe.

The INF agreement confirmed and strengthened the trend, with the conventional aspect gaining in importance in the strategies of both East and West. This accelerated trend, accompanied by the increased doubt about future American involvement, indicated that the measures France had taken in 1984 and 1985 to make it easier for its military apparatus to be used in the defense of West Germany were inadequate. The new French measures and the closer formal cooperation with Germany had undoubtedly been politically and symbolically important and in practice had also improved the availability of French army units to some extent. Given the traditional French attitude, various steps had also been fairly radical and thus important as a means of preparing the French psychologically for a possible change of French strategy and French policy. Similarly important for the future was the development of a sound institutional base, with an extensive network of regular bilateral meetings at the various decision-making levels, from the lower strata of the administration to the top government level.[3]

Nonetheless, the changed French attitude and the closer bilateral contacts did not measure up either to what the West Germans expected of France or to the real needs of Western European defense. In the first place, the French measures had not put an end to the ambiguity of solidarity with the Alliance on the one hand and France's autonomous decision-making power and *l'option de non-belligérence* on the other. France had so far done nothing to assure the West Germans that in the event of an attack French troops would immediately and automatically help to defend West German territory in sufficient numbers and with the necessary firepower. By stationing troops in the eastern part of West Germany and integrating them into the joint military command, the United States, the United Kingdom, and West Germany's other allies had in effect largely renounced the possibility of determining autonomously the time at which they should join in its defense. Their solidarity was, in other words, an established fact, which was not true of France.[4]

In addition, the French measures were too limited to be regarded as a major contribution to the defense of Western Europe and West Germany. The military relevance of the *Force d'Action Rapide* (FAR) to the defense of West Germany as a whole also seemed limited. For one thing, the formation of the 47,000-man FAR did not signify the expansion of the French army to include new units or military equipment: Various existing units had simply been placed under a single new command. Furthermore, as the FAR is extremely heterogeneous in its composition, there are in fact two or three smaller FARs. Some units of the FAR are intended primarily for defensive missions in France, others mainly for military operations outside Europe (a few thousand men being in fact stationed overseas). Although the FAR as a whole is more flexible and better equipped and can be deployed more quickly than the average unit of the French First Army, some of its units are not yet mobile enough or are stationed too far from the Franco-German border to be deployed quickly, and not all the FAR is adequately equipped with, say, sophisticated antitank missiles with which to offer effective resistance to an enemy. Finally, except in fairly limited military operations, the FAR would be highly dependent on the NATO allies for logistical support, transport, air defense, and so on while in action in West Germany or the Benelux countries. Many arrangements and practical preparations had, moreover, yet to be made in these respects to ensure effective French action and at least some operational coordination with NATO troops.[5] It is indeed ironic that, if the FAR went into action in West Germany, France would be more dependent than other allies on NATO and West Germany for support simply because Paris has refused to deploy sufficient equipment on West German soil in advance and to make necessary logistical and other preparations on the grounds that such measures would erode France's independent position.[6]

Although one of the aims of setting up the FAR was to overcome the ambiguity of autonomy and solidarity, this ambiguity and, above all, its untenability have thus been accentuated even more clearly. France consequently had enough reasons to go a step further in rapprochement with Germany and to take greater account of the requirements of Western European security. For Bonn too it seemed wise to strengthen the links with Paris, given the doubts about the American attitude. In late February 1986 another Franco-German summit meeting was held, attended by two leaders who had been meeting almost monthly since the beginning of 1985, without, however, making any real progress in Franco-German cooperation. This time, however, they did take practical action on the basis of the decisions and reforms of 1983/84.

It was no coincidence that this should happen just after the first signs of détente between the two superpowers had emerged. In November 1985 Reagan and Gorbachev had had their first meeting in Geneva. In January 1986 the Soviet leader had launched the idea, as the apotheosis of a whole series of disarmament proposals, that all nuclear weapons should be eliminated from the world by the year 2000. And, to the surprise of many, President Reagan announced that he thought this was a good idea and proposed that the first step should be the removal of American and Soviet medium-range weapons from Europe within three years. His disarmament proposal made the Western European leaders look rather ridiculous in the eyes of the peace movement and those sections of their public who had opposed the deployment of the INFs. It was also feared in Bonn, London, and Paris that the removal of the recently deployed medium-range weapons would result in the decoupling of American and Western European defense.[7]

The fact that the two world leaders were suddenly able to agree put sufficient pressure on the two Western European leaders to take new and more radical steps. Chancellor Kohl and President Mitterrand came to various practical arrangements to strengthen diplomatic cooperation at all decision-making and executive levels. The measures concerning military cooperation attracted the most attention, however. First, it was decided to increase operational cooperation between the armed forces of the two countries and to consider how better use could be made of the French forces, and especially the FAR, in Germany. It was agreed that this accord should lead to joint maneuvers, beginning in 1986/87, which was seen as an important new step by Paris. A second measure concerned the joint training of officers. A third remarkable element concerned one of the most delicate aspects of Franco-German relations, the French nuclear deterrent. The president of the French Republic expressed his willingness to consult the Federal chancellor on the possible use of French prestrategic weapons on German soil, but "subject to the limits imposed by the exceptional speed with which it must be possible for such decisions to be taken." The same text reiterated, however, that the decision on the use of prestrategic weapons could not be shared and so continued to be entirely the French president's responsibility.[8]

The French assurance that the Federal chancellor would be consulted under certain conditions was seen as a success for Bonn, though it was not regarded by the West Germans as an "historic gesture" from their former archenemy. This in turn led to disappointment in France, where it was seen as yet another demonstration of the West Germans' lack of appreciation for French efforts. After all, Mitterrand's assurance went a very long way, according to the French, given their traditional view that the national element of the *force nationale de dissuasion* must in no way come under pressure.[9] The West Germans, on the other hand, had mixed feelings about the conditions attached to the French assurance relating to "the limits imposed by the exceptional speed..." One West German commentator remarked: "There is agreement on consultation that cannot take place in time."[10] This seemed somewhat excessive, but skeptics were able to find authoritative support for their arguments in a statement that President Mitterrand made barely three weeks before the Franco-German summit:

The only one who can give the order for nuclear engagement is the President of the Republic. The decision has to be taken in a matter of seconds. It will be very difficult to deliberate, to have consultations. If you try to reach agreement in circumstances like this, the war will be over, and you will have lost.[11]

The decisions on conventional cooperation were important for Germany because they showed that the measures the French had taken in 1983 and 1984 were not intended merely to placate their neighbor to the east for a while, but could actually be regarded as the beginning of a further change in West Germany's favor. The joint maneuvers announced in the declaration were held in December 1987, with fifty thousand West German and twenty thousand French troops participating. The scenario for these Franco-German maneuvers predicted that the *Bundeswehr*'s position would be threatened by the enemy in the first few days of "forward defense" and that France would then come to its aid by deploying the FAR as a strategic reserve. The maneuvers, the code name for which was Cheeky Sparrow (*kecker Spatz—moineau hardi*), revealed that France was more prepared than before to commit itself to the defense of West Germany.

In various important respects the maneuvers differed, after all, from the annual Franco-German exercises held in the past. The Cheeky Sparrow maneuvers saw the first involvement of units of the French FAR (until then FAR units had been active only in Chad, Lebanon, and French Polynesia). During the operations in the Federal Republic the twenty thousand men of the FAR were under the command of a West German general. The scenario also called for the French troops to intervene in the military conflict in West Germany at a very early stage, which was an important sign to a potential enemy that Paris would do the same in a real crisis. It was also important for NATO since it meant that there would be a better chance of beating off an attack and more time to bring in reserves from the United States and elsewhere. It was also the first time that French troops had penetrated so far east into West Germany. While most military exercises had previously been held west of the line joining Dortmund and Munich, some FAR units now came as close to West Germany's eastern border as seventy kilometers.[12]

The time and place of the French intervention clearly revealed the development in French strategic thinking, with the idea of *la première bataille* and *la bataille de France* gradually evolving into *l'idée d'une bataille unique*, with the whole area between the Atlantic Ocean and Eastern Europe seen as forming a single security zone. It also showed that, even if Paris said it would not participate in the forward defense of West Germany, in practice it still played (or could play) a very important supporting role as the largest operational reserve in Western Europe, a role that France had in fact played before withdrawing from the integrated military structure of the Alliance, since even then it had not occupied any forward positions in the Federal Republic.[13]

The Cheeky Sparrow maneuvers were important because they provided both West Germany and a potential aggressor with clearer practical proof of France's solidarity with West Germany than ever before. They were also extremely useful as a means of testing and rehearsing this solidarity in the field: the rapid transport of French units over long distances, the interoperability of French and German units, operation under foreign command, West German logistical support for the FAR, and so forth. In the process each side gained a better insight into the other's command structure, tactical codes, and communications systems.[14]

The many agreements formally reached by the supreme commands of the French and West German armed forces since the French withdrawal in 1967 now had to be put into practice on a large scale. For the maneuvers these agreements had to be elaborated in greater detail, and new arrangements had to be made. This in turn meant that the West Germans and especially the French had to adjust their own procedures and views on the defense of Central Europe both to their respective partner's and to actual circumstances. The Cheeky Sparrow maneuvers left the supreme commands of the two countries in no doubt about the shortcomings of Franco-German military cooperation, the problems connected with logistics and interoperability being more serious than expected, partly because of the enormous differences in military equipment and military concepts. The advantage, however, was that they were at least clearly revealed to all concerned.[15]

For various reasons indicated above the holding of bilateral Franco-German maneuvers was also important for NATO. This explains the positive attitude of the then NATO supreme commander, Rogers, who gave the (necessary) approval for West German troops, who were under NATO command even in peacetime, to be temporarily released from NATO's integrated military structure to take part in the bilateral maneuvers with France. Such exercises, after all, enable the split between French and NATO forces to be pragmatically and gradually healed without the delicate question of the reintegration of the French armed forces into NATO's military structure having to be broached. If in a military crisis the French president took the politically difficult decision to place French forces under the operational control of the NATO supreme commander for a specific period and task, the experience gained during such maneuvers might at least have a positive effect in the field. To many the goal therefore seemed to be to achieve the best possible "integrated nonintegration" of France into the Alliance by increasing practical military cooperation between France and the western allies.[16]

This brings us, however, to the various objections to the Franco-German maneuvers. France's nonintegration into NATO continued to be a serious obstacle to Franco-German cooperation and was, moreover, still an extremely sensitive issue in Paris. The Cheeky Sparrow maneuvers therefore took place in a fairly artificial atmosphere, since the existence of the NATO troops and structures with which there would have to be cooperation of some kind in wartime was ignored. The French did not agree to NATO military staff attending the maneuvers as observers, although observers from Eastern Europe were invited.[17] Another artificial factor was that no account was taken of French nuclear weapons, which would seriously complicate Franco-German cooperation in a real crisis.

It was also possible to sympathize with the British, who expressed surprise at all the fuss about the Franco-German maneuvers. Had they not, after all, shipped fifty-seven thousand troops across the Channel to the Federal Republic for the Anglo-German Lionheart maneuvers in 1987?[18] And, at the very time the Franco-German maneuvers were being held, had the Americans not brought over the largest number of GIs since the Second World War, thirty-one thousand of them, for the Certain Strike maneuvers in the north of the Federal Republic, when they were in fact formally responsible for the defense of Southern Germany?[19] Why, then, all the hullabaloo about these twenty thousand French brothers in arms? Perhaps it was because, as in the parable of the prodigal son, the joy was greater at the return of a member of the Atlantic family who was considered lost than over those who had always acted as worthy members of this family.

NOTES

1. C. Graf Brockdorff, "Rogers: Abschreckung ist gefährdet," *Die Zeit*, 2 March 1987.
2. Jolyon Howorth, "Resources and Strategic Choices: French Defence Policy at the Crossroads," *The World Today*, 42(5)1986, p. 77.
3. Karl Kaiser and Pierre Lellouche, "Le couple franco-allemand et la défense de l'Europe: synthèses et recommandations," in Karl Kaiser and Pierre Lellouche, eds., *Le couple franco-allemand et la défense de l'Europe* (Paris: IFRI, 1986), p. 317.
4. Franz-Joseph Schulze, "La nécessité d'une réaction de défense immédiate et commune," in Kaiser and Lellouche, eds., *Le couple franco-allemand*, pp. 159–61.
5. David S. Yost, "La coopération franco-allemande en matière de défense," *Politique Etrangère*, 53(4)88, p. 846.
6. Ingo Kolboom, "La politique de sécurité de la France: un point de vue allemand," in Kaiser and Lellouche, eds., *Le couple franco-allemand*, p. 85.
7. Bernard Weihraub, "U.S. Offers Medium-Range Missile Cut," *International Herald Tribune*, 23 February 1986; V. Markham, "Europeans Seem Cool to Arms Plan," *International Herald Tribune*, 25 February 1986.
8. "Gemeinsame Erklärungen des Bundeskanzlers der BRD, Helmut Kohl, und des französischen Staatspräsidenten, François Mitterrand, in Paris am 28. Februar 1986 nach zweitägigen bilateralen Konsultationen," *Europa-Archiv*, 41(6)1986, pp. D235–37.
9. Bernard Brigouleix, "Le sommet franco-allemand. Cinq déclarations et un nouveau développement de la coopération militaire," *Le Monde*, 2 March 1986; Pierre Ruge, "Paris will für Bonn Partner, nicht Protektor sein," *Die Welt*, 25 February 1988.
10. Kolboom, "La politique de sécurité de la France," p. 90.
11. François Mitterrand, "Quelle défense pour la France?" *Le Monde*, 11 February 1988.
12. Lothar Rühl, "Die deutsch-französische Militärkooperation ist das Kernstück der europäischen Sicherheit," *Die Welt*, 29 December 1987; Detlef Puhl, "French and Germans hold combined maneuvers," *The German Tribune*, 13 September 1987, p. 4; Jacques Isnard, "La Manoeuvre franco-allemande 'Moineau hardi' permettra de tester la capacité de la FAR à secourir la Bundeswehr," *Le Monde*, 11 September 1987.
13. Rühl, "Die deutsch-französische Militärkooperation"; Ernst Weisenfeld,

" 'Moineau hardi': la Légion à la Rescousse," *La Tribune d'Allemagne*, 4 October 1987, p. 4.

14. Isnard, "La Manoeuvre franco-allemande."

15. Yost, "La coopération franco-allemande," pp. 844–45.

16. Siegfried Thielbeer, "Paris, die NATO und die Vorneverteidigung," *Frankfurter Allgemeine Zeitung*, 29 December 1987, p. 5.

17. Yost, "La coopération franco-allemande," p. 845.

18. Michael Stürmer, "The Franco-German cooperation: A very special relationship," *Stiftung Wissenschaft und Politik*, Ebenhausen 1988, p. 12.

19. H.-J. Melder, "Huge airlift of GI's for Euro war-games," *The German Tribune*, 13 September 1987, p. 4.

9

One Cheeky Bird Does Not
Make a Summer

If the Franco-German maneuvers were seen as a positive development, then it was mainly for the following two reasons: They were regarded as proof positive that Paris was more concerned about the defense of West Germany than it had previously been, and as a first step toward the further improvement of the prospect of putting this increased solidarity into practice at times of crisis. The importance of two initiatives launched in mid-1987 must be seen in the same light: the formation of a joint Franco-German brigade and the establishment of the Franco-German Defense and Security Council.

The Franco-German brigade was proposed by Chancellor Kohl, rather unexpectedly, in June 1987. His primary concern was in some way to accommodate and also rebut the leader of the CDU parliamentary party, Dregger, and others who had been prompted by the United States' "unreliable" attitude during the INF negotiations to question continuing American involvement in the defense of Europe. He proposed that West German security policy should be reoriented, with the French nuclear umbrella extended to cover the Federal Republic as part of a Franco-German security union.[1]

In France, too, a positive attitude toward Franco-German military cooperation had emerged. In the same month, June 1987, former president Giscard d'Estaing, former prime minister Fabius, and Foreign Minister Dumas had all advocated far closer military cooperation with Germany.[2] Helmut Kohl's idea was therefore well received in France. The problem was how to put it into effect, given the continuing basic problems facing Franco-German military relations, including the nuclear factor, the difference in the two countries' relationships with NATO, and their different military strategies.

It was eventually decided to form a brigade of around four thousand men. This Franco-German brigade, the first units of which have been stationed at Böblingen near Stuttgart since October 1988, is alternately headed by a Frenchman and a West German (each for a period of two years). The West German contingent consists of units of West Germany's "territorial army," which comprises some forty-five thousand men and, unlike the majority of the Federal armed forces, is not under NATO command. One of the territorial army's main tasks is to defend those parts of West Germany (and especially airports, supply depots, pipelines, etc.) that are located behind NATO's front-line units. It is also responsible for facilitating the movement of reinforcements from the other NATO countries. The Franco-German brigade was therefore to have largely the same tasks: defending crucial locations in the hinterland and facilitating the deployment of armed forces stationed in France, undoubtedly not a bad idea, given the not wholly favorable results achieved during the Franco-German maneuvers.

The assignment of territorial army units to the Franco-German brigade meant that West Germany avoided reneging on its formal commitments to NATO and, above all, that the French units seconded to the brigade would not be formally associated with the NATO structure. Despite this, the French informally admitted that it was more than likely that in the event of a war the Franco-German brigade would be placed under the direct control of the commander of CENTAG (NATO, Central Army Group, Central Europe).[3]

The proposal for the formation of a Franco-German brigade was greeted with some skepticism and continued to invite scornful comments, since it was seen as just one more in a long line of symbolic acts. In absolute terms the 4,200-man brigade was indeed no huge military gain. It cannot, after all, take part in forward defense (nor was that the intention), it does nothing to solve the basic problems facing Franco-German military cooperation, and it cannot even be said to signify a genuine approximation of the different military concepts to which Bonn and Paris are attached. The mixed Franco-German brigade, which would not, moreover, be operational until 1991, is also far less "mixed" than its name indicates. Only the general staff and the support battalion consist of both French and West German troops, the other nine units being exclusively French or West German.

Nevertheless, if the formation of the brigade is viewed in the context of a development in which France is gradually becoming more involved in the defense of West Germany, and if it is accepted that this development can occur only step by pragmatic step, it will be realized that the new Franco-German brigade, like the joint maneuvers, may well be a vital link. Even if the brigade cannot be seen as the nucleus of a Franco-German army because of its limited military mandate, it is useful as a "laboratory" in which various aspects of Franco–German military cooperation can be put to the test in practice. Like the joint maneuvers, the brigade enables the many practical problems that exist to be accurately identified and solutions gradually proposed and tried out.[4]

The establishment of a Franco–German Defense and Security Council was first publicly suggested by President Mitterrand during the Cheeky Sparrow maneuvers in September 1987. The council was set up, together with a Franco–German Financial and Economic Council, on 22 January 1988 at the time of the ceremonies marking twenty-five years of the Franco–German cooperation agreement, or Elysée Treaty (1963).[5]

The considerable publicity surrounding these ceremonies and the establishment of the two Franco–German councils were also clearly intended as a counterbalance to the Federal Republic's intensified policy on Eastern Europe. Chancellor Kohl was thus able to show that, besides seeking rapprochement with West Germany's neighbors to the East, he was making serious efforts to strengthen relations with the West. At the same time, he retained sufficient political leeway for further improvements in relations with Eastern Europe. For President Mitterrand the new council was a means of helping to keep the Federal Republic securely in the western camp.

The establishment of the Franco–German Defense and Security Council was again brushed aside by many as yet another symbolic Franco–German initiative, presented with much decorum and nicely packaged, but without a great deal of substance. Was it much more than an upgraded version of the Franco–German ministerial meetings into which new life had been breathed five years earlier, at the time of the Elysée Treaty's twentieth anniversary? Most of the Western European allies viewed the new Franco–German initiative, like the formation of a new brigade, with suspicion, Margaret Thatcher in particular making her considerable reservations about this bilateral Franco–German cooperation abundantly clear. The main exception was Spain, just about the only country to react constructively by saying that the Franco–German initiative might be extended to include countries like itself. Washington was also inclined to welcome the initiative, U.S. Secretary of Defense Carlucci saying that the Franco–German dialogue was highly desirable and in no way weakened NATO. Washington saw this closer dialogue as a useful means of both creating a western counterbalance to West German enthusiasm for relations with Eastern Europe and involving Paris more deeply in the defense of Western Europe.[6]

Despite all the criticism of the establishment of the new Franco–German Defense and Security Council, it was a fairly logical and necessary step in Franco–German relations. Just as the creation of a European army would require some form of European government, the extension of Franco–German military relations (and especially the formation of the joint brigade) made it necessary for institutional cooperation to be raised to a higher political level. The institutional structures that already existed under the

Elysée Treaty—the regular meetings of the four foreign and defence ministers—were therefore formally complemented by the new Defense and Security Council. Besides these four ministers, and the chiefs of staff of the two countries, the French president and the German Federal chancellor sit on the council. The council also provides a firm political structure at the highest policy-making level, which may serve as the basis for further steps in Franco-German military cooperation in the future. Furthermore, the policies have been broadly defined and cover all aspects of defense and security except the nuclear element.

The months immediately preceding and following the establishment of the Franco-German council showed that, despite widespread skepticism, the two countries were indeed drawing closer together and that the aims set out in the protocol establishing the new council were thus more than finely worded, token declarations. November 1987, for example, saw the conclusion of the first agreement in fifteen years on a specific joint arms production project. After unsuccessful attempts at the joint manufacture of, among other things, tanks, fighter aircraft, and spy satellites, an agreement on the development and production of the PAH2 antitank helicopter was signed.[7]

That Paris and Bonn eventually came to an agreement in itself reflected the Franco-German rapprochement and the willingness of both countries to reconcile their differences and, in some respects, opposing security concepts and aims. One of the problems during the negotiations on joint arms production had been that the armed forces of the two neighboring countries have different objectives. While the Federal armed forces are almost exclusively concerned with deterrence and the defense of their country against an attack from Eastern Europe, their French counterparts must be able to carry out a wide variety of missions, including efficient intervention in developing countries. The two countries consequently have different requirements when procuring or developing military equipment, as became clear during the negotiations on the Franco-German helicopter. Or as Alfred Grosser, a specialist in Franco-German relations, put it: "Paris feels . . . that the helicopter should be able to operate in sandstorms, which, as you know, do not occur on the Elbe."[8]

Definite movement was also detected in Franco-German relations in 1988, where the first two objectives set out in the protocol were concerned: "establishing joint concepts in the area of defense and security" and "ensuring a growing measure of agreement between the two countries on all matters relating to the security of Europe, including arms control and disarmament." This was primarily due to the very intensive debate in France on military strategy, France's "European" role, and links with the Federal Republic. Toward the end of 1987 both President Mitterrand and his Socialist Party, now in opposition, and the center-right coalition government headed by Jacques Chirac seemed intent on outdoing each other with statements that referred to a deeper understanding of the West German position. In content, however, Mitterrand's and Chirac's "reassuring" statements were fundamentally different.

In a speech to the Institut des Hautes Etudes de Défense Nationale in December 1987 the French prime minister stated very clearly that France would assist West Germany in a crisis.

France now has the means to give expression to the European dimension of its security. . . . Who can now doubt that, if the Federal Republic of Germany was attacked, France would intervene immediately and without reservation? There cannot be a battle of Germany and a battle of France. . . . France cannot regard its neighbors' territory as a defensive *glacis*.

According to Chirac, then, Paris was no longer really free to choose not to help defend its neighbor. Despite this—by French standards—radical statement, his speech was given a rather cool reception by the West German government, principally because of something else he said: "It must be possible for France to launch its prestrategic missiles as soon as the head of state judges our vital interests to be at risk, that is to say, if necessary, some considerable time before the invasion of our national territory." As he also emphasized the growing flexibility and potential of French prestrategic nuclear weapons, this meant to many Germans that, while French involvement in the defense of the Federal Republic might have increased, there was also a possibility that French nuclear weapons would devastate part of its territory.[9]

The West Germans therefore felt far more comfortable with the way in which François Mitterrand had expressed his growing sympathy for the German situation a few months earlier. During an official visit to the Federal Republic in mid-October 1987 the French president had done his utmost to convince the West Germans that French prestrategic nuclear weapons were not meant for West German territory:

There is no truth in the statement that France's final warning to an aggressor would be aimed at German territory. . . . Who invented the story that French weapons will be aimed at German soil? . . . As the aim of French deterrence is to deter an attack, the French threat, the Atlantic threat must be directed against the aggressor, if he exists. . . . Why cause destruction by opting to strike first at one's allies and hurt one's friends?[10]

In time-honored French tradition, François Mitterrand managed to be sufficiently ambiguous and indirect in his statements. The doubts about their value grow further when we compare them with the promise he made in February 1986 to consult the Federal chancellor "on the possible use of French prestrategic weapons on German soil" and consider that a missile with a range of 120 km launched in an easterly direction will come down not in the Soviet Union but in West Germany.[11] Nonetheless, François Mitterrand's statements in West Germany were in keeping with earlier indications that he had serious doubts about the value of these "prestrategic" or "tactical" nuclear weapons and even felt that the decision to develop them had been wrong.[12]

In early 1988 he began to translate the fairly positive statements he had made to Bonn into tangible support for the West German government, thus preventing the Federal Republic from becoming isolated within NATO. In the months before the NATO summit meeting of heads of state and government at the beginning of March, U.S. Secretary of Defense Carlucci, NATO Supreme Commander Galvin, and Margaret Thatcher all called for a decision on the modernization of NATO's short-range weapons, even making it a new test of German loyalty to the western alliance. Chancellor Kohl, however, was under enormous pressure from his own public and almost all the political parties (his own CDU included) to push for negotiations on these nuclear weapons, most of which were aimed at Germany. The western allies' growing criticism of Bonn's very intensive *Ostpolitik* also seemed to point to further isolation. President Mitterrand decided not only to attend the NATO summit in Brussels but also, on the eve of the meeting, was very explicit in his support of Chancellor Kohl's views (and so opposed Prime Minister Chirac's position). This became clear when he was asked whether the modernization of short-range weapons was not imperative for the West: "No. At a time when the two blocs are engaged in a process of disarmament for the first time since the Second World War, excessive armament would be paradoxical and inopportune. Let us seek a balance at the lowest possible level."[13]

Mitterrand's intervention and, later, President Reagan's more understanding attitude were two of the factors that prevented too obvious a split within NATO, and the subtle use of language kept everyone happy. During the NATO summit it was decided not to "modernize" short-range weapons but to keep them "up to date where necessary." It was also confirmed that "in conjunction with the establishment of a conventional balance" negotiations could be held on "tangible and verifiable reductions of . . . land-based nuclear missile systems of shorter range, leading to equal ceilings."[14]

Six months later it seemed that Paris had taken a further step toward Bonn on the question of nuclear weapons, and to Bonn's great satisfaction it also changed its mind on the negotiations on chemical weapons, partly because of the international conference on these weapons that was held in Paris in January 1989.[15] In September there were reports from Paris that the Elysée was considering deferring the development of the new Hadès missile for two or three years to see if substantial reductions could not be achieved in conventional forces in Europe. It was said that France was even contemplating abandoning the Hadès program altogether if the Soviet threat waned sufficiently. Although the defense budget that had just been approved still provided for the financing of Hadès and the report was officially denied the next day, enough importance was attached to what appeared to be a leak to sound out public opinion. To some extent, after all, it reflected François Mitterrand's skepticism about short-range weapons and the financial need to cut back or postpone a number of military programs. A major constraint in Franco-German relations would also be reduced in this way. It would mean that Paris was more sympathetic to West German sensitivity about these French weapons, which would land on German soil. It would also be appreciated in Germany if France at last stopped refusing to accept a link, however indirect, between its own nuclear weapons and the disarmament negotiations.[16]

On various occasions in early 1988 the French president was also very explicit in his endorsement of West Germany's intensive *Ostpolitik*, which a number of Western European allies viewed with grave suspicion:

The French [must] realize that, given its peripheral position in Western Europe between France and the Soviet Union, it is logical that Germany should also turn its attention to the East. . . . If the Federal Republic commits itself fully to the construction of Europe, as I believe it will, why would it not play a specific role in keeping its historical background? The desires it inevitably has in this respect should not be confused with neutrality.[17]

This must have been music to Bonn's ears, especially as it was accustomed to a different tone from Paris. In their statements the West German leaders therefore made very frequent reference to what Mitterrand had said about both nuclear weapons and the *Ostpolitik* to demonstrate that Bonn was not in any way charting a separate course but could, on the contrary, count on understanding and even support on the continent of Europe. An example of these French efforts to "chaperone" the West German policy and to prevent it from becoming too isolated was the invitation extended to East German party leader Honecker to come to Paris only a few months after he had visited Bonn. France thus became the first of the three western powers in Berlin officially to receive the GDR leader. With this clear political gesture France wanted to prevent a situation where not only would Bonn's *Ostpolitik* be overly pursued in a European vacuum, which would also be to the Federal Republic's disadvantage, but also *Ostpolitik* would be Bonn's exclusive domain.[18]

President Mitterrand played a stabilizing role within the western alliance not only through his stand on the question of nuclear weapons and the *Ostpolitik* but also through the change in the French attitude toward the Atlantic Alliance itself. His presence at the NATO summit held in Brussels in March 1988 was in itself remarkable. At this meeting, after all, there was to be a discussion and possibly a decision on NATO's short-range weapons, which were ultimately of no concern to France, given its specific status.

Mitterrand's presence was, however, a consequence of a development that had been under way since mid-1987 and had marked the beginning of France's closer involvement in the Alliance's military deliberations. Paris had decided at that time to take part in the new negotiations on conventional disarmament in Europe, which meant a break with the past, since it had previously refused to participate in the MBFR negotiations. In return, it was agreed that, although the negotiations would be conducted by NATO and the Warsaw Pact, they would nevertheless form part of the Conference on Security and Cooperation in Europe. Paris could thus be credited with removing these conventional negotiations from the classical "bloc versus bloc" pattern to some extent and placing them in a more European context. It also emerged that France would be participating in an extensive NATO study on the implications of the implementation of the double-zero option and on the priorities for arms control and disarmament. During the discussion of the double-zero option France was already heavily involved in NATO's attempt to formulate a common NATO position.[19]

In September 1987 a small French military unit had also taken part in NATO's Certain Strike maneuvers, and Paris had indicated its willingness to participate in future NATO maneuvers on a limited scale. In early 1988 a thousand American troops carried out exercises of their own on French soil for the first time since 1966. Equally remarkable was the French decision to step up defense cooperation with Norway, at a time when Canada had announced it could no longer fulfill its military commitments on NATO's northern flank and none of the other allies was prepared to fill the breach.[20]

Although these developments were not earthshaking in themselves, they seemed important in that they marked the beginning of a trend in which, in addition to maintaining the strictly Franco-German contacts, Paris sought closer cooperation with the NATO allies at an operational level without, however, contemplating a return to the integrated structure of the Alliance.

A remarkable feature was that Mitterrand, unlike de Gaulle, did not try to destabilize the Atlantic Alliance by putting himself and European military cooperation forward as an alternative to American leadership in the Atlantic structure. As it took each step closer to the Federal Republic, Paris emphasized that the United States and NATO remained essential, which also implied that the hopes, or warnings, of a Franco-German or European defense system that invariably accompanied any new Franco-German rapprochement lacked any substance. As Mitterrand pointed out during his very "pro-German" period in the first few months of 1988: "It is clear that the Federal Republic depends first and foremost on the Atlantic Alliance for its security."[21] This was perhaps most clearly revealed when France reacted positively to the idea of a Franco-German brigade: "It is right to refer to a European defense system. It is a future prospect that needs to be further clarified, but one that is faced with a difficult historical situation. The Atlantic Alliance, in which the USA is the leading country, is the pillar of our security." To make it absolutely clear, he also added the following: "The other pillar is our nuclear capability. But Europe does not have this capability."[22] In other words, essential though Europe and Franco-German cooperation were, they were not (yet) pillars of French security.

As the French approach to West Germany and the Atlantic Alliance was largely inspired by the desire and the need to stabilize France's security environment (and less by the desire to create a new security framework), it was to be expected that this gradual process of rapprochement, which had begun to accelerate in early 1988, would start to flag at a given moment. Further rapprochement would result in a growing realization that even gradual steps, however taken, would lead to a more thorough review of France's own security policy, that the various initiatives primarily designed to preserve that policy would eventually erode it, and that gradual adjustments and steps would not, in the final analysis, be an adequate response to fundamental problems connected with and inconsistencies inherent in the French attitude. This was something that the West Germans, too, understood only too well.

In the months before the summit meeting to mark NATO's fortieth anniversary at the end of May 1989 these problems became abundantly clear to the French government. Barely a year after the NATO summit of March 1988 the Atlantic Alliance was again threatened with a split along roughly the same lines. This time, however, the West Germans stood their ground with even greater self-confidence. As a Dutch commentator put it:

On the one hand, our partners, especially France, are afraid West Germany will "go it alone" in an easterly direction, a fear that is rekindled by political developments in the Federal Republic. But they constantly show themselves to be incapable of changing their nationalistic spots and so avoiding a situation in which they themselves contribute to the "singularity" that is so detested in the Federal Republic. The representatives of the Eastern European countries at the Vienna conference are happy to see the western insensitivity to German sensitivities.[23]

West Germany's determination to pursue its security interests even more than before had grown further after various incidents revived the debate on the restriction of West German sovereignty. The disaster at an American air force base in Ramstein, when fifty people died during an air show, the crashing of an American aircraft near Düsseldorf, which left four dead and twenty houses destroyed, and the reluctance of the NATO forces to limit the number of low-altitude flights and the number of military exercises, which cause considerable damage, brought it home to West Germans that their country was swamped with foreign troops and bases over which they had little or no control. The 1954 and 1963 agreements between the Federal Republic and the NATO allies gave these allies, and especially the Big Three, rights concerning military bases and maneuvers which left the Federal Republic in an exceptional position in relation to the other allies. The accidents were a strong reminder of the restrictions on West German sovereignty and increased the resentment at the fact that, forty-five years after the war, West Germany still had no sovereign power over the situation in Berlin and Germany as a whole, where the Four Powers retained the last word.[24]

The resentment against the Alliance grew further when, in April 1989, the scenario of the theoretical military exercise Wintex-Cimex was revealed by the weekly *Der Spiegel*. The pattern followed by this exercise was completely inconsistent with West German security interests. NATO would be the first to use nuclear weapons; it would also use them quickly for a second attack. Almost all the seventeen nuclear weapons "launched" during this theoretical exercise, mostly from German soil, were targeted on Central European territory and would have destroyed nearly all of the GDR. Only one nuclear weapon was aimed at the Soviet Union, where the target was the important military port on the Kola Peninsula, and even it would not have been launched from an American aircraft. The Americans refused to target any more nuclear weapons on the Soviet Union. The USSR, which could reach the United States with its intercontinental missiles, was thus largely spared. During the exercise it also emerged that, although the Americans consulted their allies, as required "if time and circumstances permit," they took no notice of the fundamental objections that were raised. The exercise made it clear once again that the Americans had the final say in the use of nuclear weapons and that their view in no way paralleled West German and Western European security interests. This made the West Germans more determined than ever to ensure that their position was taken into account within the Alliance. Mrs. Thatcher's alleged remark that, as the Germans had, after all, lost the last war, they simply had to get used to the idea that the destructive response to an attack by the Warsaw Pact would be virtually confined to Central Europe, could only strengthen West Germany's resolve.[25]

Where short-range nuclear weapons were concerned, the Americans and especially the British called for an early decision on modernization and so rejected negotiations on these weapons. As the NATO summit approached, however, the Americans softened their position and agreed that a decision on modernization might possibly be deferred. The British, on the other hand, stood rigidly by their original view. This contrasted in particular with the West German position, which did, however, vary over time and depending on whether it was put forward by Foreign Minister Genscher, Chancellor Kohl, or some other CDU politician. By and large, the West Germans wanted, first, a decision on modernization postponed until 1992 and, second, negotiations on short-range weapons "as soon as possible" or at least "parallel to the conventional disarmament negotiations" (a third zero option was not advocated "in the present circumstances" but, according to some, could not be ruled out in the future). West Germany could count on support from various other continental European allies, particularly for the first aspect of its position.

Just as France had wanted to prevent Bonn from becoming isolated the previous year, it now wanted to prevent an open split within the Alliance. Although France largely agreed with the position presented primarily by Chancellor Kohl, various factors now made it more difficult for Mitterrand to take a stand and support West Germany. This may explain why France made its views publicly known only ten days before the summit meeting and tried discreetly to play the role of conciliator.[26]

Its first problem was to decide how actively it could take part in the discussions without appearing to defy its status as a member who was not integrated into the military structure of the Alliance. Its growing involvement in the Alliance again led to more allusions to France's—implicit or explicit—gradual reintegration into NATO. This resulted in Paris once again emphasizing in every statement it made that, despite everything, it continued to occupy an independent position vis-à-vis NATO. In his speech to the Institut des Hautes Etudes de la Défense Nationale (IHEDN), for example, President Mitterrand stressed "that our decision-making freedom particularly applies to NATO's integrated military bodies. Let there therefore be an end to the speculation on this matter. We consider a change of status out of the question. This does not, however, rule out military relations with the Alliance."[27] The last sentence naturally touched on what was a sore point for France. After all, it was in itself a sign that the French attitude toward NATO had indeed changed. But how far could these military relations be expanded without there being in effect a change of status?

A second problem for France was how far it could oppose disarmament negotiations on short-range weapons, given that these weapons formed part of NATO's flexible response strategy, which France rejected, and NATO, unlike France, regarded them not as the ultimate deterrent but as weapons that could actually be used. On the other hand, how actively could Paris support such negotiations when it did not accept that they should include its own short-range weapons? If these disarmament talks began, how long would the Soviets (and the West Germans, and even the Americans) agree that France's short-range weapons should not be included on the grounds that they were not "tactical" but "prestrategic"?

A third problem concerned the relationship between the negotiations on conventional weapons and those on nuclear weapons. It could be accepted that negotiations on nuclear weapons would be held only when the conventional disarmament talks had produced certain results. To what extent could the French prevent the conventional talks from being extended to include dual-capacity aircraft (aircraft capable of carrying both conventional and nuclear weapons), which Paris regarded as an essential part of its own *force de frappe*?

These three problems touched on the very core of France's security policy, its status as an independent nuclear power. This may also explain why in 1989 President Mitterrand seemed to attach more importance to Hadès, which could serve more than ever as both a symbol and a cornerstone of this independent French position.

Besides these three basic problems, a fourth area of concern emerged as it became clear that Chancellor Kohl was finding it increasingly necessary to follow Foreign Minister Genscher, who was expressing more radical views and also seemed less prepared to make fundamental concessions at the NATO summit meeting. This meant, first, that from the German point of view there was a greater prospect of a third zero option, which France opposed for some of the reasons summarized above. Second, the chance of a split in the Alliance increased, which the French also wanted to avoid. The concern about and, to a degree, resentment against West Germany was also partly due to its government's frequent failure to consult Paris on the many sudden adjustments to (and usually hardening of) its position. However, these sudden changes in Bonn's position were often the result of Chancellor Kohl's attempts to prevent his coalition coming to grief over this issue. Political survival at home always has a higher priority than diplomatic consultations with allies, however close they may be.

Ten days before the NATO summit meeting marking NATO's fortieth anniversary, and only a few days before his visit to Washington for talks with President Bush, Mitterrand at last adopted a position during a press conference devoted to France's foreign policy and labeled very important.[28] He said he was opposed to any negotiations that would result in a third zero option, but not to negotiations on short-range weapons as such. He believed, however, that priority should be given to conventional disarmament. In 1992 or so it should be considered whether any real progress had been made at this level, and a decision should then be taken on the modernization of short-range weapons in this context. The French president thus set himself apart from those who saw modernization as an imperative principle.

Although Mitterrand's statements were regarded in France chiefly as a dismissal of the German position ("German" being in France a reference mainly to Genscher's views), they were also seen in the Federal Republic as support for Helmut Kohl, who was having difficulties and trying to defend less radical views in his country than those of his foreign minister. The way in which the spokesman of Chancellor Kohl's CDU reacted to the Paris press conference pointed in this direction:

François Mitterrand has made efforts to support the Federal Republic, which is in a difficult position . . . but we must now bear in mind that France is not in favor of negotiations on short-range nuclear weapons unless progress is made at the Vienna conference on conventional disarmament. This should be food for thought both within and outside the government.[29]

In the time before the summit meeting in Brussels France appears to have discreetly helped to reconcile the differences within the Alliance and to enable West Germany and the United States in particular to reach a compromise. The success of the anniversary summit was, however, largely due to President Bush's rather spectacular disarmament and associated compromise proposal, which enabled agreement to be reached on the celebrated Comprehensive Concept.[30] Although everyone could refer to aspects of the text that reflected his or her position, it became clear that the West Germans would eventually come off best and that, for example, the new short-range weapons would never be deployed. In this respect the Comprehensive Concept stated: "The question concerning the introduction and deployment of a follow-on system for the Lance will be dealt with in 1992 in the light of overall security developments." The West Germans were fairly certain that the replacement of these weapons would be ruled out by political developments. Nor was the statement that negotiations on short-range weapons could take place only after conventional disarmament agreements had been implemented seen as an insurmountable obstacle in Bonn. Unlike the other allies, the West Germans believed President Bush when he said that these negotiations would soon produce favorable results. Bonn therefore viewed the future with some equanimity. Bush thus complied primarily with West Germany's desire for disarmament and, to some extent, trod on the sensitive nuclear toes of France and Britain, although they realized that the American compromise was the only way out of NATO's impasse.[31]

France may well have played a conciliatory role during the preparations for the NATO feast, but the American president was clearly the great entertainer during the feast itself. It was far-off American Uncle George who succeeded in reconciling the bickering European nephews and nieces and thus in preventing the birthday party and future relations within the NATO family from becoming a disaster. The NATO summit meeting was therefore primarily a reaffirmation of American leadership, a fact with which Paris was evidently able to reconcile itself without too much trouble.[32]

France clearly no longer had any great ambition to be or to become the leader of a Western European or Franco-German defense community. Had this ambition ever really been so great? It had certainly not been any greater than the hopes France pinned on the creation of a full-blown Western European or Franco-German security system, as Mitterrand's speech to the IHEDN in October, for example, had already made clear.[33] In the months before the NATO summit meeting the Europeans had indeed been openly faced with their mutual discord, which only American intervention could bring to an end. Although Franco-German relations had stood up relatively well during this period and had even played a major part in the search for a solution, the first half of 1989 had also revealed fundamental differences between Bonn and Paris, which only a radical political decision could overcome. Furthermore, there was again some disappointment in Paris over West Germany's attitude toward the European Community and the other aspects of the Franco-German relationship. This too was mentioned at François Mitterrand's press conference: "While we see that Franco-German relations are useful at both diplomatic and military level, France still has the right to expect them to be equally good at economic and monetary level. In this respect there is something of a gap. Everything needs to function simultaneously."[34]

France's ambitions also seem to have been somewhat tempered by the realization that, as a result of the change in East-West relations, it no longer held the cards it needed to play a leading role. This was reflected, for example, in its relations with Eastern Europe and its initial rejection of the West German proposal for a joint *Ostpolitik*. This in turn led to disillusionment about Franco-German cooperation in Bonn, where it could not be accepted that security and cooperation between the two countries should be largely confined to the "defense-negative" military sphere and not be extended to include the "positive nonmilitary" aspects of security. Thus the West Germans also saw something of a gap. The Franco-German relationship and, with it, the process of European integration could make progress only if balance continued to be maintained in the fulfillment of what the West Germans and the French saw as their requirements. This was to be apparent, for example, at the European Council meeting in December 1989, when the French expressed their support for German reunification and the West Germans agreed to the plans for the establishment of the Economic and Monetary Union.

In relations with Eastern Europe it was perhaps even clearer than in other spheres that "France must at last follow Bonn instead of leading it."[35] Mitterrand referred to relations with Eastern Europe as one of the top priorities of his policy and indeed greatly expanded these relations, as evidenced by various visits at the highest political level and the sizable loans granted by France. He also ensured closer consultation between Paris and Bonn on contacts with Eastern Europe. Even closer coordination, however, would make the French policy toward Eastern Europe no more than a subsidiary part of West Germany's superior *Ostpolitik*. This certainly did not befit the status of France, which, though a faithful ally of Bonn, was still one of the Four Powers with responsibility for Berlin and Germany as a whole.

The motives and objectives of the two countries' policies toward Eastern Europe also differed. The West Germans might well say that, in the final analysis, they were doing no more than the bidding of President de Gaulle, who urged Western Europe to pursue its own active policy toward Eastern Europe and to "overcome Yalta." Yet West German and French motives for a policy and objective of this kind still differed substantially. For de

Gaulle this objective was, after all, primarily a useful means of regaining France's freedom of action from the United States in the foreign policy sphere. For the Federal Republic it was not so much a means as an end in itself: overcoming the division of Europe and, therefore, of Germany. While France wanted to be part of this development to a degree so as to make Europe more independent, to "chaperone" West Germany and to prevent it from becoming isolated, it also realized that this would eventually lead to a decline in its relative influence, leaving the French with their eternal dilemma.[36]

The feeling that the "grandeur" of the French Republic was gradually being eroded was also aggravated by other factors in the first half of 1989. First, there was the fierce debate within the Rocard government in April and May on the extent to which the defense budget should be cut. In November 1987, the Chirac government and the then socialist opposition had approved an extremely ambitious modernization program, which provided for the financing of eight projects: a new tank, an aircraft carrier, short- and long-range missiles, a new generation of submarines, a fighter aircraft, an observation satellite, and a battlefield helicopter—enough, in short, for France to maintain its status and for the French armed forces to perform their four tasks of nuclear deterrence, defense of the national territory, joint defense of Europe, and presence in overseas territories. Although the socialist government quickly deferred or cut back some of these projects, it was realized barely eighteen months later that the program was still too ambitious, that the planned annual increase in the defense budget would have to be sharply reduced, and that choices would therefore have to be made. This led to heated discussions between the finance and defense ministries, the latter indignantly emphasizing that it was not right for the country's defense strategy to be determined by mere budgetary considerations. Or as someone put it: "You do not negotiate with a deputy director in the budget department on French strategic concepts for Central Europe."[37] An article in the journal *Défense Nationale* had also previously warned that "the necessary updating of the projects should be prompted not by the quest for savings but by reflection on the priority tasks."[38]

Early in June the Defense Council, chaired by President Mitterrand, approved a defense budget that struck a balance between defense and financial requirements. It was clear that during the reflection on the priority tasks fundamental choices had once again been avoided. Although the revised law on the program for 1991 and 1992 provided for cuts, it did not affect the essence of the military tasks or projects themselves or sacrifice one or more of them. The only parts of the law to escape the budgetary knife completely were such nuclear armament projects as Hadès, which thus seemed to have become an even stronger symbol of France's independent nuclear status.[39]

The failure to make any real basic choices and to ax certain tasks or projects was in keeping with what François Mitterrand stressed at his press conference and elsewhere: "La France doit tenir son rang" (France must maintain its standing), which to him meant that "France will not forgo the possession of weapons which other powers have."[40]

While the debate on the defense budget revealed France's real limitations, two other incidents were primarily of psychological importance in undermining France as an independent nuclear power. First, an opinion poll commissioned by the army showed that the French were none too keen on defending themselves. If the Red Army crossed the Rhine, one in two Frenchmen would rather negotiate than take up arms. And although the French had a very high opinion of their *force de frappe*, only 8 percent of them would want nuclear weapons used in the event of war. That of which politicians and the media in France had arrogantly been accusing the West Germans for a decade or so now seemed to be true of themselves: The French too would evidently rather be "red than dead" and, despite the trauma they suffered in 1938, they too were not immune to the "spirit of Munich" (when the Western Europeans made major concessions to Hitler). An unpleasant conclusion for proud France.[41]

Even more painful than the finding that the French did not seem very willing to make use of their independent nuclear capability was the revelation that the French nuclear force was less "independent" than had always been thought. A few days before NATO's anniversary summit meeting the contents of an article to be published in the journal *Foreign Policy* were made known.[42] It claimed that for fifteen years Paris had been receiving American help with the development of its nuclear capability and, in return, had "de facto" largely returned to NATO's integrated command. Since the time of Nixon and Pompidou, when France had had difficulty with the further refinement of its nuclear capability (during the development of MIRVs [Multiple Independent Reentry Vehicles]), the article continued, the two countries had agreed, under the personal supervision of their presidents and in utmost secrecy, that American specialists should help their French counterparts with the further expansion of the *force de frappe*. Under the "negative advice" procedure the French had not been supplied directly with technical data, but they had been given information if research connected with, say, the development of MIRVs came to a dead end. Information on other aspects of nuclear weapons such as safety, on the other hand, had been passed on directly.

One consequence of this secret program, the article claimed, was that relations between the heads of state and senior military levels of the two countries were far closer than had generally been assumed. In return (and also because the French military had never been happy with de Gaulle's nuclear doctrine and break with NATO), the French had greatly strengthened their ties with NATO's military command through the American

SACEUR (Supreme Allied Commander, Europe—the chief NATO military officer) and CINCEUR (Commander in Chief, Europe—the commander of U.S. forces). Detailed plans had been drawn up and considerably enlarged upon under Mitterrand and Reagan, not only for the Americans to make use of French lines of communication but also for French forces to occupy positions in Central Germany at a time of crisis and operate under direct NATO command, albeit after the French president had given his consent. Furthermore, the French were said to have added to their "national" plan of attack an alternative plan that was coordinated with NATO's.

The advantage of all this was that, as the practical problems posed by military cooperation between France and NATO were less serious than assumed, it would be easier to develop closer military relations between Paris and the Western European partners. An advantage for future European cooperation in the military sphere was that the Franco-American nuclear relationship would also remove an obstacle to closer cooperation between the two European nuclear powers, Britain and France. London had, after all, feared that such cooperation might lead to France obtaining information that Britain was forbidden to divulge by the Anglo-American cooperation agreements and that it would consequently forfeit its "exclusive" access to American nuclear technology. Richard Ullman's revelations in *Foreign Policy* did not therefore seem so unfavorable for the future process of European integration. They were, however, a slap in the face of those Frenchmen who still very much cherished the idea of a "France à la de Gaulle."

That the Elysée was beginning to feel concerned about the gradual erosion of this image of France became apparent during Mitterrand's press conference before the NATO summit meeting in Brussels, when he evidently thought it necessary to emphasize that he categorically rejected *"l'argument de déclin"* (which, for a head of state, ought really to be self-evident). He concluded his statement by repeating that "despite everything" France's standing must remain high.[43] The question was how long this could continue without basic choices being made.

The dilemma remained, as did French indecision. The closer cooperation with the Federal Republic revealed the Achilles heel of the French security policy. French introversion had solved nothing, because desperate diseases require desperate remedies.

NOTES

1. "Dregger für eine Neuorientierung der deutschen Sicherheitspolitik," *Frankfurter Allgemeine Zeitung*, 19 June 1987, p. 2; "Kohl will keine isolierte Sicherheitspolitik mit Paris," *Die Welt*, 20 June 1987, p. 1.

2. "In Paris wird über eine Ausweitung der 'Nukleargarantie' auf die Bundesrepublik gesprochen," *Frankfurter Allgemeine Zeitung*, 19 June 1987, p. 1.

3. Jacques Isnard, "La brigade franco-allemande aurait pour mission d'aider

l'armée française à s'engager outre-Rhin," *Le Monde*, 19 July 1987; "Getting France in by stealth," *The Economist*, 19 December 1987, pp. 38–39.

4. Alain Lavère, "La brigade franco-allemande," *Défense Nationale*, April 1989, pp. 184–86.

5. Deutsch-französischer Verteidigungs-und Sicherheitsrat, "Protokoll zum Vertrag vom 22 Januar 1963 zwischen der BRD and der Französischen Republik über die deutsch-französische Zusammenarbeit," *Bulletin*, no. 11, 27 January 1988, pp. 82–83.

6. "Tiéseur et hostilité," *Le Figaro*, 23 January 1988; C. T. & H. de B., "Un tandem qui souvent irrite ou inquiète . . . ," *Le Monde*, 21 January 1988.

7. "Frans-Duitse samenwerking krijgt twee instellingen," *De Standaard*, 14 November 1987.

8. Jan Vermeersch, "Geen zandstormen aan de Elbe," *Knack*, 29 June 1988, p. 90.

9. M. Chirac, "La défense et l'Allemagne," *Le Monde*, 13 December 1987; "L'engagement de la France serait immédiat et sans réserve dans l'hypothèse d'une aggression contre l'Allemagne fédérale, déclare m. Chirac à l'IHEDN," *Le Monde*, 13 December 1987, p. 1; L. R., "Bonn 'salue' les déclarations de M. Chirac sur l'engagement de la France en cas d'aggression contre la RFA," *Le Monde*, 16 December 1987, p. 3.

10. Jacques Amalric, "Les tentations stratégiques de M. Mitterrand," *Le Monde*, 22 October 1987, p. 1.

11. François de Rose, "L'Evangile de défense selon François Mitterrand," *Le Monde*, 2 March 1988, p. 2.

12. Amalric, "Les tentations stratégiques."

13. Jacques Amalric, "Menaces sur la consensus entre l'Elysée et la majorité en matière de défense," *Le Monde*, 1 March 1988, p. 1; "L'urgence n'est pas de moderniser mais de réduire les armements au plus bas niveau possible," *Le Monde*, 1 March 1988, p. 4; Jacques Amalric and Claire Tréan, "M. Chirac prône la vigilance à l'égard de l'Union Soviétique," *Le Monde*, 2 March 1988, p. 2; "Interview des französischen Staatspräsidenten, François Mitterrand, vom 29. Februar für die Zeitung 'Ouest France,' " *Europa-Archiv*, 43(7)1988, p. D193.

14. "Declaration of the Heads of State and Government Participating in the Meeting of the North Atlantic Council in Brussels (2–3 March 1988)," *NATO Review*, 36(2)1988, pp. 30–31.

15. Horst Ehmke, "Le rôle de la France et de la RFA dans les relations Est-Ouest," *Politique Etrangère*, 53(2)1988, p. 857.

16. "France Studying Delay in Missiles," *International Herald Tribune*, 13 September 1988.

17. " 'Ihr Deutschen seid ein grosses Volk. Bewahrt Eure Identität,' Die Welt-Gespräch mit François Mitterrand," *Die Welt*, 18 January 1988.

18. Friedrich B. Meyer zu Natrup, "Frankreich and die DDR," *Europa-Archiv*, 43(11)88, p. 315; Roger de Weck, "Honneurs für Honecker," *Die Zeit*, 8 January 1988, p. 44.

19. Mia Doornaert, "Frankrijk stapt in militair NAVO-beraad," *De Standaard*, 14 June 1987, p. 1; Kenneth R. Timmerman, "Defense Policy Shifts from Isolationism toward Europe," *International Herald Tribune*, 1 June 1987, p. 12.

20. *Mémento Défense-Désarmement 1988* (Brussels: GRIP, 1988), p. 144; David S.

Yost, "La coopération franco-allemande en matière de défense," *Politique Etrangère*, 53(4)88, pp. 844–45; Karen Fossli, "French and Norwegians to step up military links," *Financial Times*, 14 July 1987.

21. " 'Ihr Deutschen seid ein grosses Volk.' "
22. "Les réactions," *Le Monde*, 23 June 1987.
23. J. H. Sampiemon, "Houding Bonn leidt tot contradictie," *N.R.C.-Handelsblad*, 16 March 1989.
24. Karl Feldmeyer, "Air-show crash revives issue of Allied rights in Germany," *Frankfurter Allgemeine Zeitung*, 5 September 1988, in *The German Tribune*, 11 September 1988, p. 1; Hans-Herbert Gaebel, "Jet crash into houses should force NATO training rethink," *Frankfurter Rundschau*, 10 December 1988, in *The German Tribune*, 18 December 1988, p. 1.
25. "Wir Europäer sollen uns opfern," *Der Spiegel*, 24 April 1989, pp. 14–16; "Der Iwan kommt—und feste druff," *Der Spiegel*, 1 May 1989, pp. 23–27.
26. C. T., "Les premières réactions soviétiques aux propositions américaines sont positives," *Le Monde*, 1 June 1989, p. 5.
27. "Rede des französischen Staatspräsidenten, François Mitterrand, vor dem Institut des Hautes Etudes de Défense Nationale in Paris am 11. Oktober 1988," *Europa-Archiv*, 43(23)1988, p. D666.
28. "La conférence de presse du président de la République; 'Le rôle de la France est de tenir son rang,' " *Le Monde*, 20 May 1989, pp. 2–3.
29. Luc Rosenzweig, "Bonn estime que M. Mitterrand s'est rapproché sur le fond des positions américaine et britannique," *Le Monde*, 20 May 1989, p. 8.
30. "A Comprehensive Concept of Arms Control and Disarmament, adopted by Heads of State and Government at the meeting of the North Atlantic Council in Brussels on 29th and 30th May 1989," *NATO Information Service*, Brussels 1989, 15 pp.
31. Christoph Bertram, "Happy-End auf dem Gipfel des Streits," *Die Zeit*, 2 June 1989, p. 3.
32. Claire Tréan, "Les occidentaux acceptent de négocier sur les armes nucléaires à courte portée mais refusent leur élimination totale," *Le Monde*, 31 May 1989, p. 6.
33. "Rede des französischen Staatspräsidenten, François Mitterrand, vor dem IHEDN in Paris am 11. Oktober 1988," *Europa-Archiv*, 43(23)1988, pp. D671–73.
34. "La conférence de presse," p. 7.
35. Joseph Fitchett, "French Diplomacy: Taking a Back Seat to Bonn," *International Herald Tribune*, 29 April 1989.
36. Ingo Kolboom, "Ostpolitik als deutsch-französische Herausforderung," *Europa-Archiv*, 44(4)1989, pp. 116–19, 121–22.
37. Jean Guisnel, "La politique de défense sur le fil du Budget," *Libération*, 22/4/89, p. 9.
38. Maurice Faivre, "Le budget de la défense pour 1989," *Défense Nationale*, January 1989, p. 172; Jacques Isnard, "Désaccord entre M. Rocard et M. Chevènement sur la programmation militaire," *Le Monde*, 25 April 1989, p. 16; Guisnel, "La politique de défense."
39. "210,3 milliards de francs pour l'equipement en 1990 et 1991," *Le Monde*, 3 June 1989, p. 4.
40. Isnard, "Désaccord entre M. Rocard et M. Chevènement."

41. Joachim Fritz-Vannahme, "Ein Spiel auf Zeit," *Die Zeit*, 16 June 1989.

42. Richard H. Ullman, "The Covert French Connection," *Foreign Policy*, (75)1989, pp. 3–33.

43. "La conférence de presse," p. 3.

10

Erich Honecker's Visit to Bonn

Helmut Kohl's decision to allow the Pershing Ia missiles to be negotiated away under an INF agreement can be regarded as a turning point in the development of a virtual consensus on security policy, both within the Christian-Democratic family and among the leading West German political parties (as has been seen in chapter 3 on the political interpretation of the change in the West German perception of security). This decision also coincided with another important event, which would similarly prove to be a turning point in the Federal Republic's attitude toward the communist part of Europe, since it indicated a growing consensus within the CDU/CSU and among the political parties on East-West German relations and would also serve as the basis of a generally accepted policy toward the USSR and Eastern Europe as a whole.

Chancellor Kohl's decision on the "German" missiles was doubtless intended in part to clear the way for the long awaited, but repeatedly postponed visit that the East German party leader, Erich Honecker, was to pay to West Germany ten days later, from 7 to 11 September 1987. The two Germanys had, after all, gone out of their way to create the most favorable possible inter-German climate in preparation for the historic summit meeting, as it was not permitted to be called, and to prevent some incident or other from leading to a further postponement of the visit. East Berlin made concessions on various issues about which the West Germans were sensitive: It became the first Eastern bloc country to abolish the death penalty, it proclaimed an amnesty for prisoners, it withdrew the order to shoot would-be refugees at the inter-German frontier (it transpired later that it had simply been suspended), it eased the restrictions on travel to West Germany, and so on. The two Germanys agreed on an exchange of spies and at last concluded a scientific and technological agreement, which they had been negotiating for ten years.[1]

Ten days before Honecker's arrival Helmut Kohl was able to advance the most important argument of all, one that was bound to make the East German leader's visit palatable: In 1987 a total of around a million East Germans under retirement age would be permitted to visit the Federal Republic, double the number in 1986 and twenty times more than in 1982.[2] The chancellor was certainly able to make very good use of the GDR's various concessions as proof that his *Deutschlandpolitik* was really paying dividends and benefiting the East Germans, even though some of his party supporters did not find it psychologically easy to accept this policy. This was not surprising, given that the CDU/CSU was the spiritual architect of the Hallstein doctrine, which not only ruled out any contact with the GDR but also rejected diplomatic relations with third countries by which it was recognized. In contrast to earlier attempted visits, however, there were this time no disruptive statements from CDU/CSU politicians that might have jeopardized Honecker's visit. In its attitude toward the GDR the party as a whole had clearly changed, partly as a result of the CDU's poor showing in the 1987 elections.

That it was possible for the East German leader's visit to go ahead in September 1987 was, of course, due not only to East German concessions and the change in the CDU's attitude but also to the more relaxed East-West relationship, which formed a better basis for delicate inter-German meetings than the cold war atmosphere that had prevailed a few years earlier. Improved inter-German relations were also commensurate with the foreign policy and the philosophy of the common European house that the Soviet leader who had come to power in 1985 was beginning to proclaim with growing vociferousness. In May, at its meeting in East Berlin, the Warsaw Pact (i.e., the Kremlin) decided that the various member countries might have some freedom in their foreign policies.[3] The Soviet leaders had realized that not even Erich Honecker's go-it-alone attitude in 1983/84 had had an untoward effect on the West German party-political scene. Furthermore, President von Weizsäcker and Foreign Minister Genscher had been able to put West German-Soviet relations, upset by Helmut Kohl, back on the right track during their visit to Moscow in early July 1987. Now that the West German politicians had shown the leaders of the communist world that they were of good faith and had no malicious ulterior motives, Comrade Erich could make his visit to the other Germany with an easy conscience. Or was it sheer coincidence that the news of Honecker's visit was announced less than a week after von Weizsäcker's visit to Moscow?

The East German leader's visit to Bonn was also facilitated by being one of a series of contacts between the Federal Republic and other Eastern European countries. In the first few years of his term of office Kohl had made the mistake of pursuing a *Deutschlandpolitik* that did not form part of a broader *Ostpolitik.*[4] This was perhaps not really surprising, since his CDU/CSU had had little experience with the *Ostpolitik* and, indeed, had always rejected it. From 1969, when relations were first established with Eastern Europe, until 1982, the two sister parties had, after all, been in opposition. The result, however, was growing suspicion of German intentions in the surrounding countries, which was one reason for the open rejection of Honecker's *Deutschlandpolitik* by the leaders in Warsaw, Prague, and Moscow. In 1987 Honecker's visit was preceded by trips by von Weizsäcker to Moscow and by the Bulgarian party leader, Zhivkov, to Bonn. Honecker had, moreover, already been received in Italy and the Netherlands.

Another feature of the change both in the attitude of the Christian Democrats and in inter-German relations was that the visit canceled in 1984 would have been completely unsatisfactory for Honecker in terms of protocol, whereas almost all the requirements in this respect had been met by 1987. In 1984 West Germany's greatest concern was that the East German party leader's visit should not be interpreted as official recognition of the GDR. If Honecker had made his visit in 1984, protocol would therefore have required that he be placed more or less in quarantine: He would have arrived not in the Federal capital, Bonn, but at Frankfurt airport; he would have had political discussions not in Bonn but in Bad Kreuznach, 150 km away; he would have had a meeting with the Federal president, but not at his official residence.[5] Three years later it was possible to reduce these symbolic niceties to a minimum. The East German head of state arrived in the capital of the Federal Republic, was given an official reception, met von Weizsäcker in his official residence, inspected a military parade, and so on. Although the foreign ministers were not formally included in the official delegations (the Federal Republic did not regard East Germany as a foreign country) and, according to the official program, not the "national anthems" but the "anthems" were played, it was clear nonetheless that the East German leader was being received in the same way as other heads of state visiting the Federal Republic.

As the East German regime saw it, Honecker's arrival in Bonn on 7 September to be greeted "de facto" as the head of state therefore put the final seal on the recognition of the German Democratic Republic by the Federal Republic of Germany, not in the legal but in the political sense.[6] It was also a victory over the CDU/CSU's official doctrine, which did not accept the existence of two separate Germanys. His arrival in Bonn therefore signified for Honecker the end of the difficult struggle for recognition in which he had been engaged for sixteen years. Two years later, however, this recognition was to contribute to the developments that marked the end of the East German regime itself.

Honecker's visit was greeted with mixed feelings in West Germany. For many it was the coming of "one of our brothers," as Helmut Schmidt put it,[7] another important step in the normalization of relations between the two Germanys. It would facilitate contacts between ordinary people on either side of the Wall, and it would enable the division between the two societies to be overcome. Overenthusiastic dreamers were brought back to earth, however, by Honecker's initially rather flat and unspectacular statements and by his famous remark that "socialism and capitalism are as compatible as fire and water."[8] In so saying, the East German leader forgot that, incompatible though these two elements are, water can put out fire (but not vice versa).

For others in the Federal Republic Honecker's visit was a rather painful experience. The few minutes the two German heads of state spent side by side in front of Chancellor Kohl's official residence, listening to the two German anthems and with two German flags before them, one with and one without the hammer and sickle, were, for instance, more difficult to cope with than had previously been thought when the rational decision was taken to agree to Honecker's visit. Clearly, not everyone appreciated that the Germans on the other side of the Wall could be helped with this tribute to the very man who had been responsible for its construction in 1961. For the Christian Democrats the visit also implied de facto recognition both of the failure of their former *Deutschlandpolitik* and of the existence of two Germanys, even though they had denied the existence of East Germany for four decades. Two years later they would be able to triumph. The prospect of a single German nation, however, had become possible only by the apparently inconsistent, indirect route of recognizing the GDR. In many cases, ideals can indeed be achieved only if they are qualified or set aside for a time.

While Honecker's visit might imply de facto recognition of his regime, the West Germans did not renounce the basic goals that Federal governments had always pursued and which were also enshrined in the constitution. In his welcoming address the Federal chancellor explicitly referred to this:

This visit can and will do nothing to change the difference in the views of the two states on such fundamental issues as nationality. The preamble of our constitution is not open to amendment. . . . It seeks a united Europe and calls on the German people to achieve the unity and freedom of Germany in free self-determination.

Nevertheless,

we know from experience that conflicting positions on fundamental issues must not prevent practical cooperation between the two states in Germany. . . . Let us concentrate in the next few days on what is feasible, and let us also continue to agree that we should not place the emphasis on the problems that cannot be solved for the moment.

From this he concluded that "the German question remains open, but a solution is not on the agenda of world history at the moment, and we will also need our neighbors' approval of any solution."[9]

However, the two German statesmen also made statements that indicated a possible further change in their policies that would help to put "the German question" on the East-West agenda sooner than expected. For the West Germans this concerned policy toward Eastern Europe as a whole, and for the East Germans, moves to make the border between the two Germanys more penetrable. In his statement Helmut Kohl referred to a goal that Foreign Minister Genscher, the FDP, and the SPD had strongly advocated in the past. "We are called upon to play our part in a larger task, the task of shaping a European peaceful order which overcomes the division of Europe."[10] If he actually intended to take this statement as a guideline for government policy, the Federal government could be expected to adopt a different position on the international and especially the European stage in the future. So global an objective would, after all, require a more active and more radical *Ostpolitik* than one primarily designed to protect inter-German relations against any adverse effects of global East-West relations.

The East German party leader, who had been fairly noncommittal in his various statements, regaled his hosts with an unexpected and hopeful address during his brief stay in the village of Wiebelskirchen, the place of his birth, to which he was returning for the first time since 1949. This part of his visit clearly revealed the human dimension of the division of Germany, since the situation of the Honecker family from Wiebelskirchen could be regarded as symbolic of the fate of many millions of Germans. This, then, was the feeling when seventy-five-year-old Erich Honecker arrived at the place where he had spent his youth, met his sister, and visited the grave of his parents, who had died at a time when relations between the two Germanys had even made it impossible to attend the funeral of one's own parents. It was not therefore surprising that he should say on this particular occasion, "If we act together in accordance with the communiqué we have agreed on in Bonn and bring about peaceful cooperation in this connection, the day will come when the frontiers no longer separate but unite us, as the frontier between the GDR and Poland unites us."[11]

Whatever the reason for this surprising statement—to increase the pressure on the West German politicians, to polish up his image, sullied by the Wall, or to give vent to his emotions—it certainly made an impact and caused a wave of subdued hope to flow through the political ranks in the Federal Republic. This more than any other statement was seen by the proponents of an active and far-reaching *Deutschlandpolitik* and *Ostpolitik* as a sign that they were on the right track.

Both the East German and the West German leaders realized, however, that there was in fact little chance of the frontier being opened while the prosperity and economic potential of the two Germanys differed so markedly. This was indeed openly admitted by those accompanying Honecker on his visit.[12] The Wall was still performing the economic function of preventing East Germany from losing its best-trained and most talented workers and West Germany from being confronted with a growing mass of unemployed people looking for homes. The GDR might call itself the "Japan of Eastern Europe" and have the strongest economy and highest standard of living in the Eastern bloc, but it did not compare with the other Germany in any way. The standard of living in East Germany was about half that in West Germany, and East German economic growth was no longer as high as it once was.[13] As a considerable proportion of the East German population had been given the chance to visit West Germany in the first half of 1987, East Germans were also more aware of the disparity than before. For the GDR leaders it was therefore essential that better political relations with the Federal Republic should be accompanied by increased West German economic support for the East German economy.

For Bonn too it was important that economic development and living standards should improve in the GDR, so that political dreams of a more open frontier and even closer inter-German relations might more easily come true. If the difference in economic development was less pronounced, less damage would, after all, be done to the East German economy and labor market when the frontier was opened, and the Federal Republic would not be flooded with so many East Germans wanting to turn their talents into money in the rich West. Even in 1987 it became clear that the native West German population was far from enthusiastic about the rising, though still limited, number of "compatriots" looking for work in their country, and least of all about their being given preferential treatment in the housing market. In purely economic terms, West German industry was also well aware of the enormous potential to be tapped in the GDR, as in the whole of Eastern Europe and the USSR, and of the considerable lead their geographical location and traditional economic links gave them over most other western partners and competitors. In 1987 inter-German trade accounted for only about 1.5 percent of all West Germany's foreign trade, as much as trade with such countries as Spain, Yugoslavia, and South Africa, and a sixth of that with the Netherlands or France.[14]

This in itself puts in perspective the contention that the Federal Republic might one day prefer the Eastern European to the Western European market. West Germany's economic relations with its eastern neighbors might have considerable potential for growth, but compared to trade with Western Europe they continue to be of secondary importance, particularly now that the completion of a single market in the European Community is opening up new prospects of trade.

Given the importance to both Germanys of more economic contacts, this aspect of inter-German relations attracted considerable attention during Honecker's visit. The party leader and twenty-three directors of East German export firms met the representatives of three hundred or so West German companies and umbrella organizations. Both East and West Germans clearly wanted to increase trade and, above all, to improve its quality and to widen its range. Both sides therefore urged more exchanges and cooperation in the field of modern technologies. Hence, for example, Foreign Minister Genscher's proposal that Eastern European countries should be permitted to participate in the Western European EUREKA program for the joint development of technological projects.

The possibility of penetrating the technological "wall" between East and West was, however, still restricted by COCOM (Coordination Committee of Western Nations on Technology Transfer), the committee formed by NATO (and Japan) which limits and monitors the export of western technologies to the communist world. In the discussions during Honecker's visit to the Federal Republic it was noticeable how a kind of "German" consensus had emerged on the reduction of the COCOM restrictions on technology transfer. Bonn was therefore to become increasingly outspoken in its defense of this position within the Atlantic Alliance, especially as two economic and, therefore, political heavyweights in the Federal Republic, the Federal Association of German Industry (BDI) and the German Industrial and Trade Association (DIHT), were increasing the pressure for a more flexible attitude.[15]

Like the West German political community, West German industry was thus prepared to respond to the rapid developments when the communist regime in East Berlin began to collapse toward the end of 1989 and closer economic relations between the two Germanys suddenly became possible. Both had, after all, the backing of an existing network of economic and personal contacts. The discussions during Honecker's visit to Bonn on increased cooperation were indeed important more for the closer contacts they brought between the East and West German partners than for actual agreements and achievements. The practical results of Honecker's stay in the Federal Republic were, after all, relatively limited, especially when it is considered how many drumrolls and warning shots preceded his arrival.

What, then, did this "historic visit" achieve? The signing of three previously negotiated and agreed treaties on science and technology, environmental protection, and the exchange of information on the danger of nuclear radiation; the improvement of rail and road links with West Berlin and of telephone and postal links between the two countries; an assurance that GDR citizens who had fled to the West before 1982 might visit their own country again; permission for medicines and West German technical journals to be sent to the GDR; and so on. The results thus tended to be modest, and as most were based on existing agreements, they certainly did not warrant the adjective "historic." This was indeed even more apparent from the proposals on which agreement was not reached, such as Bonn's attempt to obtain permission for West German visitors to spend the night in East

Berlin and for cyclists to enter and tour the GDR (as a compromise it was agreed that people visiting East Germany by car might take a bicycle with them).[16]

The high-level East German visit was therefore primarily important for helping to lay the foundations for future developments. Existing political and economic contacts were intensified, and new contacts were established, contacts that could be further developed over the next two years and that ensured that, despite the initial surprise at the speed of events, West Germany was able to respond quickly to internal developments in the GDR in 1989 and 1990. The way was, moreover, partly paved for this East German revolution by the sharp increase in confidence and familiarity between the heads of the two countries, prompting the party leaders in East Berlin to take the "West German option" in solving their internal problems so as to avoid the "Eastern European option."

The East German leaders clearly faced a serious dilemma. They were confronted with growing dissatisfaction among their own people and increasing internal pressure, which somehow had to be eased. The dissatisfaction continued to grow because more GDR citizens than before were able to travel to rich West Germany and so became painfully aware of the shortcomings of their own regime. The internal pressure similarly increased because East Berlin refused to apply Comrade Gorbachev's philosophy of glasnost and perestroika to East German society, even though two other communist countries, Hungary and Poland, were slowly beginning to do so. The realization that the leading country in the communist world was pursuing objectives that might in some ways produce the ideal that East Germans believed they had seen on their visit to the Federal Republic could not fail to increase the pressure on the regime. A good example of this combination and interaction of what was for the GDR leaders unfavorable influence from both East and West was provided by the disturbances that occurred in East Berlin in June 1987. When young East Germans took up position near the Brandenburg Gate to hear the western pop concerts given by David Bowie, the Eurythmics, and Genesis on the other side of the Wall and clashed with the riot police, they chanted both "Down with the Wall" and "We want Gorbachev."[17]

As even the Kohl government led by the Christian Democrats had now de facto recognized the Honecker regime and was adopting a relatively positive approach toward it, there appeared to be a growing conviction among the East German leaders that, as the West German politicians would not go beyond certain acceptable limits, they knew where they stood with their West German counterparts, something that could not be so easily said of their Eastern European colleagues. It was also realized that a change in the East German communist regime might undermine the very existence of the GDR. It would appear that the GDR leadership therefore chose to offer East Germans greater "transparency to the West" as a substitute for undesirable internal reforms. This gave rise to the paradoxical situation in which the East German leaders saw greater advantages, a better chance of exercising control, and less danger in offering its citizens increased access to capitalist West Germany than in adopting remedies proposed by their ideological fellow-believers in the East. Honecker thus faced a dilemma from which there was no way out. The interaction of the two negative influences, from East and West, was bound to have a destructive effect on the East German regime.

After Honecker's visit the number of East Germans allowed to travel to the Federal Republic increased further. Chancellor Kohl was therefore able to announce proudly in early 1988 that Honecker had sent him the following figures on travel between the two Germanys: 5,062,914 visits by GDR citizens to West Germany, including 1,286,896 by people under retirement age.[18] This was, respectively, some 4,000,000 and 550,000 more than the previous year. When the number of visits by West Germans to the GDR is then added, the total comes to over thirty million movements between the two parts of Germany and Berlin: The "feeling of togetherness" could not fail to grow.

This feeling, which had been given an additional boost on political and human levels by Honecker's visit, was also enhanced by the more flexible attitude that the authorities in East Berlin took in other respects (or were forced to take in return for further West German aid). While they had agreed to only two "partnerships between towns" in 1986, for example, and were still very suspicious of this phenomenon in early 1987, by the end of that year they had agreed to some twenty East German towns and by mid-1988 forty or so establishing relations with towns in West Germany.[19] And while they had initially been at pains to ensure that only officials took part in mutual visits between two towns, they increasingly allowed ordinary citizens to participate. In early February Honecker also made a concession he had been unwilling to make a few months earlier in Bonn: West Berliners were permitted to spend the night in the eastern part of the city.[20] This measure was important to Bonn not only because of the human aspect but also for other, more fundamental reasons. It was seen as a fresh sign that, as with the treaties signed in Bonn, the East German leaders were also beginning to depart in practice from their former principle that West Berlin was not to be regarded as a normal part of the Federal Republic (spending the night in East Germany had, after all, been possible for some years in the "normal" border region between the two countries).

Although Honecker had chosen to alleviate the adverse consequences of the Wall for his people by adopting a more flexible policy on travel and establishing closer relations with the other Germany, he was increasingly confronted with the logic of the Wall. The number of "refugees" in 1987 was almost twice that in 1985. Most managed to escape by simply not returning to their official fatherland after visiting West Germany, but a small minority of 288 reckless or desperate East Germans were forced to take the extremely dangerous course of going over the Berlin Wall or the Iron Curtain. Although the number of refugees—6,252 according to official West German statistics, about 12,000 according to East German religious leaders—might not seem so high compared with the total number of travelers, it was particularly alarming to East Berlin that after Honecker's visit to West Germany the number of disloyal citizens should suddenly rise. In December 1987, for example, 1.5 percent of all East Germans visiting the Federal Republic stayed in the West, many of them, moreover, highly trained people like doctors, who found the difference between their own and their West German colleagues' income and affluence too blatant. The relaxation of the travel restrictions led to a rise not only in the number of "traitors" but also in the number of East Germans who, after returning from a trip to West Germany, had the courage to make official applications to the East German authorities for permission to leave the country with their families. The policy of more open frontiers, intended, among other things, to offset the growing frustration with life in the GDR, was thus in fact extremely counterproductive.[21]

Critics of the East German regime also had the courage to express their frustration in public on a limited, but growing scale. This was apparent, for example, from the blossoming of ecological and other protest movements attempting to achieve some unofficial room to maneuver under the protective wing of the church. This had begun in the months before Honecker's visit to West Germany, when the authorities took a fairly tolerant line by East German standards. A remarkable occurrence in this context was the disruption of the official ceremony in memory of Rosa Luxemburg in early 1988 by demonstrators demanding more freedom of speech and travel and carrying banners bearing Rosa Luxemburg's own words: "Freedom is always the freedom of others to think differently."

This was a painful confrontation for the East German leaders and ideologues, and they became increasingly nervous in the course of 1988. The popular glasnost-inclined Soviet magazine *Sputnik* and various films from the USSR were banned. Party ideologue Hager explicitly rejected political and economic reforms like those being undertaken in the USSR and emphasized that "just because your neighbor puts up new wallpaper, you do not have to do the same." Party leader Honecker described the reinterpretation of the history of the Soviet communist party then under way as "claptrap of the petty bourgeoisie gone wild."

The burgeoning protest movements were attacked with greater ferocity, and members of dissident movements were arrested. In the process the East German authorities made the mistake of not only expelling these public enemies to the Federal Republic, to the supposed and, for many, unattainable paradise, but also, initially, giving them permission to return to the GDR later. This could hardly be called serious punishment of people who in most cases had joined the protest movement after vainly applying for exit visas. This measure therefore came as something of a surprise both to the man in the street and to the disillusioned supporters of the regime. "You have to be a criminal before the state courts you like this." The general unrest continued to grow, the ranks of the protest movements swelled, and a new flood of would-be émigrés followed. The authorities took increasingly tough measures against these expressions of protest, and as a deterrent they also began to arrest applicants for exit visas.

In early 1989, however, various East German refugees had discovered a new escape route: moving into the West German mission in East Berlin and the embassy in Prague to insist on being admitted to the Federal Republic. The refugee problem that was to prove to be the GDR regime's undoing had begun.[22]

The self-confidence and euphoria that had prevailed among the East German leaders after Honecker's visit to Bonn had thus turned very quickly into alarm and despondency. The price they had had to pay to make that visit possible and to overcome the CDU/CSU's traditional refusal to recognize the GDR proved to be much higher and to have far more serious implications than they had ever assumed. Their decision to take the "West German option" by permitting more visits to the Federal Republic rather than the "Eastern European option," which would have meant reforms, had simply increased the internal pressure for the latter option. The foundations had thus been laid for a massive protest movement and exodus, which was to erupt with great intensity shortly afterward.

NOTES

1. Articles in *De Standaard* (21 and 22 July 1987, 13 and 27 August 1987, and 19 September 1987), *The German Tribune* (23 August 1987), and *La Tribune d'Allemagne* (13 September 1987).

2. Helmut Kohl, "Chancen für die Menschen in Deutschland und für Abrüstung und Rüstungskontrolle, Erklärung zum Besuch von General-Sekretär Honecker," 26 August 1987, *Bulletin*, 27 August 1987, p. 681.

3. Peter Bender, "Keine Frontstaaten mehr. Bundesrepublik und DDR als Lobbyisten der Entspannung," *Die Zeit*, 24 July 1987, p. 4.

4. Ibid.

5. Carl-Christian Kaiser, "Ein Schritt auf langer Strasse. Bonn warnt vor allzu grossen Hoffnungen und Forderungen," *Die Zeit*, 24 July 1987, p. 3.

6. Carl-Christian Kaiser, "Viel Wahrheiten, kein Augenzwinkern," *Die Zeit*, 11 September 1987, p. 3.

7. Helmut Schmidt, "Einer unserer Brüder," *Die Zeit*, 24 July 1987, p. 3.

8. "Offizieller Besuch des Generalsekretärs des Zentralkomitees der SED. Vom 7. bis 11. September 1987. Empfang in der Redoute," *Bulletin*, 10 September 1987, p. 707.

9. Ibid., pp. 705–6.

10. Ibid., p. 706.

11. "Rede des Generalsekretärs des ZK der SED und Staatsratsvorsitzenden der DDR, Erich Honecker, in Neunkirchen/Saar am 10. September 1987," *Europa-Archiv*, 42(19)1987, p. 549.

12. Carl-Christian Kaiser, "Eine Investition in die Zunkunft," *Die Zeit*, 18 September 1987, p. 7.

13. A. H., "Honecker voor Bonn een 'moeilijke gast,' " *De Standaard*, 7 September 1987.

14. Joachim Nawrocki, "Wichtige Klammer," *Die Zeit*, 24 July 1987, p. 3.

15. "Ne pas se brûler, ni se mouiller. Entretiens économiques en marge de la visite d'Erich Honecker," *Handelsblatt*, 10 September 1987, in *La Tribune d'Allemagne*, 27 September 1987, p. 7.

16. "Rede des Bundeskanzlers vor dem Deutschen Bundestag," *Bulletin*, 11 September 1987, pp. 742–43; Luc Rosenzweig, "Rapprochement à petits pas entre les deux Etats allemands," *Le Monde*, 10 September 1987, p. 3.

17. A. H., "Persbureau DDR ontkent rellen rond rockkoncert," *De Standaard*, 10 June 1987, p. 4.

18. Helmut Kohl, "Stand und Perspektiven der Politik der Bundesregierung," *Bulletin*, 13 January 1988, p. 31.

19. "Bundesregierung: Deutschlandpolitik 1987 war ausserordentlich erfolgreich," *Frankfurter Allgemeine Zeitung*, 28 December 1987, p. 4; Albrecht Hinze, "Mécontentement croissant en RDA. Mais les relations intra-allemandes restent satisfaisantes," *Süddeutsche Zeitung*, 18 September 1988, in *La Tribune d'Allemagne*, 7 September 1988, p. 4.

20. "Ein Anfang," *Frankfurter Allgemeine Zeitung*, 15 February 1988, p. 4.

21. Leslie Colitt and David Marsh, "Familiarity with the West breeds enthusiasm for escape," *The Financial Times*, 19 January 1988.

22. "Positive Leistungen," *Der Spiegel*, 13 February 1988, p. 22; A. H., "Kandidaat-emigranten gearresteerd in DDR," *De Standaard*, 7 March 1988, p. 4; Claus Wettermann, "East Berlin begins bullying again," and X., "An old Stalinist screeches against reform," *The German Tribune*, 11 December 1988, p. 4; "Herber Rückschlag," *Der Spiegel*, 16 January 1989, p. 23; Henry Kamm, "East Germans Dismiss a Moscow-Style Renewal," *The International Herald Tribune*, 1 March 1989.

11

Two Streams in One Channel

The consensus among the various West German political parties on the Federal Republic's *Deutschlandpolitik* continued to grow after Honecker's visit. The CDU/CSU in particular became more flexible and more attuned to the policy that had been earlier proposed by the FDP and SPD. A growing part of the West German political and ideological spectrum accepted, implicitly at least, that the "unity of the German nation," defined as a goal in the West German constitution, did not necessarily mean the formation of a single German state. In other words, it was not the political "division" of the two Germanys but human and social "separation" that lay at the heart of the German question. This implied that policy must be geared to healing this human and social rift rather than overcoming the division and achieving reunification.[1]

The debate within the Christian-Democratic family was rekindled in late January 1988 by the Federal minister for intra-German relations, Dorothee Wilms, when she said that "the division of Germany is unlikely to be overcome in the near future since Europe too is still divided."[2] As her words were sharper than Helmut Kohl's statement that the resolution of "the German question" was not on the agenda of world history for the time being, Mrs. Wilms was criticized by the CSU and some members of her own CDU. A few weeks later, however, it emerged that the discussions of a party committee in preparation for the CDU congress in June had to some extent pointed in the same direction. This committee, chaired by Heiner Geissler, proposed, moreover, that the political dialogue with the GDR should be intensified and that contacts and cooperation with the other Germany should be stepped up in every area. It suggested, for example, that the various ministers of the two Germanys should hold regular discussions and that new forms of cooperation should be introduced. The Geissler report was extensively amended after being fiercely opposed by an—albeit small—section of the rank and file, a small minority led by Todenhöfer causing a stir with their criticism of the report's failure to use the word *reunification* and its claim that the Germans could achieve the unity of Germany only after obtaining the approval of their neighbors in East and West.[3]

This does not alter the fact, however, that the sometimes heated debate within the CDU took place in a year when political contacts between the GDR and the Federal Republic continued to develop at a practical level, with Federal Transport Minister Warnke, for example, visiting his counterpart in East Berlin at the time of the CDU congress.[4] The paradox of the reunification issue is indeed that the pragmatists, having at first been prepared to set aside the goal of reunification, in fact paved the way for its achievement, and that it was basically more realistic than their opponents and they themselves had assumed.

Although the CDU did not accept the fairly explicit proposals put forward by the Geissler committee, it was clear that, for the moment at least, the Christian-Democratic leadership was increasingly prepared to abandon the goal of reunification for a new objective: to reunify Europe and so bridge the dividing line between Eastern and Western Europe. There was growing awareness of the truth of what Dorothee Wilms had emphasized: "The division of Europe must be overcome if the division of Germany is also to come to an end."[5] In other words, closer relations with the Eastern European countries must be sought as a means of overcoming the division of Europe and so creating the conditions for bridging the frontier between East and West Germany. Implicitly at least, this philosophy, long held by the FDP and the SPD, was adopted by all the factions of the CDU/CSU in the months after Honecker's visit. It was also to be one of the central elements of the policy pursued by Bonn in late 1987 and throughout 1988 and 1989.

The course that had been mapped out by Foreign Minister Genscher, wandering, like some Don Quixote, through Eastern Europe and seeking more dialogue and closer cooperation between the two parts of Europe, was thus accepted by his coalition partners, who had previously been so skeptical. In late 1987 and early 1988 the political community in Bonn (and Munich) launched an extensive political and economic offensive on Eastern Europe.[6] Barely a month after Honecker, Hungary's Prime Minister Grosz arrived in Bonn, and Genscher visited Romania and, shortly afterward, Germany's neighbor Czechoslovakia. In late 1987 the leader of the Bavarian CSU, Strauss, treated himself and the world to an unexpected visit to Moscow. In mid-January 1988 Genscher flew to Poland, and Soviet Foreign Minister Shevardnadze spent three days in the Federal Republic. In February Chancellor Kohl himself paid a visit to Prague, and it was the turn of Baden-

Württemberg's prime minister, Lothar Späth of the CDU, to go to the Soviet Union.

Particularly important for the future direction of West Germany's policy on Eastern Europe was the visit to Moscow by Franz-Josef Strauss, the man who had always had considerable influence on Bonn's policy and in 1983 had also played a crucial role in the new Federal government's future *Deutschlandpolitik* by supporting the billion-mark loans granted to the GDR. The CSU chairman had been a stubborn opponent of the Soviet regime for more than two decades and had also taken an extremely negative view of Gorbachev's plans for reforms. It therefore came as a great surprise when he visited the Soviet capital and adopted a very positive attitude toward his host. The man who had previously been known for such statements as "Visit the Soviet Union before it comes to you" now took a completely different tone: "The postwar period is over. We have begun a new chapter. The Soviets have nothing to do with foreign adventures. We must make it clear to them that we have every faith in their desire for détente." And on a somewhat more personal note: "It was one of the greatest moments in my life to see myself on the front page of *Pravda*."[7]

That the Soviet leaders invited Strauss of all people to be the first politician in the CDU/CSU family to visit Moscow indicated that they were aware that, while this rather melodramatic exterior concealed the man within the ruling coalition who formed the greatest obstacle to the further development of Soviet-West German relations, he could, with his political influence and his links with the economic and industrial world, ensure that the West German *Ostpolitik* at last entered a new phase.

After Strauss's sudden about-face, Foreign Minister Genscher and the SPD certainly felt satisfied, since he had largely accepted their views, having previously so vilified them. With the CSU leader's change of heart, there was a wide measure of agreement across party lines in the Federal Republic in early 1988 on the need to pursue an active and dynamic *Ostpolitik*. Helmut Kohl's reference during Honecker's visit to the task of "giving shape to a European peaceful order which overcomes the division of Europe, unites nations and states, and opens the frontiers to the people" had proved to be more than mere words and indeed to indicate a specific policy that was to be pursued.

That such a policy could have serious advantages in political, economic, and human terms had already been revealed to the doubters among the West Germans in October 1987 during the visit of the Hungarian prime minister, to which the Federal government devoted an abnormal amount of publicity.[8] Bonn wanted both its own rank and file and the other Eastern European countries to see its relations with Hungary as a model. In the economic sphere, relations with Budapest were indeed exemplary by comparison with relations with other COMECON (Council of Mutual Economic Assistance) countries: There were already 330 cooperation agreements and 27 joint ventures between the two countries, and the Federal Republic was Hungary's second most important trading partner after the USSR. This already outstanding economic cooperation was given an additional boost during Prime Minister Grosz's visit by agreements on technological and scientific cooperation and on the protection of investments and above all by a West German guarantee for a bank loan of DM 1 billion.

In return, Hungary was also showing itself to be the undeniable leader in Eastern Europe in humanitarian terms. Budapest decided to grant the German minority in Hungary wide-ranging cultural independence and to liberalize travel for all Hungarians from 1 January 1988. Genscher had been pressing the Hungarians for this measure for some time. His attempts to have the restrictions on travel between Hungary and Western Europe relaxed had, however, long had to contend with the reluctance of the NATO partners, for whom stemming a potential flood of spies was more important than implementing one of the basic western principles, the freedom to travel. Consequently, the German proposal that Hungarians should be allowed to enter the Federal Republic without a visa, a concession they enjoy when traveling to Austria, was rejected by the allies for some considerable time. (Poles similarly had great difficulty traveling to Belgium because of the reluctance not of the Polish but of the Belgian authorities.) The Hungarian decision was naturally considered extremely important by Bonn, since it meant that travel had become a right, not a favor as it was in the GDR. The first formal breach had thus been made in the Iron Curtain, and as the demands for freedom and reforms in Hungary grew, it was eventually to become a real breach in August 1989, which would prove to be of crucial importance for the relationship between the two Germanys.

West Germany's growing interest in Eastern European countries other than the GDR became even more intense as a result of the rigid and constrained attitude of the East German regime in 1988. The East German leaders' tough line on the protest movements in their own country, their increasingly negative attitude toward Bonn and reforms in the USSR, Poland, and Hungary, and their refusal to undertake reforms themselves led to growing awareness among politicians in the Federal Republic that their *Deutschlandpolitik* had reached its limits and that no further progress of any significance was possible. The step-by-step policy seemed to be doing more to permit the Honecker regime to preserve the status quo than to encourage it to make radical changes.[9] The *Deutschlandpolitik* was therefore gradually incorporated in a broader, dynamic policy on Eastern Europe, with priority given to the opportunities arising for West German diplomacy in the other communist countries.

The fact that the goal of actively seeking closer relations with the communist countries of Europe enjoyed almost universal support in the Federal Republic and was also being translated into actual policy undoubtedly put

West Germany in a unique position in Europe and the western alliance. Nowhere else was this goal so high on the political agenda. Nowhere else was there sufficient political vision, perseverance, and experience for a purposeful response to the emerging process of reform in the USSR and the Eastern European countries to ensure that it developed to the advantage of Western Europe and western aims and values. Nowhere else were the real implications of the policy proposed by the Federal Republic appreciated. When Chancellor Kohl referred in the *Bundestag* to "the phase of the *Ostpolitik* now before us," he was not using empty words.[10] This indirect reference to the "second *Ostpolitik*," which Foreign Minister Genscher and the SPD had been advocating for two years, completed the circle. The CDU, CSU, FDP, and SPD, having been at loggerheads over all manner of policy decisions in early 1988, now all agreed on the policies on security and Eastern Europe that West Germany should pursue.

This national consensus naturally strengthened West Germany's position in relation to the western allies. Bonn was able to make it clear to them that its policy on Eastern Europe was not just the outcome of a chance coalition but was openly supported by all the West German political parties. It must therefore at last be taken seriously by the allies and also seen as a normal aspect of West German policy. This was not so self-evident, given the traditional western suspicion of any West German rapprochement with Eastern Europe. The West German government was therefore well aware that its *Ostpolitik* could succeed in the long run and have far-reaching consequences only if it was accompanied and backed by at least as active a "*Westpolitik*." Only then could the suspicion of Bonn's *Ostpolitik* be prevented from becoming too strong again and so weakening the Federal Republic's position in the western camp. With a dynamic *Westpolitik*, on the other hand, it could seek understanding and support for West Germany's own policy options and, moreover, attempt to persuade its partners to adopt some aspects of that policy, which would further increase its impact.

On the disarmament question Bonn again realized that, for its "divergent" position on nuclear modernization to have any influence, it needed the support of other allies, and it must be made clear to the western partners that the West German position was not a sign of growing neutralist tendencies but a normal vision cherished by a state that, though firmly entrenched in the western camp, had its own security interests stemming from its geographical position.

In late 1987 the West German government did indeed begin to pursue an extremely active policy on Western Europe. Military cooperation with France was stepped up; Bonn finally agreed to the elaboration of the originally French, now Western European, space projects of the European Space Agency (and, together with France, agreed to meet a major portion of the costs); and, above all, the great dedication and achievements of the West German presidency of the European Community in the first six months of

1988 were clear evidence that the Federal Republic attached considerable importance to Western European integration. Bonn gave a decisive boost to the still fledgling 1992 project and succeeded in resolving various disputes that had long paralyzed the EC, even though this often entailed substantial financial sacrifices by West Germany. The Federal Republic, which had frequently been regarded as the most difficult member state in 1986/87 and had made it clear on several occasions in this period that it was tired of always having to play banker for the Community (which was, moreover, growing southward, when the Eastern European countries were of primary importance to West Germany), emerged in 1988 as the driving force behind the process of European integration, along with the commission headed by Jacques Delors, with whom Bonn had previously clashed so often.

In 1988 the benefits of the West German policy on Western Europe gradually came to light. At the NATO summit meeting in March 1988 the French supported both Bonn's *Ostpolitik* and its position on the modernization of nuclear weapons. And particularly as regards its attitude toward Eastern Europe, this verbal support gradually developed into active support and even into the adoption of the main lines of its policy on Eastern Europe by various other member states of the Community. The West German presidency succeeded in bringing the negotiations between the Community and COMECON to a satisfactory conclusion. By signing a joint declaration, the Community and COMECON recognized each other and—above all—COMECON and the USSR recognized that economic contacts would be developed primarily between the Community and the individual communist countries, not between the Community and a COMECON controlled by Moscow. From mid-1988 the pace in the development of relations between the Community and the Eastern European countries therefore quickened.[11]

The closing months of 1988 were characterized by a major "Eastern Europe offensive" by the Western European countries. The Italian and Austrian Prime Ministers and President Mitterrand visited Moscow; French, Italian, British, and West German banks offered the USSR enormous loans; Western European industry concluded major contracts with the Soviet Union (with considerable technology transfer involved); and France, among other countries, began to step up contacts with not only the USSR but also the smaller communist countries in Eastern Europe.[12] There were many reasons for this rather sudden general "rush to the East" by the Western European countries: They were finally beginning to believe that the reform process in the Soviet Union and a few other Eastern European countries was serious and had a chance of succeeding; they did not want Bonn to have the exclusive right to establish political contacts with the communist countries; and above all, they could hardly accept that German industry in particular should derive economic advantage from the opportunities emerging as a result of the policy of perestroika.

It was clear, however, that most Western European countries were pursuing economic and short-term objectives through their increased contacts with the East and—unlike Bonn—were less interested in a long-term strategy. This indeed was to remain the major difference between the Federal Republic and the other Western European countries. All the Western European leaders would make statements advocating further rapprochement between East and West, a more secure Europe, and so on. For most of them, however, this was little more than reiteration of general objectives, which they trotted out in statement after statement. For Bonn, on the other hand, these were prime objectives, to which its policy was specifically geared.

One of the consequences of this Western European move eastward was that Helmut Kohl's visit to Moscow in late October 1988 and the consolidation of relations between the Federal Republic and the USSR no longer raised such a stir abroad or the uneasiness it would undoubtedly have caused in the past (although Kohl's visit still attracted far more international attention than visits by his Western European counterparts). The Soviet leaders gradually succeeded in making their country and western relations with it "ordinary," and Bonn increasingly managed to do the same with its policy on Eastern Europe.

The western fear of too close a relationship between West Germany and the Soviet Union and of Moscow possibly playing its "German card" (of offering reunification in exchange for neutrality) was largely allayed by the Soviet leaders during Kohl's visit.[13] On the first day of his visit the Federal chancellor placed great emphasis both on fundamental western principles and on German unity and the need to overcome the division of Germany, but his host was no less unequivocal. Gorbachev said not only that the Federal Republic and the GDR happened to belong to different systems and to different political and military alliances, but also that the status of Berlin (not regarded by the USSR as a normal part of the Federal Republic) would not be changed. And on "the so-called German question": "The attempts to disturb what is the outcome of history or to strike at it with an unrealistic policy could have unpredictable and even dangerous repercussions." The limits to a possible understanding between Bonn and Moscow had thus been defined from the outset.

This brief reiteration of principles, and thus of the fundamental differences between the two sides, had major advantages for both leaders. CDU leader Kohl showed the conservative section of his rank and file that efforts to establish better relations with the communist countries did not mean that he saw reunification as any less of a priority. He also showed them, however, that as reunification was still impossible in practice, they would have to accept his method of achieving this long-term objective: taking the indirect route of first improving relations with the Eastern European countries and the USSR, backing their reforms and endeavoring to steer them in the right direction, and so supporting tendencies that would make changes to the very system in these countries possible. At the same time, the Federal chancellor made it clear to the other part of the political spectrum, which suffered from exaggerated "Gorbimania," that as there were limits to Gorbachev's spectacular policy, improved relations between East and West could not be expected to produce everything. This also enabled him to alleviate the concern felt by the western partners, and in this he was helped by Defense Minister Scholz's uncompromising lecture to Soviet military personnel on the threat emanating from the superiority of the Warsaw Pact forces. In this way Chancellor Kohl gave himself more scope for improving relations with the Soviet Union without attracting too many suspicious looks.

The Soviet leader had similarly been able to show his allies, who were also becoming skeptical, that, despite everything, he remained inflexible on the "German question" and that in this respect at least the communist leaders of the Eastern European countries, and especially the GDR, could therefore continue to count on him. By also succeeding in refuting most of the arguments advanced by western skeptics, he prevented the Federal Republic's allies from impeding Bonn's policy toward Eastern Europe and West German-Soviet relations, which were becoming increasingly important to Moscow. During Kohl's visit the two countries had, after all, indicated numerous areas of cooperation, which they intended to discuss in greater depth in the ensuing period.

While it was still being said during Chancellor Kohl's visit to Moscow in October 1988 that the two countries were prepared to give their relations a "new quality," it was clear this goal had already been achieved by the time Gorbachev visited the Federal Republic in June 1989. Eleven agreements were signed, putting into effect the declarations of intent made eight months earlier. The agreements also covered a very wide range, from the protection of West German investments in the USSR and West German training for Soviet economists to the installation of a "hot line" between the Federal Chancellery and the Kremlin. The high point for the West Germans was the Joint Declaration signed by Chancellor Kohl and President Gorbachev in Bonn, since it confirmed principles that they had long advocated, and so paved the way for even more radical changes in Eastern Europe, which not even the GDR could now escape.

The Joint Declaration included the following statements: "The right of all peoples and states freely to determine their destiny and to shape their mutual relations on the basis of international law must be ensured"; "the Federal Republic of Germany and the Soviet Union consider it to be a priority task of their policies . . . to help overcome the division of Europe"; "the Helsinki Final Act in all its parts and the final documents of the Madrid and Vienna conferences will determine the line followed in achieving these objectives"; and "[each state] has the right freely to choose its own political and social system." The declaration also confirmed the involvement of the United States and Canada in Europe's future and referred to the protection of the legitimate rights of national minorities in Europe.[14]

What was remarkable was that, while Gorbachev's visit and especially the Joint Declaration were considered very important in the Federal Republic, even a milestone, the general view abroad was that neither could be described as "historic," dramatic, or surprising. For many the declaration was no more than a summary of principles that, though "western" in nature, had already been accepted by the Soviet Union and so contained nothing new. Most were indeed vague and not clearly worded. Apart from the fact that the Soviet leader had been received by the West German public with great enthusiasm, nothing spectacular or disturbing was, on the whole, seen in Gorbachev's visit. American officials praised the Federal chancellor himself for the way in which he had received the Soviet leader and at the same time reassured the NATO allies.[15]

The fact that the rapprochement between Moscow and Bonn was not viewed with any great suspicion was largely due to the changes in the political situation in Eastern Europe. As Gorbachev's visit came at a time when Poland and Hungary were actually carrying out fundamental internal reforms, it was becoming clearer that the Kremlin's fine words were not just intended to entice the Federal Republic out of the western camp. This, however, was one of the reasons for the declaration being seen in Bonn as significant and setting the trend for the future.[16] That the Soviet leader was prepared to put his signature to these principles at a time when developments in Poland and Hungary were beginning to assume ambitious proportions and so to bring growing pressure to bear on their non-reform-minded communist neighbors was seen by West Germany as a sign that the Kremlin might also accept more sweeping changes in the other Eastern European countries. The events in late 1989 certainly showed that most of the principles endorsed in the declaration were actually being respected by the Kremlin and that the GDR too was being swept along by developments.

Gorbachev's visit to the Federal republic was also considered highly significant because it again confirmed West Germany's recently acquired status of most important Western European country. In the previous months it had become clear that both the United States and the USSR saw the Federal Republic as *the* essential European state, with which the best possible relations had to be established. Both superpowers realized, after all, that it was not France or the United Kingdom but the Federal Republic that formed the nucleus of both the European Community and the "new Europe."[17] The economic giant was clearly no longer a political dwarf.

It cannot have escaped the Soviet Union's attention that the weight carried by the increasingly self-assured Federal Republic within NATO had grown significantly. Bonn had been able to bring considerable influence to bear on the decisions NATO had recently taken: The door to negotiations on short-range weapons had been opened, despite the United States' and especially the United Kingdom's previous categorical refusals to entertain the idea; no decisions on the modernization of these weapons would be taken before 1992; and far-reaching proposals on conventional disarmament had been put forward. Bonn was also able to persuade the NATO allies and particularly the European Community to accept its views on Eastern Europe and the reforms in communist Europe.

Given its economic power and its growing influence in the Community, NATO, *and* the Eastern European countries, West Germany was able to play a crucial role by helping to ensure that Western Europe reacted appropriately and calmly to the drastic reforms being undertaken in communist Europe. Hence Gorbachev's willingness to join with his West German counterpart, Kohl, in reaffirming western and, above all, West German principles and rules. Hence, too, the emphasis placed on economic aspects during his visit; the fact that he made his most important statements not in Bonn but in Düsseldorf, Cologne, and Stuttgart, in West Germany's industrial heartland; and the fact that he concluded his visit not in the Federal capital but in the Ruhr.[18] Here again, then, the traditional link in West German diplomacy between money and principles was forged. The Soviet leader's visit also marked the end of a period in which the Kremlin had to some extent ignored and belittled Bonn diplomatically (the atmosphere had become even worse after Kohl compared Gorbachev to Goebbels), in which it had tried almost everything to remove the Federal government from the straight and narrow western path, and in which West Germany had promptly been labeled "revanchist" whenever it reaffirmed its own principles.[19]

Bonn's success in giving Gorbachev a favorable reception without compromising its own values and its attachment to NATO and the European Community, and without aggravating western fears that West Germany was drifting eastward, also enhanced its status and increased its importance in the West.[20] The Federal Republic's greater influence had already been apparent in previous months. The United States began to realize that West German knowledge of, experience with, and influence in the "Eastern bloc" were very important if it was to react as appropriately as possible to developments in this region, of which its own knowledge was very one-sided and limited. When some kind of positive reaction to the upheaval in the communist camp was expected by the public in the Atlantic Alliance and was made necessary by the new situation, West Germany was the only NATO partner to be ready with a constructive response to the reforms in the Eastern bloc and to the constant flow of disarmament proposals from the USSR. The determination of the West Germans during the debate on NATO's short-range weapons had also shown that Bonn was no longer willing simply to accept the positions of the allies and that its interests and opinions had to be taken seriously.

President Bush's reference to the Federal Republic as a "partner in leadership" during his visit to Mainz in late May 1989 was not therefore intended as mere flattery.[21] As Foreign Minister Genscher remarked, not only German-Soviet but German-American relations too had taken on a new and higher quality.[22] This was clearly demonstrated by the fact that Genscher, who had been constantly criticized and treated with suspicion in Washington in previous years, was received very favourably and listened to attentively in mid-1989, to the considerable dismay particularly of the British, who suddenly found that not they but the West Germans were seen by the Soviets *and* the Americans to be the privileged and essential negotiator. Bonn had succeeded in the delicate balancing act of improving relations with Eastern Europe and the USSR without adversely affecting its relations with Western Europe and the United States. The two streams were able to develop neatly in the same bed, with no danger of one breaking its banks and flooding the other.

NOTES

1. Marion Gräfin Dönhoff, "Ein Dach für ganz Europa," *Die Zeit*, 11 April 1988, p. 1.
2. Dorothee Wilms, "Konzept der Deutschlandpolitik im Rahmen der europäischen Einigung," *Bulletin*, 27 January 1988, p. 103.
3. "Unsere Verantwortung in der Welt. Christlich-demokratische Perspektiven zur Aussen-, Sicherheits-, Europa- und Deutschlandpolitik, Diskussionsentwurf der vom Bundesvorstand eingesetzten Kommission," *CDU-Dokumentation*, 6/1988; Dönhoff, "Ein Dach für ganz Europa"; "Unsere Verantwortung in der Welt. Christlich-demokratische Perspektiven zur Aussen-, Sicherheits-, Europa- und Deutschlandpolitik, Beschluss des 36. Bundesparteitages der CDU," *CDU-Dokumentation* 19/1988.
4. Herbert Wegener, "Jürgen Warnke à Berlin-Est," *Nordwest Zeitung*, 1 July 1988, in *La Tribune d'Allemagne*, 17 July 1988, p. 4.
5. Wilms, "Konzept der Deutschlandpolitik."
6. Claus Gennrich, "Die Mienen glätten sich. In Bonn spricht man von neuer Dynamik in der Ostpolitik," *Frankfurter Allgemeine Zeitung*, 9 January 1988, p. 10.
7. Theo Sommer, "Reisen bildet," *Die Zeit*, 8 January 1988, p. 1; "Wir werden niemals das Schwert erheben," *Der Spiegel*, 4 January 1988, pp. 18–24.
8. "Besuch des Ministerpräsidenten von Ungarn," *Bulletin*, 14 October 1987, pp. 881–83.
9. Claus Wettermann, "East Berlin begins bullying again," *The German Tribune*, 11 December 1988, p. 4; Hermann Rudolph, "Critics say Bonn is getting little in return for its Deutschlandpolitik," *Süddeutsche Zeitung*, 16 January 1989, in *The German Tribune*, 29 January 1989, p. 4.
10. Helmut Kohl, "Erklärung der Bundesregierung zum 25. Jahrestag der Unterzeichnung des Vertrages über die deutsch-französische Zusammenarbeit und den offiziellen Besuch des Bundeskanzlers in der CSSR," *Bulletin*, 5 February 1988, p. 162.

11. "Joint Declaration on the establishment of official relations between the European Community and the Council for Mutual Economic Assistance," *Official Journal of the European Communities*, 1988, no. L 157/35; Arie Bloed, " 'Doofstommen horen en spreken weer': normalisering van betrekkingen EEG-COMECON," *International Spectator*, 1988(10), pp. 661–66; Jacques Bel, "Les relations entre la Communauté et le Conseil d'assistance économique mutuelle," *Revue du Marché Commun*, no. 318, June 1988, pp. 313–16.

12. "L'Europe se bouscule au portillon du Kremlin," *Libération*, 27 October 1988, pp. 2–6.

13. "M. Gorbatchev: la situation allemande est le fruit de l'Histoire," and "M. Kohl: la division de l'Allemagne est contre nature," *Le Monde*, 26 October 1988; "Kohl in Moscow," *The Guardian*, 27 October 1988; Thomas F. O'Boyle, "Soviet Response to 'German Question' Brings Bonn's Dreamers Back to Earth," *The Wall Street Journal*, 28 October 1988.

14. Horst Teltschik, "Die Reformpolitik Gorbatschows und die Perspektiven der West-Ost-Beziehungen," *Aussenpolitik*, 40(3)1989, pp. 211, 221–23; Helmut Kohl and Mikhail Gorbachev, "Gemeinsame Erklärung," Bonn, 13 June 1989, *Bulletin*, 15 June 1989, pp. 542–44; "Abgestimmte Pressemitteilung," *Bulletin*, 15 June 1989, pp. 544–545.

15. Robert J. McCartney, "An East-West Balancing Act: Bonn Gains in Gorbachev Trip," *The International Herald Tribune*, 16 June 1989; Georges Suffert, "Elégance diplomatique," *Le Monde*, 14 June 1989; "Bonn has both money and position," *The Independent*, 14 June 1989.

16. Horst Teltschik, "Auf dem Weg zu einem neuen Europa? Perspektiven einer gemeinsamen westlichen Ostpolitik," *Frankfurter Allgemeine Zeitung*, 9 September 1989.

17. "This Week's Appeal," *The Times*, 16 June 1989.

18. Ibid.

19. Serge Schmemann, "Parting Words from Gorbachev on Berlin Wall: 'Nothing is Eternal' " and McCartney, "An East-West Balancing Act," *The International Herald Tribune*, 16 June 1989.

20. McCartney, "An East-West Balancing Act."

21. "Bush declares Berlin Wall 'Must Come Down,' " *USIS Wireless File*, 1 June 1989, p. 3.

22. " 'Worten müssen auch bei uns Taten folgen.' Gespräch mit Aussenminister Genscher über das Ost-West-Verhältnis und die Deutschen," *Der Spiegel*, 12 June 1989.

12

The Growing Political Role of the European Community

The Euro-pessimism that characterized the first half of the 1980s gave way to uncommon euphoria with surprising speed. The problems that had paralyzed the Community in the first half of the decade were overcome in 1984 and 1985, and Spain and Portugal were at last able to accede. The Single European Act and the 1992 objective set the course to be followed and provided the means for the next stages in the process of European integration.

This reborn European Community seemed, however, to have no solution to the security problems with which Western Europe had had to contend since the late 1970s. Security and defense were virtually left aside in the process of renewal, as if all the antimissile demonstrations, all the heated debates on whether or not to deploy nuclear weapons and then to dismantle them, the problems between the United States and the European members of NATO, the changes in Eastern Europe, and so on had taken place on another planet and were of no concern to the European Community and Western Europe.

One of the main pillars of the new dynamism, the Single European Act signed in 1986, gives little cause for enthusiasm on the subject of security. Article 30(6)(a) of the European Act reads:

The High Contracting Parties consider that closer cooperation on questions of European security would contribute in an essential way to the development of a European identity in external policy matters. They are ready to coordinate their positions more closely on the political and economic aspects of security.[1]

This does not differ so very much from what was adopted in the Solemn Declaration on European Union by the European Council in Stuttgart in June 1983, which made the first reference to the "coordination of the positions of the Member States on the political and economic aspects of security."[2] At the time the Stuttgart declaration was regarded as a nonevent and was symptomatic of the malaise then prevalent in the European Community. It stemmed from an initiative of Emilio Colombo, then Italy's foreign minister, and above all Hans-Dietrich Genscher, who had envisaged something quite different. Genscher therefore had every right to feel deeply disappointed with the results of this attempt to refloat the Community and to add the security dimension. The failure to have the Community play a larger role in the security field was to stick in Genscher's mind and influence his choice of forums for discussions on this aspect. A broader approach to the security problem than that adopted in the Stuttgart declaration also proved impossible when the Single European Act was drawn up.

This was indeed to be expected, given the line taken in the discussions of the Dooge Committee. This ad hoc Committee on Institutional Affairs, which consisted of the personal representatives of the heads of state or government, was set up by the European Council at its meeting in Fontainebleau (June 1984) to formulate proposals for the improvement of the functioning of the European Community and European Political Cooperation (EPC). The report that it submitted in March 1985 contained some far-reaching proposals in the section on "security and defense" (the heading alone could be called revolutionary). This section was not approved by the Danish and Irish representatives, and the Greeks too had reservations about some parts of the text.[3] It must therefore be inferred from the findings of the Dooge Committee that the Community of the Twelve was not considered a suitable forum for the development of a common security policy and, more specifically, a common approach to the defense aspect of security. This does not, however, alter the fact that, as nine member states did accept the text, future initiatives could well have the support of some of their number (although it is clear that certain other member states would similarly have voiced reservations if it had come to more than noncommittal proposals and if they had not been certain that two member states would reject the text).

The Treaty of Luxembourg, which put the seal on the Single European Act, brought European Political Cooperation within the Community's institutional structures, albeit with special provisos. It continued to be entirely intergovernmental, and its range of activities was not formally extended. In this respect the Single European Act did not in any way live up to the European Parliament's expectations and the proposals it had made, for example, in the Draft Treaty on European Union, better known as the Spinelli report.[4] In this document the European Parliament had said not only that EPC should be empowered to consider "matters relating to the political and economic aspects of security," but also that "the European Council may extend the field of cooperation, in particular as regards armaments, sales of arms to nonmember States, defense policy, and disarmament."

The European Parliament's definition of the Union's global security objective was far broader: "The Union shall gear its efforts in international relations toward the achievement of peace through the peaceful settlement of conflicts and toward security, the deterrence of aggression, détente, the mutual balanced and verifiable reduction of military forces, and armaments." The Draft Treaty on European Union was approved by an overwhelming majority of parliamentarians from all member states and of all political complexions. It formed the basis of the decisions taken at the European summit meeting in Fontainebleau, the activities of the Dooge Committee, and the convening of an intergovernmental conference to amend the Treaties of Rome, which gave rise to the Single European Act. The proposals it contains must be taken seriously, and it is no exaggeration to say that any future amendment of the Treaties and adjustment of the Community will be to its credit.

Even earlier, when approving the Haagerup report by adopting the Resolution on European Security and European Political Cooperation, the European Parliament had emphasized that "the Member States share a number of vital security concerns even if the Community has no military dimension of its own," and that "these shared security concerns should be fully explored and elaborated, particularly within the context of EPC, in order to give substance to . . . a true European peace and security concept." In the resolution Parliament also stresses that "the concept of European peace and security goes beyond those issues which are related to military defense and embraces nonmilitary aspects of security," and that genuine security can be achieved only "by creating the basic conditions for peaceful relations between nations and solving not only the military problems but also the nonmilitary difficulties facing these nations."[5]

These remarks now seem self-evident. In the very early 1980s, when security appeared to be synonymous with the decision whether or not to deploy medium-range weapons, this was far from being the case, and such an approach to the security problem was evidence of broad perception and long-term thinking. The personality of the rapporteur, the Dane Niels Jürgen Haagerup, was of decisive importance in this respect. The European Parliament also avoided succumbing to naive faith in peace or lack of responsibility. The Haagerup report also pointed out, for example, that it would perhaps be advisable for EPC to consider more complex subjects, such as weapons systems, troop levels, arms control, and disarmament, rather than simply leaving them to NATO.[6]

The European Parliament's resolution indicates the emergence of a much broader concept of European security, which differed from the strictly

military concept to which the Atlantic Alliance adhered. At a time of considerable uncertainty and discord about western security policy and the
European security situation, the Haagerup report made the European Parliament the only institution to remind Europeans of the need to take on
responsibility for themselves and to propose European adjustments to the
western security system, which was being questioned. In European circles,
however, the Haagerup report was not given the reception it deserved.

What "positions on the political and economic aspects of security" referred to in the Single European Act ultimately means is primarily a political
decision. The inclusion of EPC in the Community framework makes a
broad interpretation easier. A broad interpretation is indeed possible and
also more logical. While the text of the Treaty may well make explicit
reference only to the political and economic aspects of security, it does not
say or imply at any point that the Member States may not coordinate their
positions on the military aspects of security or, for example, that they should
not play a more active part in the disarmament negotiations. Nor does the
third paragraph of Article 30(6), which says that nothing in this Title shall
impede closer cooperation in the field of security within the framework of
the Western European Union or NATO, detract from this in any way. A
broad interpretation seems even more plausible if we read the article in the
spirit of what the twelve Member States declare in the preamble of the
Single European Act:

Aware of the responsibility incumbent upon Europe to aim at speaking ever increasingly with one voice and to act with consistency and solidarity in order more
effectively to protect its common interests and independence . . . so that together
they may make their own contribution to the preservation of international peace
and security.

The authors of the European Act seemed aware that their wording of the
provisions on EPC were extremely conservative. In the twelfth and final
paragraph of Article 30 they explicitly state that five years after the entry
into force of the Act the Member States will examine whether any revision
of the provisions on EPC is required. This means that the evolution in
practical EPC activities and the proposals previously made by a majority
of the Dooge Committee must be reviewed in 1992. The developments in
international politics and the resulting emphasis on the untenable distinction
between the various aspects of security and on the Community's need for
its own comprehensive security policy have, however, placed this issue on
the political agenda even earlier.

Another reason why a broader interpretation must eventually prevail—
unless EPC as a whole is pushed aside —is that the various aspects of security
are in practice inseparable, as the European Parliament indicated, for example, in the Galluzzi report. Galluzzi also emphasised that "politics should

be more important than arms, in other words, they should be seen in the context of a network of political relations and acts." Consequently, if a full-fledged security policy that takes account of all aspects of security is to be developed in Western Europe and if the political aspect determines and controls the other aspects, the European Community/EPC framework, which, along with the Member States and NATO, is competent for the political and economic aspects of security, must eventually be involved in one way or another in western policy on the military aspects of security. In the Galluzzi report the European Parliament therefore called for the more active involvement of the Twelve in the disarmament negotiations.[7]

As they had done before the Single European Act was adopted, the Twelve continued to ensure that formally no military aspects of security were considered during consultations within the framework of EPC, and formally this field continued to be regarded as the exclusive preserve of NATO and WEU. Initially, it seemed in fact as if not only the military aspects but also at times the political aspects of security were being avoided for fear that military matters would unwittingly be broached (it was evidently realized, then, that the various aspects of security cannot be separated).

This extreme caution was apparent in 1987, when Commission President Delors proposed that, in response to the Soviet Union's disarmament proposals, the European Council should hold a special meeting devoted to security problems, adopt a common position, and lay the foundations for a common security policy. Delors's initiative was a reaction not only to the unremitting flow of Soviet proposals but also equally to the absence of a constructive response from NATO and WEU, which are, however, explicitly empowered to consider defense questions. If these organizations, which are generally recognized as being competent for defense questions, did not accept their responsibility and so left the Western European public without an effective champion, was it not the European Community's task to step into the breach? Delors's proposal was supported by President Mitterrand, the president of the European Parliament, Lord Plumb, and the then president of the European Council, Prime Minister Martens, who rightly pointed out that "if expression is given to the political will for a European Community summit on security, it is not the legal structure that will stop us." In this he disagreed with his Foreign Minister, Tindemans, although the latter had himself proposed in his report on European Union in 1976 that it should be decided "regularly to hold exchanges of views on our specific problems in defense matters and on European aspects of multilateral negotiations on security" and "to reach a common analysis of defense problems." The disagreement over this aspect within the Belgian government, which held the presidency of the Council at the time, and British pressure resulted in the proposal being dropped.[8]

In practice, however, there was no escaping the defense question. Even as EPC came into being, it had been clear that defining powers is an extremely equivocal matter, given the possibility of a significant difference between formal and real powers. From the time of the discussions in preparation for the Helsinki negotiations in late 1972 the Six, and later the Nine, played a not unimportant role in the Conference on Security and Cooperation in Europe (CSCE), even though it concerned not only economic cooperation (Basket 2) and humanitarian and cultural cooperation (Basket 3) but also "questions relating to security in Europe" (Basket 1). The West defined its position on the "confidence-building measures" (such as the prior announcement of military maneuvers), which formed part of the first basket, within the NATO framework. The three-part structure of the CSCE, and the inclusion of confidence-building measures in the CSCE package, was, however, largely based on a detailed proposal that the Community countries, to the surprise of the other delegations, had put forward acting as a single entity. By adopting and jointly defending common positions, the Community countries were successful in steering the agenda and the mandate of the conference in a direction that was favorable for Western Europe and, with the group of neutral and nonaligned countries, showed themselves to be *the* driving force. The member state holding the presidency of the Community during the conference always acted as spokesman for the Nine and, in so doing, also touched on military matters. Another remarkable feature was that NATO experts from the member states attended EPC meetings, thus facilitating the coordination of EPC and NATO meetings. The Helsinki agreements (including confidence-building measures) were signed by Aldo Moro on 1 August 1985 in his dual role of prime minister of Italy and president of the Community's Council of Ministers.[9]

The equivocal nature of the dividing line between military and nonmilitary aspects of security is also apparent from other examples. Where the major political options are concerned, disarmament and arms control appear in practice to be regarded by EPC as a "nonmilitary aspect" and are considered within the EPC framework. The Member States' delegations to the United Nations (UN) consult each other so that as far as possible they may adopt joint positions in all areas of negotiation and thus in UN debates on arms control and disarmament.[10] One of the members of the small EPC secretariat in Brussels is responsible, among other things, for disarmament and "questions of security in general."[11] The Twelve have also stated their opinion on the disarmament negotiations on numerous occasions. In 1986, for instance, they emphasized—despite American skepticism—the importance of the Stockholm Conference on Disarmament in Europe and welcomed the 1987 INF agreement. And in December 1988 the European Council meeting in Rhodes stated in a Declaration on the International Role of the European Community that its goal was "the establishment of a secure and stable balance of conventional forces in Europe at a lower level, the strengthening of mutual confidence and military transparency, and the conclusion of a global and verifiable ban on chemical weapons."[12] Although it was still insisted that EPC was not concerned with military aspects of security, "conventional forces," "military transparency," and "chemical weapons" sound like little else. It is clear that such general declarations reveal no more than the tip of the iceberg and fail adequately to reflect the wider and far more comprehensive discussions on defense and security questions during EPC meetings. Moreover, the regular informal meetings of the foreign ministers provide an opportunity for confidential discussions on highly sensitive security questions.

Although the schizophrenia that characterizes the attitude of the Twelve toward military questions can certainly be criticized, it also has potential. Whatever may be formally claimed, the Twelve not only have a treaty basis that permits them to discuss military aspects of security, but also they are in fact already doing so. As the importance of the nonmilitary aspects within a global security concept continues to grow, although security will always include military components, the European Community may become the main forum for mapping out decisions on the positions of the Twelve in the 1990s, unlike the 1980s.

This trend was already apparent during the Helsinki follow-up conferences. In Madrid, from 1980 to 1983, the role and impact of EPC was far more limited than at the Helsinki conference itself. The détente of the early 1970s had given way to yet another cold war period, resulting in the various provisions in the Helsinki agreement on East-West cooperation being pushed into the background and in NATO putting itself forward as the organization for the coordination of the western position. In contrast to the previous decade, the Americans were now interested in the CSCE forum, seeing it as an excellent instrument for recently elected President Reagan to denounce the Soviet presence in Afghanistan, the suppression of Solidarity in Poland, and communism in general. This led to an appreciable narrowing of the European room for maneuvering. The European Community was in the midst of a serious internal crisis at this time and for this reason alone was unable to make its voice heard on the international scene.[13]

EPC came into prominence again during the third CSCE follow-up conference held in Vienna from November 1986 to January 1989. At this conference a mandate also had to be adopted for the negotiations on reductions in conventional forces in Europe (to replace the defunct MBFR negotiations) and on the link between these negotiations and the CSCE. The second phase of the Vienna discussions in particular took place in a completely different atmosphere from the previous follow-up conferences in Belgrade (1977/78) and Madrid. East-West relations were relaxed, the reforms in the USSR, Poland, and Hungary were assuming a more distinct shape, and the European Community was demonstrating fresh vigor. With the Twelve increasingly forming a politically and economically strong and coherent entity, their impact on the other countries and on the negotiations grew.

As the conference continued, it became clear that, in contrast to the previous ten years, during which the attempt had been made to limit the debate on European security and East-West relations to a few specific aspects, both East and West now wanted progress made in all three baskets of the Helsinki agreement and new courses charted in East-West relations. January 1989 saw the signing of a final document that greatly exceeded initial expectations. The way was cleared for fresh negotiations on conventional disarmament. The communist countries signed new undertakings concerning, among other things, legal protection, freedom of religion, and freedom to travel. They agreed to the creation of a mechanism to monitor respect for human rights. And it was decided to hold conferences within two years to consider, for example, human rights, information, the environment, and economic cooperation, thus opening up new prospects of even closer contacts between Eastern and Western Europe.[14]

The global and updated nature of the Vienna discussions further enlarged the European Community's role. During the discreet EPC activities both in Vienna and at the EPC secretariat in Brussels it was evident that in practice the formal division between politico-economic and other aspects of security was no obstacle to the discussion of the military aspects. Member states traditionally opposed to greater Community involvement in security on political or constitutional grounds tacitly permitted EPC meetings to consider all the subjects discussed in Vienna, including, for example, the mandate for negotiations on conventional forces. It seemed that, while the representative of a country like Ireland stood aside on constitutional grounds, he was now nonetheless happy to be present for this important debate. As these internal EPC discussions attracted very little attention from the international and especially the national press, the heads of government in Dublin, Copenhagen, and Athens had no real need to fear domestic criticism of their "pragmatic" and "tolerant" attitudes. It is in any case through such pragmatic diplomacy in the field that the member states concerned are becoming increasingly aware that in practice the artificial barriers between the various aspects of security cannot be maintained.

The declaration of the European Council meeting in Madrid in June 1989 showed that the reticence to comment on the European security problem had meanwhile diminished:

The Twelve, who are gradually strengthening their cooperation as a contribution to preserving their security, seek to enhance stability and security through lower levels of forces and armaments as well as through greater transparency and predictability in military matters. . . . In this framework, they attach great importance to the negotiations on conventional forces in Europe . . . and will strive for their early and satisfactory conclusion.[15]

We also see a parallel development in the relationship between European Political Cooperation and the Community's other policies. The European Parliament has always advocated the incorporation of EPC in the Community's institutional framework. The fact that this eventually happened in Luxembourg did not in itself have any immediate consequences, since EPC remained intergovernmental and the decision was little more than formal confirmation of existing practices.[16] Nonetheless, it opened up a number of prospects.

It is perhaps important at this juncture to refer to the European Monetary System (EMS) and what has happened in this sphere since 1986. The EMS in its then form was similarly incorporated in the Treaties through the Single European Act. This prompted quite a few questions from various quarters. Until that time the EMS had been able to evolve and grow into what it signified in 1986 and had really restored monetary stability, because it was not covered by the Treaties and so did not need to comply with various of their imperative rules, such as the requirement that decisions be unanimous. Now the Treaties contained the provision that any further development should be the subject of a Treaty amendment and would therefore require unanimous approval. Would this not paralyze the EMS? Could the EMS continue to evolve? Despite this skepticism, it was decided in December 1989 to convene an intergovernmental conference with a view to developing the EMS into a genuine monetary union with a European Central Bank. And this may have been possible precisely because EMS had been thrown into the Community's maelstrom, which has demonstrated a dynamism all its own. And, as 1989 and 1990 showed, Britain was unable, despite the unanimity rule, to prevent this development toward a European Monetary Union, while the other member states decided to press on.

The same argument applies to EPC. The Treaties of Luxembourg have given EPC a structured form, and it has rightly become part of the Community's sphere of influence. The Community's centrifugal force can now act upon it. This largely subjective fact counts for far more than textual arguments and formal logic. Even though the European Community and EPC continue to apply their own particular methods and procedures, at institutional and policy levels, the interaction between the Community's other policies and EPC is steadily growing, and in practice the distinction between the two is slowly fading.

At one time, for example, it was the custom for the foreign ministers meeting as the European Community's General Affairs Council to move to a different venue for discussions within the EPC framework. The first departure from this custom occurred in February 1990, when the General Affairs Council met in Dublin. Ironically, it was the Irish presidency that managed to moderate this formal distinction at the meetings of the Twelve, and introduced the new procedure whereby the president is accompanied by representatives of the Council secretariat and the EPC secretariat and allowed wide-ranging discussions on security at the meeting of the European Council. The foreign ministers and a member of the Commission now discuss foreign policy at least once a month (as against the formal practice of only twice a year in the case of the NATO Council). At the twice-yearly meetings of the twelve heads of state or government both internal policy and external relations within the EPC framework are similarly on the agenda.

As a result of the internal momentum of the process of European integration the external aspect is also becoming more important. The European Community's new strength does after all increase the possibility of the Twelve taking action at the international level. The implications of internal developments, and especially the establishment of a single market, for the non-Community countries are also growing, and they are consequently turning to the European Community as an entity with increasing frequency. Furthermore, the country that holds the presidency for six months does so for both the European Community and EPC, and for both internal activities and the representation of the Twelve in the outside world. From the fact that one person represents the Community, be he or she the head of state or the leader of the government of the country holding the presidency, the foreign minister, or a diplomat, it is clear that matters considered in a Community or EPC context form, in the final analysis, a single entity. It is also the presidency that is responsible for initiating activities that come under the heading of EPC. Nineteen eighty-eight and 1989 saw a remarkable increase in the interest shown by the West German and French and even the Greek and Spanish presidencies in Western Europe's external relations and security.

The link between the European Community and EPC is also strengthened by the part in EPC activities played by the Commission, which was made responsible by the Single European Act for seeking, with the presidency of the Council, cohesion between the European Community's policy and EPC. The requirement in the Act that the Commission be fully involved in EPC does not mean that the member of the Commission who attends the Council's meetings is the equal of the foreign ministers or has the same powers and functions as he or she has in a strictly European Community context. It is not the Commission but the presidency that must take initiatives. Nor may the Commission formally participate in EPC decision making. However, informally, the Commission does take initiatives, and it influences the decision-making process through its own activities. Sometimes it also acts more quickly than the foreign ministers, who as a general rule meet only once a month. This was already apparent, for example, after the Soviet invasion of Afghanistan in 1979, when it suspended food aid to that country almost a week before the Council met to discuss the question.[17] As most positions adopted in the EPC framework also have economic causes and implications, the link with the Community institutions is indeed necessary. As EPC does not have ad hoc instruments to lend weight to the Twelve's declarations, apart from the conventional methods of diplomacy, it is logical that, to retain its credibility, it should use the instruments that the Community derives from its economic strength. Particularly since the crisis in Poland in 1982 the Commission has been called upon to propose and possibly implement Community measures to back EPC decisions. This was true, for example, of the sanctions imposed on South Africa and on Argentina during the Falklands crisis and of economic aid to the Central American countries (in support of the Contadora initiative) and recently to the Eastern European countries.

With its resources, infrastructure, and experience, the Commission is the only body capable of implementing measures effectively. As the Commission is represented at all EPC meetings and its president also attends the meetings of the European Council (and the summit meetings of the seven richest western countries), the Commission also has an understanding of the wider political context in which Community activities take place. The Commission indeed has played a distinctly political role, especially since President Delors took office.

The European Community has sole responsibility for the Twelve's external economic relations. It is the Commission that, through the Directorate-General for External Relations headed by its own commissioner, conducts the negotiations with other countries. It also has a network of a hundred or so diplomatic missions abroad (as many as a medium-sized member state). Negotiations with third countries are an important tool for the Commission, since it ensures continuity in relations between the Twelve and third countries and is the Community's only constant negotiator. As the presidency of the European Community changes every six months, so does the "face" of the Twelve. It is therefore important, for instance, that a member of the Commission should always be present during foreign missions undertaken by the "troika" (the foreign ministers or lower-level representatives of the previous, current, and next presidency).

When the Commission negotiates cooperation agreements with third countries or groups of countries (on the basis of a mandate it has received from the Council), the political dimension of these agreements is often just as important as the commercial aspects. Indeed, certain cooperation agreements would never have been concluded solely on commercial grounds, examples being the agreements with China, Central America, and ASEAN (Association of Southeast Asian Nations).[18] The importance of the political dimension was apparent from the Commission's attitude toward the Eastern European countries. In 1988/89 cooperation agreements were concluded with Hungary and Poland, the two most reform-minded countries in Eastern Europe, granting them far more favorable conditions and covering a wider field than the agreement between the Community and Czechoslovakia. And in April 1989 the Commission suspended the negotiations with Romania on a trade and cooperation agreement. The reason given for this suspension in a joint statement by the Commission and the Council of Ministers was "the Romanian Government's continued failure to meet its commitments under the Helsinki process, in particular in the field of human rights." They explicitly added that the negotiations could be resumed only when clear evidence emerged of a significant improvement in the Romanian authorities' attitude in this respect.[19]

These various cooperation agreements with Eastern European countries could not have been concluded had it not been for the political dimension of the Community's external relations. This dimension became possible, after all, only because the Community had adopted a position of principle during the negotiations with COMECON on relations between the two very different economic organizations: Relations between the European Community and the communist countries must be developed not through Soviet-dominated COMECON but with the individual countries. In the end this was also accepted by the Soviet Union in the Joint Declaration on the establishment of official relations of June 1988.[20] The way was thus cleared for a Community policy that could take account of the political and economic situation and reforms in each individual country.

An important sign of recognition of the Community and the Commission's role by the member states *and* the western countries was the mandate that the Commission received from the seven richest countries in July 1989 to coordinate western aid to Poland and Hungary.[21] Although this mandate is primarily economic in substance, it is also politically important both for the relationship between the European Community and Eastern Europe and for the European Community's position in the West.

Like the changes in the communist countries, the question of the relationship between East and West Germany gave the Community and the Commission an opportunity to show what they are capable of. On 18 November, a week after the Wall collapsed, the twelve heads of state or government met at the Elysée Palace for emergency talks on the new situation. This was symbolic of how the member states' attitude had evolved: Something happens that may change the European geopolitical situation radically, and it is decided to hold a meeting immediately. Despite the problems that arose after Chancellor Kohl had presented his ten-point plan, the European Community partners approved Germany's reunification at the summit meeting in Strasbourg (8 and 9 December 1989). At the same meeting they also succeeded, partly by putting moral pressure on the Federal Republic to adopt a positive attitude toward the Community, in taking new steps in the process of integration by deciding to convene an intergovernmental conference on European Monetary Union.

As regards West Germany's and the Community's future relationship with East Germany, it was again the Commission that took the lead in the political debate and in political action. In January 1990, while the debate on the possibility and manner of German reunification was still very much in progress, Commission President Delors declared that the Community must prepare itself to absorb an East Germany united with West Germany. To this end, a special monitoring group chaired by Vice-President Bangemann was set up to make the practical preparations. In a statement to the European Parliament on 7 January 1990 Delors also proposed that a special European Council meeting should be held after the East German elections in March to discuss inter-German relations and their implications for the Community. This idea was accepted by the General Affairs Council meeting in Dublin in February 1990, which promised support, albeit after a heated discussion, for the reunification process and also decided that a special summit should be held in Dublin on 28 April for the sole purpose of discussing German unification. It was therefore possible for this meeting to be properly prepared, which again indicated that the Community was looking ahead and not succumbing to frantic crisis management.

Various elements of the Community's policy toward the USSR and Eastern Europe in 1989 had already been set out in the report drawn up for the European Parliament by Klaus Hänsch on "political relations between the European Community and the Soviet Union" (1988).[22] Although it does not have the same formal right to participate in decision making or even to advise on EPC matters as it does in the Community, the European Parliament has also shown itself to be a harbinger and driving force in foreign policy and European security issues. After an initial period of disagreement within Parliament on whether or not security might be discussed, it set to with conviction and a knowledge of the facts. Although the controversy over medium-range weapons accentuated the dividing line between right and left for a time, the members of parliament from the twelve member states and the various political groups gradually succeeded in defining their own security thinking and a strategy, as evident, for example, from the Haagerup, Galluzzi, and Hänsch reports. The ideas, strategies, and global concepts proposed by Parliament then slowly filtered through into the Community's policy, as they also did in the case of the institutional reforms and the single market. In this way Parliament helped to ensure that the security question was put on the Community agenda and that the broadest possible view was taken of the substance of the security concept. Besides mapping out the broad lines for the development of a European security policy, Parliament also paid close attention to specific aspects of European security, such as the implications of the CSCE, the Conference on Disarmament in Europe (Stockholm), EUREKA and SDI, arms limitation, industrial production, and security in the Mediterranean region and in Northern Europe.

The debate on the nuclear deterrent, which split the political parties in the various member states, also influenced the European Parliament. The Penders report (1989) on the security of Western Europe did not therefore say anything new.[23] For the time being at least this debate is unlikely to divide Parliament, and it can therefore be expected to perform its task as a think tank to the full again.

The Single European Act gave the European Parliament a power that enables it to bring direct influence to bear on foreign and security policy: Association agreements with third countries or groups of countries require the approval of an absolute majority of its members.[24] It can thus help to determine relations between the Community and Eastern European countries and encourage or sanction certain developments. Parliament clearly does not view the situation solely from the economic angle, but also considers the general political context. The Commission has presented its plans for second-generation agreements with the Eastern European countries, which will certainly require Parliament's approval. As these future association agreements will determine the political framework of relations between the Community and the countries of the former Eastern bloc, they are a particularly effective means for Parliament to consolidate its influence on the Community's foreign policy. It should not be forgotten in this context that the U.S. Senate is so important precisely because all treaties concluded by the president require its approval. And although in the European Parliament's case this power is (provisionally) limited to association agreements, it undeniably forms the nucleus of far-reaching powers with regard to foreign issues.

Just as important for future relations with the Eastern European countries and Parliament's part in them is that its approval is also needed before new member states may accede. In other words, the European Parliament may demand that certain economic, political, and security requirements be satisfied before such countries join the Twelve. Awareness of this may in turn influence the policy pursued in the former Eastern bloc countries.

This network of interinstitutional relations, embedded in the stabilized entity which the Community may justifiably be called, may form the basis of a second-generation European security policy, in which not only are statements made on the policy that is formally pursued in other bodies, but the policy is also formulated and, increasingly, implemented.

NOTES

1. "Single European Act," *Bulletin of the European Communities*, Supplement 2/ 1986, p. 18.

2. "Solemn Declaration on European Union," *Bulletin* 16(6)1983, p. 31.

3. Jean de Ruyt, *L'Acte Unique Européenne* (Brussels: Editions de l'Université de Bruxelles, 1987), p. 224.

4. European Parliament, "Draft Treaty on European Union," 14 February 1984,

Official Journal of the European Communities, C 77/83, 19 March 1984, pp. 33–52, Articles 63, 66, and 68.

5. European Parliament, *Resolution on European Security and European Political Cooperation*, adopted on 13 January 1983, PE 82.486, pp. 68–71.

6. Niels Haagerup, *Report drawn up on behalf of the Political Affairs Committee on European Political Cooperation and European Security*, European Parliament, 3 December 1982, Doc. 1–946/82, pp. 28–29.

7. G. Galluzzi, *Report drawn up on behalf of the Political Affairs Committee on the political dimension of a European security policy*, European Parliament, 2 July 1987, A1–110/87, pp. 6–8.

8. "Commission européenne: le président Delors pour un sommet européen sur les relations est-ouest," *Agence Europe*, 16 March 1987, p. 3; "Anniversaire du Traité de Rome; le président Delors illustre la stratégie de la Commission et réaffirme qu'un sommet spécial devrait être consacré aux problèmes de sécurité," *Agence Europe*, 20 March 1987, pp. 3–4.; Mia Doornaert, "Martens, Mitterrand laten proefballon op over EG-defensieraad," *De Standaard*, 20 March 1987, pp. 1, 10; "Plumb voor defensietop," *De Standaard*, 21 March 1987, p. 4; Leo Tindemans, "The European Union: Report to the European Council," *Bulletin of the European Communities*, 1/76, p. 18.

9. H. van der Velden and H. A. Visée, *Ontspanning in Europa. De Conferentie over Veiligheid en Samenwerking in Europa* (Baarn: Het Wereldvenster, 1975), pp. 113–114, 127; Alfred Pijpers, "EPC and the CSCE-process," *Legal Issues of European Integration*, (1)1984, pp. 140–42.

10. Philippe de Schoutheete, *La coopération politique européenne* (Brussels: Editions Labor, 1986), pp. 209–11.

11. Pedro Sanchez da Costa Pereira, "The Use of a Secretariat," in Alfred Pijpers, Elfriede Regelsberger, Wolfgang Wessels, eds., *European Political Cooperation in the 1980's: A Common Foreign Policy for Western Europe?* (Dordrecht: Nijhoff Publishers, 1988), p. 89.

12. "Verklaring van de Europese Raad over de internationale rol van de EG," *Europa van Morgen*, 8 December 1988, p. 578.

13. Pijpers, "EPC and the CSCE-process," pp. 143–46.

14. Michael Groth, "Fortschritte im KSZE-Prozess. Das dritte Folgetreffen in Wien," *Europa-Archiv*, 44(3)1989, pp. 95–102.

15. "Europese Raad, Conclusies van de Voorzitterschap. Madrid, 26–27 juni 1989," *Europa van Morgen*, 29 June 1989, p. 357.

16. For an overview of the institutional structure of EPC and of its relationship with the European Community see de Ruyt, *L'Acte Unique Européenne*, pp. 238–48, and Gianni Bonvicini, "Mechanisms and Procedures of EPC: More than Traditional Diplomacy?" in Pijpers et al., eds., *European Political Cooperation in the 1980's*, pp. 53–61.

17. Simon Nuttall, "Interaction between EPC and the EC," *Yearbook of European Law*, vol. 7, 1988, p. 235.

18. Reinhardt Rummel, "*Speaking with One Voice—and Beyond*," in Pijpers et al., eds., *European Political Cooperation in the 1980's*, p. 127.

19. "Communauté/Roumanie: La communauté annonce formellement la suspension des négociations en vue d'un nouvel accord," *Nouvelles Atlantiques*, 26 April 1989, p. 4.

20. Arie Bloed, " 'De doofstommen horen en spreken weer': normalisering van betrekkingen EEG-COMECON," *International Spectator*, (10)1988, pp. 661–70.

21. "La fin de la réunion à Paris des pays les plus industrialisés. Les déclarations économiques et politiques," *Le Monde*, 18 July 1989.

22. K. Hänsch, *Report drawn up on behalf of the Political Affairs Committee on political relations between the European Community and the Soviet Union*, European Parliament, 18 July 1988, Doc. A2–155/88.

23. J. Penders, *Report drawn up on behalf of the Political Affairs Committee on the security of Western Europe*, European Parliament, 24 February 1989, Doc. A2–410/ 88.

24. L. Planas Puchades, *Report drawn up on behalf of the Political Affairs Committee on the role of the European Parliament in foreign policy under the Single European Act*, European Parliament, Doc. A2–86/88, 26 May 1988, pp. 10–12.

13

Necessity and Conviction

In the late summer of 1982 Mikhail Sergeyevich Gorbachev, the secretary of the Central Committee responsible for agriculture, realized that the harvest would again be a disaster. For the fourth consecutive year since he had assumed responsibility for this sector he would fail, despite his major efforts to achieve satisfactory results, despite the creation of new structures, despite the action taken to ensure strict adherence to the plans and the methods of orthodox communism. It was also clear that Brezhnev could not accept the latest agricultural disaster so readily and allow it to pass without political repercussions as he had done in previous years, when poor weather conditions were blamed for everything. The fifty-one-year-old secretary, who had been made a full member of the Politburo two years earlier, realized that this time he could be made the scapegoat since he was responsible for agriculture and above all because he had sided with his protector, Andropov, in recent internal discussions. By Soviet tradition any decision to remove him from the Politburo would not, however, be taken until after the celebrations to mark the anniversary of the October Revolution. Brezhnev, wanting to nip rumors about his very poor health in the bud, spent several hours watching the parade that bitterly cold 7 November. The effort was too much, and three days later Leonid Brezhnev died of a heart attack. The political future of the secretary for agriculture was safe for the time being.[1]

Brezhnev was succeeded by Andropov, whose former post as head of the KGB gave him a better insight than anyone into the disastrous consequences of the protector-protégé relationship between party and government and of the resulting corruption, incompetence, abuse of power, and growth of privileges for the elite. Andropov therefore appreciated how extremely negative an impact the rampant abuses under Brezhnev had had on the economy, discipline, public morals, academe, intellectual life, and other aspects of Soviet society. He therefore launched an anticorruption campaign and attempted to steer younger and more competent politicians and technocrats into the Central Committee and a more independent government in order to break the vicious circle. The enterprising but ailing Soviet leader was, however, to die barely eighteen months after taking office.[2]

In a final show of strength the Brezhnev clan succeeded in forcing their candidate for the succession on the innovators within the party apparatus. The fact that Chernenko, who was three years older than Andropov, was eventually accepted by everyone was principally due to his only positive trait in the eyes of Andropov's disciples: his terminal illness. On 10 March 1985 the third Soviet leader in less than two and a half years died. The American expert on Soviet affairs, Seweryn Bialer, who left Moscow a week before Chernenko's death, described the situation as follows:

The mood was one of gloom, frustration, impatience and embarrassment—gloom about the country's huge problems, frustration with the inactivity of those who were supposed to lead, impatience with an "old guard" of party leaders who refused to yield power and embarrassment that a great nation and great power was essentially leaderless.[3]

On the very day that Chernenko died Gorbachev was appointed the new secretary-general, advantage being taken of the chance absence of three members of the Politburo, who were confronted with a fait accompli on their return. Had they been present, the decision on the succession would in all probability have favored Gorbachev's rival and Chernenko's protégé, Grishin. And if Chernenko had died a month later, Gorbachev would have had little chance, since Grishin's protectors, sensing that the party leader was soon to die (but not expecting him to go so quickly), were making preparations for an orderly transfer of power in the latter half of March.[4]

March 1985, then, saw the appointment as the new leader of the Soviet empire a man who had a few months earlier, despite the traditional orthodox line he took, aroused the hopes of many intellectuals in Moscow with his statement that "openness is a compulsory condition of socialist democracy and a norm of public life."[5] He was indeed to launch fundamental reforms in the Soviet Union. And abroad he would be referred to as the man who made a fundamental change in East-West relations possible, who after forty years at last enabled wide-ranging disarmament negotiations to begin *and* to be brought to a successful conclusion, who enabled Eastern Europe simply to become part of Europe, and who paved the way for the unification of the two Germanys. But what if, by some whim of fate, Brezhnev had survived the military parade and Chernenko had died a few months later, as planned? Would we then have simply commemorated the 1789 revolution without witnessing one ourselves?

There is no denying that, through his political skill, his intellectual capacities and flexibility, and his dynamic and attractive appearance, Gorbachev has played a key role in the various fundamental changes that have been made. It is also clear, however, that these reforms are attributable not only to Gorbachev and his personal political choices and skills but also to a whole new, well-educated middle class that no longer has any direct links with the Soviet state's early revolutionary period, that was instead seeking a new order based on intelligent analysis, rational debate, and cooperation and that found in Gorbachev a highly skilled spokesman and leader.[6] It was a new generation that had long been waiting in the wings, but had until recently been prevented from moving on stage by the USSR's political system. It was a new class of Soviet leaders that, because of this belated entry, now faces the enormous task of adjusting the country to the social, economic, and scientific advances that have been made in Europe and elsewhere in the world in the last decade, but that have passed the Soviet Union by because its system is essentially based on nineteenth-century conditions. Gorbachev and his supporters are, in other words, being carried along on a wave of change that is not of their own making but was set in motion by deep historical forces and the resulting problems, to which the new generation of Soviet leaders must find solutions.[7]

Gorbachev's awareness, due partly to his own failure in the colossal Ministry of Agriculture, of the poor state of all sections of Soviet society was evident from his address to the 27th Congress of the Communist Party in 1986:

Difficulties began to build up in the economy in the 1970s, with the rates of economic growth declining visibly. As a result, the targets for economic development... were not attained. Nor did we manage to carry out the social program charted for this period. A lag ensued in the material base of science and education, health protection, culture, and everyday services.... There are serious lags in engineering, the oil and coal industries, the electrical engineering industry, in ferrous metals and chemicals, in capital construction. Neither have the targets been met for the main indicators of efficiency and the improvement of the people's standard of living. Acceleration of the country's socioeconomic development is the key to all our problems, immediate and long-term, economic and social, political and ideological, internal and external.

The difference from the traditional addresses at previous congresses, when the praises of all achievements were sung, was rather striking. And the euphoric self-assurance of a Khrushchev, who had said in the 1950s that the USSR would overtake the United States economically and bury capitalism, belonged to the distant past.[8]

A collection of extracts from Gorbachev's book *Perestroika*, which was published in 1987, puts the crisis in the Soviet system in even sharper focus:

At some stage—this became particularly clear in the latter half of the seventies— something happened that was at first sight inexplicable. The country began to lose momentum. . . . A kind of "braking mechanism" affecting social and economic development formed. . . .

An absurd situation was developing. The Soviet Union, the world's biggest producer of steel, raw materials, fuel and energy, has shortfalls in them due to wasteful or inefficient use. One of the biggest producers of grain for food, it nevertheless has to buy millions of tons of grain a year for fodder. We have the largest number of doctors and hospital beds per thousand of the population and, at the same time, there are glaring shortcomings in our health services. Our rockets can find Halley's comet and fly to Venus with amazing accuracy, but . . . many Soviet household appliances are of poor quality.

This, unfortunately, is not all. A gradual erosion of the ideological and moral values of our people began. . . .

Many Party members in leading posts stood beyond control and criticism, which led to failures in work and to serious malpractices. At some administrative levels there emerged a disrespect for the law and encouragement of eyewash and bribery, servility and glorification. . . .

An unbiased and honest approach led us to the only logical conclusion that the country was verging on crisis.[9]

Thus, the remarks of the leader of a superpower on his own country. The new generation of Soviet leaders realized full well that the economic, political, and social problems were closely linked and that fundamental changes were needed in all these areas. In contrast to earlier attempts in the communist countries, it was appreciated that radical and sustained structural economic changes were possible only if they were backed by social and political renewal. The policy of perestroika (restructuring the economy) was therefore accompanied by the policy of glasnost (political and social openness) and, toward the end of the 1980s, after most of Brezhnev's protégés had been ousted, by political reforms. From the haste with which he launched structural political reforms at the turn of the decade it was evident that Gorbachev was aware how right he had been to write in *Perestroika* a few years earlier: "Perestroika itself can only come about through democracy. . . . Democratization is also the main guarantee that the current processes cannot be reversed."[10]

The process of political reform and glasnost produced results more quickly than perestroika, which can only bear fruit in the long term. For the moment, the economic reforms are in fact having primarily an adverse effect on the people and the economy, mainly because most of these structural reforms have been fairly half-hearted. This is true, for example, of the agricultural reforms, the granting of greater autonomy to enterprises, the legislation on joint ventures, and the possibility of private ownership. The result is that the disadvantages of the economic reforms are already being felt by the people, without there being any sign of improvement. As unemployment rises sharply and the number of basic products that can be bought in the shops continues to fall, patience and confidence are slowly running out. Glasnost is increasing the opportunities for voicing dissatisfaction and even having it expressed in the political forum through the election of representatives. The strikes have been another example of the consequences of the combination of successful glasnost and unsuccessful perestroika. Another problem is that, unlike the political reforms and glasnost, the economic reforms have yet to set in motion a process that has its own momentum.[11]

It became increasingly difficult in practice for Gorbachev to abide by one of his other statements, where he said that the USSR would be "looking within socialism, rather than outside it for the answers to all the questions that arise" and that "those (in the West) who hope we shall move away from the socialist path will be greatly disappointed."[12] As events in the Eastern European countries have shown, reforming socialism means abolishing socialism. The initial illusions about the possibility of fundamental reform that does not necessarily culminate in the death of socialism must surely have disappeared with the developments in Eastern Europe and on the outskirts of the empire. The reforms, which even then they continued to propose—abolishing the monopoly of the communist party—showed, however, that the leaders in Moscow realized the eventual abolition of the communist system was ultimately preferable to the disappearance of the Soviet Union as a superpower or, put another way, the abolition of their own system was the only way left to retain superpower status also at the end of the twentieth century. They fully appreciated, however, that the criteria for superpower status that apply at the end of the twenthieth century will no longer be the same as those that applied at the beginning and in the middle of this century.

This also establishes the relationship between the Soviet Union's domestic and foreign policies. Like the domestic reforms, the radical changes of course in foreign policy stemmed from the realization that they were essential if the USSR was to survive as a state and a superpower. Above all, the foreign and security policies that Moscow had pursued in previous decades could no longer be sustained financially and economically and were in fact sapping the country. The enormous array of military power within and outside the USSR meant that the percentage of the GNP spent on defense was extremely high. Maintaining this military apparatus therefore became increasingly difficult to finance. In addition, the large number of skilled workers and scientists and the vast quantities of high-tech equipment assigned to the defense system put civil industry at a serious disadvantage, resulting, among other things, in goods important to the people being in short supply and of a poor quality.[13]

Not only the array of military power but also support for wars and lesser conflicts in various parts of the world could no longer be financially sustained. Furthermore, this strategy had failed to have positive effects. The system of satellite states in Eastern Europe and other parts of the world was also becoming an increasingly intolerable drain on economic resources. After all, these countries not only had to have military assistance, often involving the presence of Soviet troops on their soil, but most also needed economic assistance and supplies of raw materials and energy. As their Marxist economies had not succeeded in producing significantly better results than the USSR's, various communist satellites found themselves in a real economic predicament.

While the communist system may have been useful to the Soviet Union itself as a means of quickly transforming a semifeudal and agrarian society into an industrialized and, economically, relatively strong society, the same could not in any way be said of the Eastern European countries. Nor did the communist model permit any kind of efficient response to the technological revolution of the 1970s and 1980s, making the adverse implications of central planning even more apparent. Eastern Europe increasingly became a museum of industrial archaeology and gradually sank to the economic level of the developing countries. This was alarming principally because various fledgling industrialized countries in the so-called Third World were raising their economies to First World levels with the help of the most advanced technologies and so overtaking the communist countries. While the Eastern European countries had previously been able to rely on a relatively sound industrial base and low wages to fill the gaps in western markets, the city-state of Singapore, for example, with its 2.5 million inhabitants, exported more machinery to the West in 1988 than the six Eastern European countries together, with their population of 112 million. Half of the exports from the six Eastern European countries that had still been competitive in the world market in 1980 were no longer so in 1985.[14]

The decline in exports to the West and the consequent loss of foreign exchange revenues made it more difficult for the Eastern European countries to modernize their industries and to pay the interest on their debts to the West. Some governments in the Eastern bloc tried to remedy this situation by introducing austerity programs, which pushed already low living standards even lower. A country like Hungary, as the *New York Times* put it, imposed Swedish taxes on Ethiopian wages. Furthermore, the communist system was simply incapable of producing sufficient consumer goods, when they could be obtained in the West without difficulty. The people were also confronted with growing pollution, which began to assume dramatic proportions in certain areas. Hence, for example, the unflattering comment that Czech factories are competitive only in the production of pollution. In addition, and partly as a result of this, it became clear that the health of the people as well as the economy was declining. In five of the six countries life expectancy had fallen since 1970 and was on average three years less than in the European Community countries. Infant mortality was almost twice as high. The result was that the dissatisfaction of the people became even more pronounced and led to public clashes in Hungary, for example, and even in Romania. Growing public dissatisfaction with the serious economic situation, the consequences of which were becoming increasingly tangible in everyday life, helped to form a sound basis for the protest movement that erupted in 1989.[15]

In most Eastern European countries some attempt was made to reform the economy, but without affecting the communist model. Generally speaking, political control of production, prices, and enterprises was retained, making it impossible for the reform measures to have the intended effect and often exacerbating existing problems. When, to stimulate a given sector, the enterprises in that sector were given greater economic independence, they came up against a totally unchanged economic environment that prevented them from making efficient use of their new freedom, an example being the difficulty regularly encountered in obtaining supplies of raw materials. The countries that went furthest with what were nonetheless partial reforms were therefore most directly confronted with the inevitability of a fundamental and total reform of their economic system and with the need for western assistance in carrying out these reforms. They were also the countries that owed the West most and had therefore become largely dependent on it since, in return for rescheduling or granting a moratorium, it insisted on major sacrifices and fundamental reforms.

This was one reason why Poland and Hungary sought the closest contacts with the West and were the first in Eastern Europe to undertake political as well as economic reforms. Fundamental economic reforms would, after all, lead to even more price rises, import restrictions, reorganization of loss-making state-owned enterprises, even lower wages, and unemployment. As a representative of the Hungarian Free Democrats rightly pointed out in the early part of 1989: "No wonder the present government would have liked to see the opposition sharing responsibility at that time." In the latter half of 1989 Solidarity, the party in the Polish coalition government with most "economic" ministerial portfolios, must already have realized how impossible its task was. If this feeling had also begun to overtake the Soviet leaders, it may partly explain the ever more extensive political reforms, including the abolition of the communist party's leading role.[16]

The Soviet Union's inability to continue giving its satellite states economic support and its awareness that the economic situation in these countries might eventually pose even greater problems, possibly culminating in revolt, is therefore one explanation for Moscow's decision to let the Eastern

European countries go their own way economically and, in the end, politically. They were thus given the freedom and, ultimately, the explicit advice to undertake economic and political reforms and to seek economic assistance in the West, so that they would not come to form an economic and political vacuum, which would have been dangerous for the USSR. Granting them this freedom, however, had long-term political implications for the USSR, since western economic assistance would have western political and other conditions attached and give the Eastern European countries even more room to maneuver in their relations with the USSR. This is something of which the Kremlin must surely have been aware.

This brings us to another reason for the fundamental changes in both domestic and foreign policy. The Soviet leaders must have begun to realize that the USSR had failed to turn its increased military capacities and military presence in third countries to permanent political advantage simply because it is a one-dimensional superpower, one whose strength is based primarily on its military potential. It is unable, as a model of society, to offer the same leadership or achieve the same dominance politically, economically, technologically, and ideologically.[17] In the ideological sphere it was clear not only that Marxism-Leninism was crumbling in the Soviet Union but also that the revolutionary attraction that the Soviet model had previously had for various countries, peoples, and resistance groups had now largely vanished. Foreign communist parties dissociated themselves from the party in Moscow and from the Soviet model.[18] Communist parties in the Eastern European countries and even in some of the Soviet republics had been distancing themselves from the communist party in Moscow. So unattractive an ideology and model of society were not, of course, the ideal basis for a superpower that wanted to exercise continuing influence throughout the world. This, then, was the major difference between the USSR and the United States, which was not only more attractive to third countries but also whose model of society was accepted and becoming dominant even in countries where anti-American feeling was rife.

Even many of the countries that formed part of the Soviet sphere of influence or maintained friendly relations principally with the USSR were gradually turning to its superpower rival, the United States. The Soviet Union might be generous with military aid, and was indeed the largest supplier of military equipment to the Third World, but if serious economic, financial, and technological assistance was needed, little could be expected of Moscow, and it was better to look to Washington or the European capitals. Countries such as India and Algeria therefore turned to the United States for support and closer economic cooperation. And when the Marxist-Leninist and extremely pro-Soviet regime in Ethiopia was faced with widespread famine in 1985, most of the aid came from the western countries, and only a very small proportion from the Soviet Union.[19]

To make matters worse for the Soviets, the Americans had even succeeded in developing a world economic and financial system that it dominated through international institutions and thanks to the commanding role of the dollar, a system that had most developing countries in its grasp and could not be simply ignored by the communist countries. The absence of a sound economic base was thus hardly conducive to the maintenance of Soviet influence in the world and, for this reason alone, called for structural economic changes in the USSR. The Soviet leaders had never seen dialectical materialism in this light.

In the end, it must have become clear to the Soviet leaders that, despite their enormous military potential and spread of power, they had relatively little influence on developments in the world and, moreover, could still not feel really secure. The military structure and domination of various surrounding countries, which was in itself intended to increase the USSR's security and to prevent a recurrence of painful past experiences, eventually gave rise to a feeling of reduced security.[20] The surrounding European and Asian countries and the rival superpower felt even more threatened by this show of strength, closed their military ranks, and stepped up their military efforts, often leaving the Soviet Union feeling more than ever surrounded by hostile countries. Furthermore, although the USSR had various allies or friends throughout the world, they remained a minority by comparison with the number of western-oriented countries. The Soviets knew only too well that the widespread contention in the West that there was no getting rid of the Soviet Union once it had a hold on a country was a myth and, sad to say from their point of view, did not tally with the facts. Although it had been able to extend Soviet influence in previous decades to embrace a number of countries, Moscow had lost its foothold in various others, among them very important countries like China, Egypt, and Indonesia.[21]

That the militarization of its foreign policy and its unwillingness to accept political compromises, cooperation, and reconciliation had not increased but in fact reduced the USSR's influence was very clear in Europe. Moscow had, after all, been able to exercise very little influence on the foreign policies of the Western European countries, as the crisis over the deployment of medium-range missiles in the early 1980s had shown. A more aggressive and more threatening posture had in fact led the Europeans to close ranks and look more to Washington for instructions. In addition, the Soviet presence in Eastern Europe had certainly not made the Eastern European peoples more Soviet minded. A change of course was thus needed. Fairly soon after the new Soviet leaders had taken the first steps toward a more conciliatory and détente-oriented policy, it became apparent that Moscow's influence on the western countries and on the developing countries was growing.

The USSR was an overextended superpower not only because of its domination of Eastern Europe and distant countries, but also because of its commitments that could not be permanently sustained by its own financial and economic resources and structure; the USSR was therefore condemned to losing its superpower status.[22] This statement is universally valid, but in a communist country it takes on a highly ironic undertone. The Soviet Union was also increasingly overextended as a superpower because of its enormous size. The inefficiency of its economic structure and its poor economic and agricultural performance made it extremely difficult to provide the whole empire with more than the minimum of services. The size of the Soviet empire, with its ten time zones, and the resulting major internal disparities also created a situation that could not be endure forever.

A review of what the Soviets placed under one central authority in Moscow is very revealing. This review of the formal and informal ingredients of the Soviet brew also shows that the results cannot be predicted when the brew begins to ferment. It shows how simplistic our picture of the Soviet empire has been in recent decades, with Moscow and Leningrad often the only cities known in the West. Even the three Baltic republics were virtually unknown to most Western Europeans until a few years ago.

The Union of Soviet Socialist Republics comprises fifteen republics: Estonia, Latvia, Lithuania, White Russia or Belorussia, Moldavia, and the Ukraine in the European part; the three Caucasian republics of Georgia, Azerbaijan, and Armenia; the Asian republics of Kazakhstan, Uzbekistan, Turkmenistan, Tadzhikistan, and Kirghizia; and, finally, the Russian Soviet Federal Socialist Republic itself. The republics differ widely in language, religion, traditions, external influences, traditional political structures, economic development, population, and so on. In the last respect, Russia itself is preponderant with its 145 million inhabitants, compared with the 1 to 7 million of most other republics. The Ukraine, with a population of 51 million (almost as large as France), falls between the two extremes, revealing the importance of this agriculturally and industrially rich republic.[23]

Besides these fifteen republics, there are twenty Autonomous Soviet Socialist Republics: Karelia (formerly part of Finland but seized after the First World War), Komi, Yakut, Buriat, Tuva, Udmurt, Tartar, Mari, North Ossetia, Bashkiria, Kara-Kalpak, Kabardino-Balkar, Kalmyk, Checheno-Ingush, Mordvinia, Chuvash, Abhazia, Adjaria, Nahichevan, and Dagestan; eight Autonomous Regions (or *oblasti*): South Ossetia, Nagorno-Karabakh, Adygei, Karachayevo-Cherkess, Gorno-Badakhshan, Gorno-Altai, Khakass, and the Jewish *oblast* far away in Asia; and ten National Areas (*okrugi*): Aga-Buryat, Nenets, Komi-Permyak, Khanty-Mansi, Yamalo-Nenets, Taymir, Evenki, Ust-Ordyn Buryat, Chukot, and Koryak.[24] Most of these last three categories were created to cater to the presence of larger or smaller minorities and demarcations brought about by history. Behind all these official names stand people, such as six million Tartars, of whom only 1.5 million, however, live in the eponymous republic; almost two million Khivates; more than one million Mordvins; the Komis and Komi-Permyaks, Maris, Udmurts and Avars, of whom there are about half a million in each case; and the many other peoples, a few of them very small in number, like the 440 Aleuts.[25]

As most of the republics, autonomous republics, *oblasti*, and *okrugi*, many of which were created to cater to existing minorities, themselves include minorities, there is a serious risk of nationalist and ethnic conflict, with all that it entails, as was first shown by the problems in Nagorno-Karabakh. The above list reveals, however, that these ethnic conflicts and appeals for greater independence and self-government were likely to increase sharply as the once strict central authority in Moscow slackened the reins. The snowball effect this may have is evident from the case of the Gagauzis. These 180,000 Turkish-speaking orthodox Christians live in Moldavia, which is totally alien to them in terms of language, culture, and traditions, and was part of Romania until annexed by the USSR in 1940 and oppressed by the cultural and economic hegemony of the Russians. The Moldavians, who form one of the fifteen republics, followed the example of the Baltic nationalist movements, demanded more independence and managed, among other things, to have Moldavian declared the principal language of the republic. This, however, led to a reaction from the Gagauzis, who were now expected to learn the alien Moldavian language as well as the equally alien Russian and, as a minority, felt even more oppressed. Just as the Moldavians demanded more freedom from the Russians, the Gagauzis were becoming increasingly explicit in their demands for greater independence from the Moldavians, and at its first congress in May 1989 the nationalist movement, Gagauzi Khalki, approved the proposal for the formation of an autonomous republic, consisting of various southern districts of Moldavia, with Komrat as its capital. In 1906 the Gagauzis had indeed proclaimed their independence, but were crushed two weeks later.[26]

The problem for Moscow is not only the great diversity of the Union controlled from the Russian capital but also the fact that many of these peoples are traditionally anti-Russian. Just as Soviet dominance of the Eastern European countries failed to change their attitude toward the USSR and toward each other, the absorption of the many peoples into the Soviet Union has not resulted in their having a more positive attitude toward Moscow and each other. Unlike the United States, Moscow can also be said to have failed in the latter respect, the creation of friendly relations among different peoples traditionally hostile to each other, and has thus further undermined its long-term security. The Americans have indeed achieved remarkable results in Western Europe by forcing the countries dependent on them to cooperate since the Second World War, even though it must be admitted that the situation in Western Europe was far less complicated than in the central and eastern parts of the Eurasian continent. Nevertheless, while nationalist tensions have largely disappeared in the West, they have not been resolved in Eastern Europe and the USSR itself even after forty-five, seventy, or more years. They have simply been glossed over and suppressed.

Hence the great dilemma for the Soviet leaders, who realize that they cannot possibly keep their extensive empire permanently under control and are incapable of administering this huge country properly, but are aware of the problems and violent or nonviolent conflicts that may arise if they relax their central control. There is also the dilemma that, while perestroika, glasnost, and political reforms are needed if the Soviet Union is to be restored to health, these reforms are bound to give rise to nationalist feelings and greater demands from the various peoples, republics, and regions within the USSR, demands that in most cases have but one explicit or implicit objective—independence. The Baltic and Caucasian republics and regions showed the way, and in this respect they were also able to point to the constitution of the USSR, Article 72 of which says that "each Soviet Republic retains the right to secede from the USSR."[27]

The various, ever larger concessions the Kremlin made after mid-1989 indicated that Moscow, the last colonial power, realized that it too should begin the process of decolonization and that the peoples and areas it had conquered, not across the seas as the Europeans had done, but across its own Eurasian continent, should be allowed to go their own way to some extent. This would mean a reversion to the original ideas of Lenin. At the seventh pan-Russian conference in 1917 the Bolsheviks led by Lenin demanded "for all nations which form part of Russia . . . the right freely to secede and to establish independent states." Six months later the rebel government formed by the Bolsheviks also adopted a "Declaration of the rights of the peoples of Russia" on a proposal from the Georgian Stalin, then commissioner for the nationalities. Indeed, in 1901 Stalin had already referred in a pamphlet to the unacceptable situation of the peoples in Russia, as the following fine prose shows:

They sigh, the oppressed nationalities and religions, especially the Poles and the Finns, driven from their native soil, their most holy feelings trampled underfoot. . . . They sigh at the ceaseless persecution and humiliation, the Jews, who have been deprived of even the insignificant rights that other Russian subjects enjoy. . . . They sigh, the Georgians, the Armenians and the other peoples.[28]

When he ruled the country, however, this same Stalin was to be responsible for the ruthless suppression of the national minorities, for massacres, and for the many compulsory resettlement programs that created the problems to which the present Soviet leaders must now find solutions.

Like Lenin in 1918, Gorbachev may eventually be forced by circumstances (then military, now political and economic) to adopt the same strategy to achieve the same goal: Give up part of the empire so that at least its heartland may be retained. Against the will of some of his comrades the first Soviet leader agreed in 1918 to the Peace Treaty of Brest-Litovsk with the Germans, under which he made major territorial concessions from which not only the Germans benefited. The areas surrendered at this time included the Ukraine, White Russia, the Baltic states, the three Caucasian and various Asian regions,[29] an event that is still deeply impressed on the memories of these states.

NOTES

1. Zhores Medvedev, *Gorbachev* (Oxford, Eng.: Basil Blackwell, 1986), pp. 117–118. For Gorbachev's agricultural policy see chapters 5, 6, 7.

2. Ibid., pp. 121, 135.

3. Ibid., pp. 7, 12.

4. Ibid., pp. 3–7.

5. Ibid., p. 159.

6. Michael Howard, "1989: A Farewell to Arms?" *International Affairs*, 65(3)1989, p. 407.

7. Ibid.

8. Paul Kennedy, *The Rise and Fall of the Great Powers* (London: Unwin Hyman, 1988), pp. 489–490.

9. Mikhail Gorbachev, *Perestroika: New Thinking for Our Country and the World* (London: Collins, 1987), pp. 18–24.

10. Ibid., pp. 31–32.

11. P. L., "Prof. Gorlé vreest voor Russisch nationalisme; 'Help Russen Bedrijven leiden maar pomp geen geld in Sovjet-ekonomie,' " *Financieel Economische Tijd*, 7 March 1990, p. 4; Richard Hornik, "Winter's Bitter Wind," *Time*, 4 December 1989, p. 42.

12. Gorbachev, *Perestroika*, p. 36.

13. Kennedy, *The Rise and Fall of the Great Powers*, pp. 498–499.

14. "Oost-Europa is de nieuwe Derde Wereld," *De Standaard*, 18 January 1988.

15. Ibid.; *Basic statistics for COMECON (Europe)*, European Parliament, Directorate for Committees and Delegations, PE 137.061, 5 December 1989, p. 4.

16. "Oost-Europa is de nieuwe Derde Wereld," *De Standaard*, 18 January 1988; H. M. van den Brink, "Democraten Hongarije klaar voor verkiezingen," *N.R.C.-Handelsblad*, 21 March 1989.

17. Zbigniew Brzezinski, *Game Plan: How to Conduct the U.S.-Soviet Contest* (Boston: The Atlantic Monthly Press, 1986), pp. 130–131, 134, 137.

18. Ibid., pp. 125–126.

19. Ibid., pp. 136–137.

20. Kennedy, *The Rise and Fall of the Great Powers*, pp. 488–489.

21. James Chace, "A New Grand Strategy," *Foreign Policy*, no. 70, Spring 1988, p. 9.

22. Kennedy, *The Rise and Fall of the Great Powers*, pp. xv–xvi.

23. Dominic Lieven, "Gorbachev and the Nationalities," *Conflict Studies*, (216)1988, pp. 15–16.

24. *Great Soviet Encyclopedia*, vol. 31 (New York: Macmillan, 1982), pp. 2–6.

25. Werner Adam, "Von den Abchasen bis zu den Zachuren," *Frankfurter Allgemeine Zeitung*, 6 January 1988, p. 9.

26. "Gagaoezen eisen autonome republiek," *De Standaard*, 9 August 1989, p. 5.

27. Zbigniew Brzezinski, "Postkommunistischer Nationalismus," *Europa-Archiv*, 44(24)1989, p. 736.

28. André Fontaine, *Histoire de la guerre froide. Vol. 1, De la révolution d'Octobre à la guerre de Corée. 1917–1950* (Paris: Fayard, 1965), p. 35.

29. Ibid., pp. 34–42.

14

The Year of Upheaval

Early 1988. Within the Hungarian communist party there is a heated debate on whether or not to permit noncommunist youth organizations. Hungary is again showing itself to be one of the most liberal countries in the Eastern bloc. In Poland the government is trying to recover from the defeat it suffered in the referendum in late November 1987. General Jaruzelski had proposed economic and political reforms, which would benefit "everyone who has not excluded himself."[1] In other words, the banned Solidarity trade union stayed banned. In the referendum no credence was given to the reforms, and they were rejected out of hand. In the USSR all attention is focused on the laborious process of reforming the economy. Skepticism about Gorbachev, however, continues to dominate in East and West. The East German party leader, Honecker, his Czech counterpart, Jakes (who replaced Husak in December 1987), and Romania's Ceausescu observe with suspicion, even hostility, the unorthodox behavior of Kadar, Jaruzelski, and Gorbachev. The Bulgarian party leader, Zhivkov, also displays some unorthodox tendencies (for a time).[2]

Early 1989. Honecker, Jakes, Ceausescu, and now Zhivkov are feeling increasingly concerned about attitudes in Moscow, Budapest, and Warsaw. The communist parties of Hungary and Poland are actually beginning to give serious consideration to the possibility of introducing political pluralism, and in Moscow a genuine election campaign has even been launched. What is more, in Hungary reformist Kadar has been replaced with the even more liberal communist leader Grosz, and Bruno Straub becomes Eastern Europe's first noncommunist president. Zhivkov, on the other hand, reverts to the familiar old line and removes reform-minded fellow communists. The new Czech party leader, Jakes, who was responsible for expelling half a million would-be reformers from the party in 1968, is frightened of a new Prague Spring and, as early as October 1988, replaced the reformist Prime Minister Stroegal with Adamec.[3]

Early 1990. The time when a change in the group photographs of communist leaders made the headlines is clearly over. At the meetings of the former communist countries held within the framework of the Warsaw Pact and COMECON, which still formally exist, there are many new faces: the Catholic prime minister of Poland, Mazowiecki, once adviser to Solidarity; Vaclav Havel, former dissident and now president of Czechoslovakia; Miklos Nemeth and Marian Calfa, heads of the governments in Budapest and Prague, which also include noncommunists; the East German Prime Minister Modrow, who, like Calfa, is thinking of leaving the communist party before the elections; the Romanians Iliescu and Roman. Jakes and Grosz, having been in power for barely a year, have already had to step down. And like Husak and Kadar before them, Honecker, Zhivkov, and Ceausescu have disappeared from the political stage. In precisely two years, the five men who for twenty, thirty-two, nineteen, thirty-five and twenty-four years respectively helped to determine the face of Eastern Europe as leaders of their countries have been ousted. Furthermore, in only a year communism, after dominating Eastern Europe for almost forty-five years, has been toppled from its throne. Eastern Europe suddenly seems to be just another part of Europe. And in the USSR there are growing signs that the mounting nationalist tensions and the growing self-confidence of the republics will turn the Soviet Union back into Russia again.

This very rapid change in the European political and ideological scene did not, of course, just happen: It was the outcome of various long-term developments. In the past decade, and particularly in its latter years, the inherent inconsistencies and shortcomings of the system itself had steadily increased the pressure in the communist boiler. Moscow was, moreover, steadily loosening the nuts designed to keep the lid on. And the West was pulling at this lid in all kinds of ways. Thus, as soon as the pressure inside found a way of escaping, the whole system was bound to burst apart.

In the past both East and West had underestimated the strength of the simple fact that people simply do not want to live under an authoritarian regime that restricts their freedom and denies them their national self-awareness and individuality. Despite the apparent stability of the regime and passivity of the people, they retained the necessary keenness of mind even after several decades to find the strength and courage to rid themselves of the communist leaders once the opportunity arose. Despite decades of official desecration of history and denial of the past of the various Eastern European peoples, their memories of what had preceded communism were even clearer than had been assumed.

It was therefore no accident that various high points in the history of the Eastern European countries and peoples were used as a front and a lever in the opposition to Soviet dominance and the communist regime.[4] The mounting Polish pressure for an explanation of the massacre at Katyn was one of the first examples of this. At Katyn the Red Army had murdered over four thousand Polish officers when it invaded Poland in 1939, although Moscow blamed the Nazis. This issue was a very useful means of further strengthening national awareness and of mobilizing the elite and the people. It was also used to exert pressure on the Polish leaders to proclaim the truth both in this particular case (as they eventually did in March 1989) and more generally, and it gave them considerable bargaining power in their discussions with the Soviets.

The Baltic republics demanded the reexamination and repeal of the non-aggression pact signed by Stalin and Hitler in August 1939. The Party Congress in Moscow was indeed subsequently to declare the pact illegal, thus giving the Baltic states a further strong argument for independence. Sometimes, then, rewriting history has its advantages as a means of legitimizing changes that are difficult to accept. Other republics and peoples in the USSR were also surprisingly quick to recall their history and use it as a lever for achieving greater independence.

In June 1989 a million Serbs gathered in Kosovo to commemorate the 600th anniversary of the death of seventy thousand soldiers of the Serbian Prince Lazare in the struggle against the Turkish Sultan Murad I. The present Serbian leader, Milosevic, the "Lazare" of the late twentieth century, succeeded in using this symbol of Serbian resistance to intensify the Serbian struggle against the western-oriented Croats and Slovenians and the alleged oppression of the Serbs in Kosovo, an autonomous province in the Serbian republic 90 percent of whose population is Albanian. This also gave Milosevic an excuse to restrict Kosovo's independence and increase Serbia's power.

The funeral in Vienna in early April of Zita, the last empress of Austria and queen of Hungary, and the visit by her son (and member of the European Parliament) Otto von Hapsburg to Hungary in May brought crowds into the streets in both parts of the former Austro-Hungarian dual monarchy and also caused unrest among the German and Hungarian minorities in Romanian Transylvania. Like various other "details," this in itself rather insignificant event further strengthened the feeling of togetherness. It was therefore no coincidence that the Hungarians were the first ostentatiously to cut down a few kilometers of the Iron Curtain, thus giving the starting signal for the removal of the whole East-West dividing line. Nor was it a coincidence that the arrest of a priest of Hungarian extraction in the Romanian town of Timisoara and the ensuing protest by the Hungarian minority should trigger the events that led to Ceausescu's fall.

On 16 June 1989 the remains of Imre Nagy, the Hungarian leader executed in 1958, were ceremonially reburied in Budapest, an event at which the victims of the crushing of the Hungarian uprising by Soviet troops in 1956 were also commemorated. Three weeks later, on 6 July, Nagy was officially rehabilitated in public esteem by the supreme court. The same day saw the death of Janos Kadar, the man who had succeeded him in 1956 after the Soviet invasion. History has an eye for detail.

A chronological record of February 1989 sets the scene admirably for a review of the year of the great changes.[5] The shortest month of the year included virtually all the elements that were to help determine developments in Eastern Europe in the rest of the year. The twenty-eight days also embraced various turning points that heralded the end of the past, formed a basis for future developments, and so indicated an acceleration in the collapse of the communist Eastern bloc.[6]

Thursday, 2 February 1989. A chapter in the period of intractable East-West relations is closed. After more than fifteen years of discussions the MBFR negotiations on troop reductions in Europe are concluded without any worthwhile results being achieved. As agreed at the final session of the third CSCE follow-up conference in Vienna two weeks earlier, completely new negotiations on conventional disarmament will begin in early March, and the new principles on which they are to be based this time offer the prospect of results being achieved in the relatively short term. This prospect, and the unexpectedly positive conclusions drawn at the follow-up conference in Vienna, now provide a favorable East-West setting for the changes in the various Eastern European countries.

Thursday, 2 to Saturday, 4 February 1989. For the first time in thirty years a Soviet foreign minister visits China. The end of the break between the two communist giants is marked by the decision that Gorbachev will visit Beijing from 15 to 18 May. There is nothing to indicate that on his arrival in the Chinese capital, and also as a result of his visit, Gorbachev will be confronted with a horrifying scene, which is also hanging like the sword of Damocles over the Soviet Union and Eastern Europe: a massive uprising, followed by bloody military suppression, and the crushing of the incipient process of reform.

Monday, 6 February. The beginning of the "round table" talks in Warsaw, attended by representatives of the government, the opposition, and the church. With Walesa, as leader of the banned trade union Solidarity, permitted to take part in late November in a unique televised debate with his official counterparts, and Prime Minister Rakowski, who had helped to ensure the suppression of the free trade union from 1981, describing him as a compromise figure, Solidarity is again accepted as a body with which discussions cannot be avoided. The spread of the strikes makes it even clearer that the communist leaders are in dire need of Solidarity's cooperation. The round table talks concern the reintroduction of trade unions and political pluralism and the holding of parliamentary elections in which the opposition may participate. There is little to indicate that barely six months later Poland's prime minister will be a former Catholic adviser to Solidarity. There is nothing to indicate that less than a year later serious discussions will also be going on at round tables in all other Eastern European countries.

Friday, 10 and Saturday, 11 February. These are difficult times for loyal communists. A week that began for them as a nightmare also ends as a nightmare. The Central Committee of the Hungarian communist party accepts the principle of the multiparty system and so puts an end to the communist party's monopoly on power. The reformists in the communist party, with Imre Pozsgay as their figurehead, also say that the insurrection suppressed by the Soviets in 1956 was not a counterrevolution but a popular uprising. The reformists clearly do not want to give the emerging opposition the chance to be alone in using the nationalist theme. The government therefore moves the national holiday to 15 March, to commemorate the 1848 uprising against the Austrians. On 15 March both the government and the opposition will celebrate this new holiday with massive demonstrations. As it is to become clear six months later, the Austrians do not take this amiss in any way.

A few days later, Wednesday, 15 February. Again an embarrassing page in Brezhnev's history book is turned. Waiting for General Boris Gromov as he crosses the Amou-Daria river between Afghanistan and the USSR is his small son Maxim. The Red Army's presence in Afghanistan has come to an end. The flowers the general receives from his son cannot conceal the fact that the Soviet invasion in December 1979 was an enormous blunder, which helped to make Ronald Reagan American president, put a damper on Soviet relations with the West and many developing countries, and led to economic bloodletting, over a million dead, and a bad military hangover. Even the withdrawal of the troops appears to be a difficult military operation. Above all, the Afghanistan blunder has made it clear that, despite its superpower status and its enormous military potential, the USSR has been unable to eradicate an armed resistance movement with resources and a structure that are fairly primitive, notwithstanding the foreign assistance it receives, and to keep a country like Afghanistan permanently under control. It had evidently not learned a great deal from the American experience ten years earlier. One of the major obstacles to the further development of relations with the West and China has thus been removed. The live television pictures shown worldwide of the Soviet troops withdrawing across the Amou-Daria send out another important message that contradicts a persistent myth: The Soviets are able to withdraw from occupied territory.

The next day, Thursday, 16 February. The Lithuanians have long understood this message, and the Sajudis nationalist movement, which has emerged as a genuine second force after being officially in existence for four months, calls for Lithuania's right of self-determination. It also demands the publication of the secret protocols that accompanied the Soviet-German pact of 1939, with the aim of showing that Lithuania is an occupied country. Three months earlier the Estonian parliament, the Estonian communists in other words, decided that the republic's own laws took precedence over Moscow's. The measures approved by the Presidium of the Supreme Soviet in early December increasing the rights of the republics were considered inadequate. The struggle for the independence of the Baltic states continues and will assume far-reaching proportions barely a year later.

Tuesday, 21 February. In Prague the sentences on the participants in the banned ceremony held to commemorate Jan Palach, the student who burned himself to death twenty years earlier as a protest against the Soviet invasion of his country, are announced. The ceremony was violently disrupted by the police, as befits an orderly communist state. Polish and Hungarian conditions are, after all, as welcome as the plague. Vaclav Havel, cofounder of Charter 77, who has already spent five years in prison as a dissident, is sentenced to nine months. Another troublemaker out of the way. A year later Havel is president of Czechoslovakia.

Tuesday, 28 February. After exceptional measures are taken in Kosovo in response to the general strike by the Albanian population, hundreds of thousands of Serbs demonstrate in Belgrade in solidarity with the Serbian minority in this autonomous province. Tito's legacy is coming under growing attack.

The same day, the same problems. Hundreds of thousands of Armenians gather in Erevan to commemorate the first anniversary of the anti-Armenian pogrom in Azerbaijan. The nationality problems centering on Nagorno-Karabakh have since led to repeated disturbances, refugees, many dead, and political tensions, and a state of emergency was therefore declared in November. The commemoration is a clear indication that the end of the nationalist and ethnic tensions is still a long way off.

Finally, another two important elements that partly dominated the month of February. Since the beginning of the year many East Germans have sought refuge in West Germany's mission in East Berlin and its embassy in Prague, in the hope of reaching the "real" German fatherland. The refugee problem is vexing to both the East German and the West German governments, who can hardly imagine what enormous proportions it is yet to assume and what implications it will ultimately have for both Germany and Europe.

Still in February, the first genuine election campaign launched in January continues in the Soviet Union, with candidates from the various tendencies within the communist party and from the independent Memorial movement competing for seats in the Congress of Deputies. As the electorate will really be an electorate this time, it will have to choose from several candidates, an unprecedented event in the Soviet Union. The comrades in Moscow are thus setting for their fellow believers in Eastern Europe a bad example. Is it then in any way surprising that the Genius of the Carpathians, Ceausescu, should be disparaging about the alarming course of events in the communist mother country?

The broad lines for 1989 are thus drawn, the main themes being political reforms and nationalist demands. Events in the rest of the year will be variations on the same interrelated themes, although these variations will produce some very surprising and radical results.

The next five months are particularly important for the further elaboration of the political reforms launched earlier. At both the first and second rounds of the "free" elections in late March and early April Soviet citizens opt for reforms and democratization. Various official candidates put up by the communist party who hold important political posts do not win enough votes and are thus rejected by the public. Reformist and nationalist candidates, on the other hand, win a surprisingly large number of votes. Boris Yeltsin, who was removed from the Politburo in late 1987 under pressure from the conservatives in the Kremlin for criticizing what he saw as the excessively slow pace of Gorbachev's reforms, gains almost 90 percent of the votes in Moscow and is consequently rehabilitated by the public. Andrei Sakharov, father of the Soviet hydrogen bomb, dissident, and Nobel Prize winner, exiled to Gorki by Brezhnev and recalled by Gorbachev in 1986, is one of the new deputies. Party leader Gorbachev uses the poor election results of many official candidates to dismiss 110 members or candidate members of the Central Committee and so to strengthen his position in relation to the conservatives in the party.

In late May there is a further sensation in Moscow, when during the debate of the Congress of Deputies, which is televised live, reformers dominate the rostrum and fight a verbal battle with the conservatives, and various entrenched taboos become a thing of the past. As the reformers and nationalists are, however, clearly in the minority, the best known (and thus most feared) of them are not elected to the 542-seat Supreme Soviet. Even Yeltsin is initially excluded, but then gains entry to the Supreme Soviet by the back door, when, with Gorbachev's approval, a good communist gives up his seat for him. Gorbachev also needs a somewhat progressive opposition in this body to counteract the still dominant conservatives. Despite the disappointing results for the reformers, the debate has had a serious impact throughout the country, and another step has been taken toward greater openness.

It became increasingly clear that the nationality issue was rapidly growing in import as a result of glasnost and the rejection of taboos. While the nationalist demands still appeared to be largely confined to the Baltic states and ethnic violence to Nagorno-Karabakh, the nationalist and ethnic plague was spreading throughout the USSR at lightning speed. Nationalist demonstrations in the Republic of Georgia, protesting against the attitude of the Muslims in the Abhazian Autonomous Republic, part of the Republic of Georgia, were crushed by the forces of law and order on 9 April, leaving twenty dead. Early May saw a revival of the nationalist tensions between the Christian European Armenians and the Islamic Turkish Azeris over the

Armenian enclave of Nagorno-Karabakh within Azerbaijan. In early June over a hundred Turkish Shiite Meskhets were killed in pogroms carried out by Sunni Uzbekis. Two weeks later it was the turn of the Caucasian minority in the Islamic Republic of Kazakhstan, and people were killed during disturbances on the eve of the visit by the Iranian leader, Rafsanjani, to Moscow. In mid-July there were again reports of ethnic clashes and twenty dead in Georgia and Abhazia.

Many republics and peoples, whose very existence was known to very few people in the West and that had always been ignored in Moscow, were suddenly alive and kicking and standing up for their rights. And such measures as the granting of some autonomy to the Baltic states were systematically rejected as insufficient. The disturbances and protests would therefore continue in the future, spread further geographically, and lead to ever growing demands. Problems aplenty, then, for Moscow. This was not really surprising, however, when the aim was to unite fifteen republics, numerous autonomous republics, autonomous regions, and national regions, and over a hundred nationalities and ethnic groups in one country and under one central authority.

In Poland three months of round table discussions between the government and the opposition were concluded on 5 May with the signing of an historic agreement. Trade union pluralism, the democratization of the political institutions, and the opposition's entry into Parliament, now split into two chambers, were the most important results. Two weeks later, after Solidarity had been legalized, General Jaruzelski and Lech Walesa met for the first time since the declaration of martial law in late 1981. Walesa's appeal to the West to help Poland financially and economically and his attempts to stem the social unrest in his country showed that, by recognizing Solidarity, Jaruzelski had above all gained the support of an influential and badly needed crisis manager and someone willing to share the responsibility. The West straight away reacted positively to the political developments and promised massive aid.

The first partly free elections held in Poland on 4 and 18 June were an overwhelming success for Solidarity. It won 99 of the 100 seats in the Senate and all 161 seats set aside for independent members in the Diet, the Chamber of People's Representatives. The result was a clear demonstration of revenge on the regime, as revealed by the case of a new member of the Diet, Adam Michnik, a leading opponent of the communist rulers, who had spent several years in jail since the declaration of martial law in 1981. Most of those elected to the 199 other seats reserved for the communist and allied parties were reformist candidates. A blot on the landscape, however, was the widespread skepticism revealed by the high proportion of abstentions. It seemed that, despite the election results, not even Solidarity could simply rely on the good will of the people. This was one reason for Solidarity's rejection of Jaruzelski's proposal that it should join with the communist party in forming a coalition government. The Polish leader experienced another difficult moment when elected president by a majority of just one vote. Democracy has its dangerous sides.

A news item in early March: The UN's Commission on Human Rights in Geneva adopted a resolution condemning Romania for violations of the fundamental freedoms. Significantly, the Soviet Union and the three Eastern European countries with seats on the commission do not take part in the vote. Hungary not only voted for the resolution but also was one of its authors. Budapest had already sought support from the Western European countries within the CSCE for action against Romania because of its attitude toward its Hungarian minority. The break within the former Eastern bloc was not only growing in terms of political and economic reforms, but it was also becoming visible in the international organizations and in relations with the West. The Iron Curtain seemed to be moving. This also happened literally when, on 2 May, Hungarian border guards quite simply began to remove sections of the barbed wire on the frontier with Austria, and a month later the Romanians put up barbed wire on their border with Hungary. The first small opening in the Iron Curtain had been made; the real force of the hitherto largely obscured internal pressure within the communist countries was now at last able to find expression.

In Hungary the government and opposition followed the Polish example and began round table discussions in mid-June with a view to holding the first free elections in 1990. Ten days later Secretary-General Grosz, once respected as a reformer, found himself isolated after a reshuffle in the party and had to agree to being joined by three distinctly reform-minded party members: Reszo Nyers, Imre Pozsgay, and Miklos Nemeth, a Harvard graduate.

A few more "details" from this period. In Prague Vaclav Havel was released from prison in mid-May after four months, following a strong international protest and, among other things, the initiation by the Netherlands of the only recently adopted CSCE procedure for monitoring possible failures to respect human rights. On 1 June the expulsion of tens of thousands of Bulgarians of Turkish extraction to Turkey began. By mid-August, when Ankara made visas compulsory, over 300,000 refugees had already arrived in Turkey. In early June five hundred people were killed in the Ukraine when gas exploded beside the Trans-Siberian Railway, revealing, as the disaster at Chernobyl and the earthquake in Armenia had done, the many shortcomings and the inadequacy of safety measures in the Soviet Union. The system had failed once again. On 30 June the Union of Soviet Writers advocated the publication in the USSR of *The Gulag Archipelago* by Alexander Solzhenitsyn, who had been sent into foreign exile in 1974. Two days later the death of Andrei "Nyet" Gromyko was announced. He had been foreign minister from 1957 to 1985 and a member of the Soviet delegation headed by Stalin at the Yalta conference in 1945, but he may also have tipped the balance in the appointment of Gorbachev as Secretary-General. With his death one of the symbols of the former rigid Soviet policy disappeared. He had, however, anticipated the failure of the system. Renewal in the USSR was gaining ground. Ten days later an unprecedented massive strike began at the coal mines in the Ukraine. Only a week later the Soviet government decided to buy an equally massive quantity of consumer goods and food abroad.

August and September 1989. The Poles and Hungarians, each in their fashion, cross the Rubicon and take sides. The Polish Parliament and the Hungarian communist party condemn the invasion of Czechoslovakia, in which they themselves took part in 1968. In Prague itself two thousand courageous demonstrators take to the streets. There is, however, more to it than this in-itself highly significant act. The Poles and Hungarians are no longer reforming or adjusting: They are charting a fundamentally new course. In the still "genuine" communist capitals—East Berlin, Prague, Sofia, and Bucharest—the magnitude of the process of reform in Poland and Hungary is therefore viewed with horror and openly rejected. Even Moscow's reactions indicate greater apprehension about its reform-minded comrades.

The Poles, after all, clearly do not think it enough to accept such principles as political pluralism, to hold semifree elections, and to admit to Parliament a movement that until recently was banned. General Jaruzelski now even finds it necessary to share power with the opposition movement, Solidarity, and on 19 August to appoint one of its leading advisers as Poland's prime minister. Mazowiecki therefore goes down in history as Eastern Europe's first noncommunist premier. After taking office, he advocates the establishment of a "normal market economy of the western type" and the development of a full-fledged democratic system. In the government that is eventually formed Solidarity takes thirteen of the twenty-four ministerial portfolios, including most of the economic posts. Solidarity supporter Skubiszewski becomes the Warsaw Pact's first noncommunist foreign minister. He confirms that Poland will continue to honor its international commitments, more specifically to the Warsaw Pact, but says he is also thinking of asking the USSR for compensation for the losses suffered by the millions of Poles (including President Jaruzelski) who were forced to work for the Soviets during the Second World War. Jacek Kuron, one of the driving forces behind the strikes in 1980 and 1981, becomes employment minister, a post in which he can rack his brains over how to keep the dissatisfied Poles working.[7]

The Hungarian leaders take the opposite approach. Unlike the Poles, they provisionally chart a somewhat slower course in domestic policy, but clearly take sides in foreign policy, and this time not simply by means of a resolution but through their attitude in what is for the members of the Warsaw Pact the very delicate issue of the East German refugees, which suddenly begins to gain momentum in mid-August. The action in brief: After the Hungarians ostentatiously demonstrated in early May that for them the Iron Curtain belonged to the past, a growing number of East German "tourists" in Hungary use the gap to flee to the Federal Republic through Austria. By mid-August around a hundred East Germans are crossing the Austro-Hungarian border each day on their way to West Germany, and on 15 August the West German government finds itself obliged to open the first camps to accommodate the flood of refugees. Other GDR citizens overrun the West German mission in Budapest, as they are doing in Prague and East Berlin, to claim by legal means the right to (West) German nationality that they are guaranteed by the West German constitution. With hundreds of would-be compatriots in and outside the building, the embassy in Budapest has to be closed to the public on 14 August. On 19 and 20 August a thousand East Germans succeed, thanks to the flexibility of the Hungarians, in illegally crossing the Austro-Hungarian border, and the GDR experiences the largest exodus of its citizens to the West since the Wall was built in August 1961. The hopes of the still large numbers of would-be refugees grow. Four days later 108 refugees are able to leave the embassy in Budapest for the Federal Republic legally. It thus seems worthwhile seeking refuge in the embassy, and new candidates arrive. The flight of fifteen to twenty thousand East Germans through Hungary to West Germany in early September is therefore anticipated, and the reception camps in the Federal Republic are being prepared for them. The pressure becomes increasingly intolerable for the governments concerned.

In late August the Hungarian prime minister, Nemeth, pays an unexpected visit to Bonn, and his foreign minister, Gyula Horn, promises that the refugees will not be forced to return to the GDR, a positive attitude that Bonn will reward economically (and politically) in due course. As a result of its prompt cooperation in acting as a transit country, Austria too may be able to count on West German goodwill in the future, with regard to its application to join the European Community, for example. The pressure from the orthodox communist countries on Budapest also grows, however: Hungary must accept its responsibility as a member of the Warsaw Pact and show the required solidarity with its allies. Twenty years before, Hungary had, moreover, signed an agreement with the GDR, its most important communist trading partner after the USSR, on the return of illegal refugees, and East Berlin wanted to see this formal commitment honored. The Hungarians had, however, just signed the UN convention on refugees. Budapest thus found itself in the extremely difficult position of being forced by circumstances to make an overt choice between East and West. It vainly tried to find a way out of the dilemma by saying that a solution depended on a prior agreement between Bonn and East Berlin. By an unfortunate twist of fate it was announced that very week that West German banks were granting Hungary a DM 500 million loan.[8] Bonn and Budapest both declared that the allocation of financial assistance was in no way linked to Hungary's attitude in the German refugee question. On 10 September Budapest crossed the Rubicon, ignored solidarity with the Eastern bloc, and opened its frontiers to allow the thousands of refugees to leave for "the country of their choice." East Germany could begin to empty.

Exactly fifty years after the Hitler regime had invaded Poland and so unwittingly laid the foundations for the division of Germany and Europe and for the installation of the communist regimes in East Berlin and Warsaw, both historical events were eclipsed by fresh developments. By finally deciding to open its frontiers to everyone, Hungary overcame the strict East-West divide on its own and, in so doing, paved the way for German reunification, first on a personal, later at political levels. And two days later, on 12 September, Poland's parliament placed its trust in Eastern Europe's first noncommunist government. The first opening in the Iron Curtain and the first government not dominated by communists were facts. The snowball could begin to roll, and it moved at a surprisingly high speed. One hundred and one days later, with the fall of the Romanian government on 22 December, the process of erosion had swept through the whole of Eastern Europe, the whole length of the Iron Curtain was in tatters, and not a single communist government was still in power. Another fifty days later there was barely a party left anywhere in Eastern Europe that dared to call itself communist.

The sudden increase in the number of East Germans who achieved their private "reunification" also resulted in a spirited revival of the debate on "the German question." The West Germans themselves primarily recognized the practical problems raised by this private reunification, and their minister for inter-German relations was prompted to warn in early August that "the reunification of Germany must not take place in the Federal Republic."[9] This warning was to be often repeated in the following weeks and months. It was principally abroad, however, that the possibility of German reunification gave rise to all manner of scenarios and much doom and gloom. Like most Germans, Chancellor Kohl therefore noted with some surprise in late August that the German question was back on the agenda of international politics, which contrasted with his statements since Honecker's visits to Bonn.[10] Suddenly the German question was no longer "something for future generations to deal with" and in fact called for immediate policy measures.[11] The politicians in Bonn concluded somewhat wearily and shamefully that, although the outside world was discussing reunification for all to hear, and although they too had been putting forward the idea almost as a ritual for years, they had no recipe for achieving this objective now that circumstances suddenly no longer made it seem so unrealistic. The *Frankfurter Allgemeine Zeitung* and *Der Spiegel* were brief and to the point: "Concepts for a *Deutschlandpolitik* wanted"; "Outside world speculates on German dreams of reunification, while the Germans are at their wits' end."[12] The politicians in Bonn suddenly realized that the "policy of small steps" and their policy for the stabilization of the GDR had been overtaken by the developments in Hungary and Poland and by the attitude of the East German public.

West German politicians also realized that they had always been extremely restrained in their efforts to achieve German unity, as if, for fear of external reactions, they had been frightened to claim the generally recognized right to self-determination for themselves—even though it was one of the goals to which their own Basic Law referred, it had also been accepted by the three western powers (the United States, Britain, and France) as a goal in the German Treaty, it had been endorsed by NATO in the Harmel report, for example, and after the recent events the United States had declared its support through President Bush and its ambassador to Bonn for the re-unification of the two Germanys once free elections had been held.

In response to this awareness and to the new developments it was therefore increasingly emphasized in the Federal Republic that efforts must at last be made to achieve this formal basic objective of West German policy. It was realized that, as soon as the ailing party leader, Honecker, disappeared from the political or world scene, developments in the GDR might occur very quickly, that the sovereignty of Germany as a whole would be placed on the agenda in very concrete terms, and that neither East nor West could deny the German people the right to self-determination that had been explicitly granted to the Polish and Hungarian peoples. Or as Foreign Minister Genscher shrewdly put it in a variation on a familiar theme: "It is difficult to imagine Europe growing ever closer together, while the two Germanys grow apart; this would be a dangerous instance of Germany 'going it alone.' " And: "I do not believe that leading figures who think responsibly would want to exclude the Germans from the general process of European rapprochement."[13]

It was becoming clear to West German politicians that their policy had to be geared to encouraging fundamental political reforms in the GDR. This, however, put the German question in even sharper perspective and also indicated how plausible overcoming the division of Germany had suddenly become. After all, as the architect of West Germany's *Ostpolitik*, Egon Bahr, stressed: "When the system in Poland is changed, Poles are left. When the system in Hungary is changed, Hungarians are left. When it is changed in the GDR, Germans are left." Or as one of the ideological leaders of the East German SED said, the GDR is "conceivable only as a socialist alternative to the Federal Republic."[14] Consequently, if reforms within the GDR went too far, its very existence would be threatened. On the other hand, the flood of refugees was a sign of the considerable internal pressure from the public for reforms. The leaders in East Berlin thus faced an insurmountable dilemma. The pressure on the authorities was also increased by the rapidly growing impact of the opposition movement New Forum. The rising internal pressure surfaced when, in protest at the government's refusal to recognize New Forum and to undertake reforms, the largest demonstration since 1953 was held in Leipzig on 25 September, when eight thousand people took to the streets. The Monday evening services at the Saint Nicholas Church in Leipzig and the subsequent demonstrations, later attended by tens and hundreds of thousands, were to remain front-page news for months to come.

October 1989. The German Democratic republic has been in existence for forty years. To stem the flow of refugees, the possibility of traveling to neighboring Czechoslovakia without a visa or a passport is suspended on 3 October. The next day, to atone for this shameful decision, ten thousand East Germans in and around the grounds of the West German embassy in Prague are allowed to travel on special trains across East Germany to the Federal Republic. The same arrangement is made for six hundred refugees at the embassy in Warsaw. The measures, which are intended to calm the situation before the great festival in celebration of forty years of the GDR, lead, however, to hellish scenes: East Germans trying to jump aboard the passing "freedom trains," trains said to have run over these would-be refugees, outbursts of joy on arrival in the new fatherland. It is clear that there will not be much to celebrate in East Berlin on 6 and 7 October.

The celebrations are low-key, and Erich Honecker, the man who two years earlier, on his visit to Bonn, could note with pride that his visit also denoted the ultimate recognition of the GDR by West Germany, is now forced to realize that, while the Federal Republic may have recognized his country, his own people have not. He is perhaps already aware that the great birthday party will be his farewell party. His talks with his most important guest, Mikhail Gorbachev, will have made it clear to him that, having earlier criticized the new Soviet policy and refused to undertake reforms, he cannot count on the USSR to prop up his regime. The people commemorate the anniversary by breaking new records for the number of demonstrators: fifteen thousand on 8 October, seventy thousand the following day after the traditional Monday service in Leipzig. The demonstrations also spread to other cities. They are dispersed violently and, showing little tact, the secretary-general of the SED's Central Committee, Egon Krenz, refers to the events in Beijing's Tiananmen Square. The contrast with developments in Poland and Hungary is painfully clear.

In the USSR the political reforms continued slowly but surely. In September the party leadership had been thoroughly reshuffled, various conservatives being pushed aside and reformers promoted. On 20 September, the right of the republics to economic sovereignty was recognized. When it is considered how closely related the economic and political systems are in a communist state, it can be appreciated what such a decision may eventually lead to. The tarnished belief in the ideals of socialism was in evidence again in October, when the right to strike was recognized, an admission that the ordinary workers in a socialist country may have a reason to put down their tools.

In the meantime, the Hungarians carry on undisturbed, and on the day on which the East German communists are celebrating in East Berlin they abolish the communist party and replace it with a new socialist party, a measure that is soon to be emulated in other Eastern European countries. Reszo Nyers becomes chairman of the new party, Imre Pozsgay its candidate for the presidency. The reformists see this drastic action as the only way of still standing a chance at the elections. Sixteen days later the Hungarians decide to abolish their People's Republic, and the "Hungarian Republic" is proclaimed. Here again, Budapest is setting the trend.

On 18 October, not yet two weeks after the celebrations in East Berlin, Honecker is relieved of his post—for health reasons, it is said. Egon Krenz takes his place, resorts to some self-criticism on the SED's behalf, and tries to gain the confidence of the people with various measures, such as an amnesty for refugees and the decision to remove all restrictions on travel to Czechoslovakia from 1 November. This results in a fresh exodus, and when the Czechs decide on 3 November to open their border with the Federal Republic, the flow of refugees from the GDR can no longer be stemmed. On each of the next few days some ten thousand East Germans take this new route to flee to West Germany. Those who stay at home also make their voices heard: On 4 November around half a million people gather in East Berlin to reject Krenz's proposals for reforms as being too limited and to demand, among other things, complete freedom to travel. Diplomats in East and West wondered afterward what would have happened if this enormous crowd had suddenly moved toward the Wall.[15] Krenz's earlier reference to Tienanmen Square is recalled. Two days later 300,000 people go to church in Leipzig. The authorities promise more ambitious reforms that would have seemed spectacular only a few weeks earlier but are now simply greeted by the masses with cries of "too late, too late."

On 7 November the government resigns under pressure from the people in the streets. The next day the reformer Hans Modrow is appointed to form a new government. At the same time the atmosphere of crisis mounts in both Germanys and among the Four Powers when it becomes clear that more than a million people (out of a population of sixteen million) can be expected to attend the demonstration planned for Saturday, 11 November in East Berlin and, above all, that it must this time be assumed they will not stay near the Alexanderplatz, a good twenty minutes' walk from the border between the two Germanys, but will move toward the Wall and the Brandenburg Gate. From Moscow it is reported that Soviet troops will not intervene to rescue the East German regime, with the added warning that the USSR does not have full control over Krenz and the East German security forces and army.[16]

Thursday, 9 November 1989. The East German leaders announce that the Wall and the Iron Curtain, which have divided the two Germanys since August 1961, will be opened. Two million East Germans, most of them East Berliners, cross the border between the two Germanys over the weekend, many of them for the first time, and visit the West, so remote until now. Most return, and for the time being at least the exodus seems to have stopped. In the next few days and weeks the border police open more gaps in the Wall and the inter-German frontier, helped by many Germans with great enthusiasm and pent-up anger. The end of the postwar period is proclaimed, and when the West German chancellor, Kohl, and the East German prime minister, Modrow, together inaugurate an opening at the Brandenburg Gate, the symbol of the division of Germany, this division indeed seems to be a thing of the past.

The words spoken by Federal President von Weizsäcker a few years earlier are recalled: "The German question will be closed when the Brandenburg Gate is opened." However, the German question seemed in fact to have been suppressed for forty years only to burst forth now in all its intensity. In 1945 it had been impossible to decide on the future of Germany at Yalta and Potsdam because of general disagreement primarily between the USSR and the three western powers. And the Cold War that quickly followed had meant there had been no real discussion on the then German question, or what to do with defeated Germany, for forty years. By late 1989 the fundamental change in East-West relations and above all the about-turn in Soviet policy had created the conditions in which the German question might well be resolved. The major difference now was that the Germans themselves were taking the lead in the search for a solution.

The reaction in both the Federal Republic and the GDR and in both East and West to what had suddenly become the real possibility of the unification of the two Germanys had been extremely confused and chaotic. Positions seemed to change from one day to the next, statements were interpreted incorrectly or with bias, and many felt that the specter of a mighty German empire in Central Europe was looming again. Suspicion of the Germans again seemed very pronounced, as if they would suddenly abandon their western democratic values, were about to strike another secret bargain with the Soviets, and all at once would attach no more importance to integration into the western economy and the European Community. Evidently, outsiders still had difficulty in accepting that the Germans were increasingly determining their own future.

Thus, after Chancellor Kohl had been criticized because everyone clearly had his own idea on how relations between the two parts of Germany should develop, whereas he had yet to say anything specific himself, he presented his ten-point plan for German reunification. His proposals received almost unanimous support in West Germany, but caused a considerable stir abroad. The ten points were: immediate humanitarian and other assistance for the GDR; continuation of cooperation that benefits the people; increase in support and cooperation if fundamental reforms of the political and economic system are launched; the idea of the two Germanys forming a community governed by a treaty; the installation of confederative structures before a federation is established; the development of inter-German relations as part of Europe's future global structure; the European Community is and remains a constant factor in European development; the Helsinki process is and remains the core of this global European structure; overcoming the division of Germany requires early action on disarmament; reunification remains the government's political goal.[17]

Typical of the rapidly changing attitude of other countries toward German reunification was the sequence of reactions from the French president. On 3 November, barely a week before the Wall came down, Mitterrand broke his silence on the German question and said in reply to a question after the Franco-German summit meeting in Bonn:

Reunification should not be based on fear or approval. What is of primary importance is the decision and will of the people. . . . No one can replace this will. . . . The Germans have a legitimate desire for reunification. . . . I am not afraid of reunification. . . . History is history: I take it as it is.

As befits Franco-German relations, Chancellor Kohl responded to Mitterrand's positive statement with a strong plea for the process of European integration. Another remark by the French president was also interesting: "At the speed things are going, I would be surprised if the next ten years passed without the structure of Europe changing."

After the Wall had come down and Mitterrand had met his West German counterpart, he again referred to German reunification as a normal process. At the emergency meeting of the twelve Community leaders convened by Mitterrand as president of the EC Council and held at the Elysée on 18 November, it emerged from his statement that German reunification was not really on the agenda and that it was premature to act on this question. On his return from a visit to Moscow Foreign Minister Dumas said: "We know today that reunification is not an issue that can be considered now." In an interview with *The Wall Street Journal* Mitterrand repeated that reunification was not something to be feared, but he added:

This does not mean that I would agree, because you would then immediately have the problem of the Polish frontier. . . . But personally, I have no ideological or political objection to the idea of reunification. I merely have a number of practical arguments, and the Russians have some real strategic, geopolitical, and historical interests.

During his visit to the European Parliament with Chancellor Kohl on 22 November, President Mitterrand carefully avoided the question of German reunification. After the publication of Chancellor Kohl's ten-point plan the relationship between Bonn and Paris seemed to have been even more tense where this question was concerned, and at the NATO summit on 4 December Mitterrand endorsed the requirements for reunification enunciated by President Bush, and the reticence over the whole issue reemerged. On 8 December, at a meeting with President Gorbachev in Kiev, he adopted a very cautious tone on the question of reunification and placed greater emphasis on the strengthening of the European Community.

Three days later, at the Community summit meeting in Strasbourg, the great reconciliation between France and Germany was to emerge. The communiqué of the meeting chaired by Mitterrand refers to the Community countries' endeavors to strengthen a European peaceful order in which the German people would regain their unity through the right of free self-determination. Chancellor Kohl accepted the French proposals concerning a social charter and the Economic and Monetary Union. The balance was restored, and France gave reunification its political approval. As Mitterrand had said in November, the problem of the Oder-Neisse line was, however, to lead to renewed differences of opinion. Here again, the fast-changing attitude of the French was apparent. On the fringes of the meeting of NATO and Warsaw Pact foreign ministers in Ottawa on 13 February it was decided that the negotiations on German reunification would be conducted by the Four Powers, which are responsible for Germany, and the two Germanys. France too felt that these discussions could not be extended to include other countries. In early March, however, Mitterrand supported Poland's demand that it too be represented at the two-plus-four talks.[18]

The USSR's position was another example of how opinions abroad were at first highly critical, but as little could be done to influence actual developments, there was no choice in the end but to accept the changes. In mid-December 1989 Foreign Minister Shevardnadze, addressing the European Parliament's Political Affairs Committee, had implicitly referred to various conditions that would have to be met before reunification became possible. During Chancellor Kohl's visit to Moscow in early February, however, it was clear that reunification was already seen as inevitable.[19]

The former East German leader, Honecker, had made a dreadful mistake when in mid-1989 he insisted that the Wall would still be standing one hundred years later.[20] By early 1990 pieces of the Wall in special gift wrap and accompanied by a guarantee of place of origin were on sale in stores in Paris, London, and New York. He had been right, on the other hand, to refer to the GDR as the "front-line bastion" of communism. After the East German bastion had fallen, the remaining communist citadels in Eastern Europe could hardly survive for more than a few weeks. Like the GDR, such countries as Czechoslovakia and Bulgaria had regarded the developments in Poland and Hungary as isolated aberrations, which might be understandable in those countries, given their history, but need have no effect on themselves. Poland and Hungary had therefore simply been abandoned as parts of the Eastern European communist system. Prague and Sofia consequently turned more than ever to East Berlin, which formed the basis and keystone of communist Eastern Europe even more than before.[21] When the keystone crumbled, the whole of the remaining communist structure collapsed. The balance of Eastern European reforms, which until 9 November still favored the traditional communist countries, had suddenly shifted to the other side.

A diary of the last seven weeks of the 1980s. 10 November: A day after the East Germans announce that they will open their frontiers, the Bulgarians realize that they too must now make a start on bold reforms, and the Bulgarian leader, Zhivkov, is toppled from his throne after thirty-five years in power. His successor, Mladenov, promises reforms, although they must not affect the country's socialist system. Four days later talks are held with various Bulgarian dissidents. On 17 November a demonstration by thirty thousand students in Prague is dispersed violently by the police. While the authorities clearly intend this to have a deterrent effect, it in fact mobilizes other sections of the population. The five thousand people who took to the streets of the Bulgarian capital, Sofia, at the beginning of the month in the largest unofficial demonstration since 1945 are followed by fifty thousand demonstrating for radical reforms on 18 November. The next day, on the initiative of the writer Havel, various independent movements merge in Prague to form a new opposition movement known as Civic Forum. Civic Forum calls for mass demonstrations, and first tens of thousands, later many hundreds of thousands of people gather in Wenceslas Square each day. On 20 November, 200,000 East Germans protest in Leipzig against the new government, still dominated by the communist SED. The next day the first talks are unexpectedly held between the Czech prime minister, Adamec, and representatives of Civic Forum. Rumors in Prague about possible action by the army gain strength when, on 23 November, the police occupy the television building and the military authorities warn that they are prepared to defend socialism. The same day the first noncommunist prime minister in Eastern Europe, Mazowiecki, begins a visit to Moscow, where he has satisfactory talks with the head of the communist world, Gorbachev.

On 24 November, the great return: Alexander Dubcek, leader of the Prague Spring in 1968 and since employed largely as a bookkeeper on a state-owned farm near Bratislava, addresses around half a million of his compatriots from the tribune in Prague. The whole politburo of the communist party resigns, and party leader Jakes gives way to Karel Urbanek. At last a ray of hope for communism: Also on 24 November the Genius of the Carpathians, Nicolae Ceausescu, is reelected leader of the Romanian communist party by 3,308 votes for and none against. Romania remains an oasis of pure Stalinism. The consultations between Bucharest, Beijing, and Havana are stepped up. In the GDR the army is given a new role to play: filling the many vacancies in factories and mines left by the refugees. Over the weekend of 25 and 26 November a record number of people take part in mass demonstrations in Prague, demanding free elections and the abolition of the communist party's monopoly on power. A strange occurrence: Those who were once exiled and imprisoned by the regime generously give Prime Minister Adamec the opportunity to address the demonstration. As in East Berlin, his promise of more reforms is greeted with cries of "too late." On Monday the general strike called by Civic Forum receives tremendous support. Work throughout the country comes to a complete standstill, even the official press agency interrupts its reporting. Two days later the Czech communists decide to abolish the communist party's leading role. The historic month of November 1989 has taken its toll.

1 December. The new month begins with yet another first: The Red Pope meets the Catholic Pope in the Vatican. On the same day the East German parliament relieves the communist party of its monopoly on power. Two days later the communist SED follows the Hungarian example and announces its dissolution after the disclosures of the Honecker regime's abuse of power and its privileges have led to an outburst of public rage and attacks on the buildings of the security service, the Stasi. The same day Civic Forum and the demonstrators in Czechoslovakia reject the new government formed by Adamec, in which the communists are still in the majority. On 4 December the leaders of the Warsaw Pact countries condemn their own invasion of Czechoslovakia in August 1968. On 6 December the East German leader, Egon Krenz, resigns, and the next day the round table is set up, as in Poland and Hungary. During the very first round of talks it is decided that the first free elections in the GDR will be held on 6 May. At the same time in Prague Adamec follows his former East German counterpart's example and is succeeded by Marian Calfa.

On 8 and 9 December the SED is completely restructured, the renovated party advocates political pluralism, and Gregor Gysi, having previously accused the former leaders of corruption, is elected as the new chairman. On 10 December Calfa forms a government of national unity, in which the communists are no longer in the majority, promises to introduce a market economy and to hold free elections within six months, and the resignation of President Gustav Husak, who epitomized the restoration after the Prague Spring, is announced. Almost all the Czech opposition's demands have thus been met. Jiri Dienstbier, spokesman of Civic Forum and, for many years, of Charter 77, for which he spent three years in prison, is appointed foreign minister. Vaclav Klaus, an eminent economist employed mostly as a tram conductor from 1968 to 1988, becomes finance minister. The Czechs clearly have a sense of irony.

On the same day in Sofia 100,000 demonstrators demand that the process of reform be accelerated. The next day the Bulgarian leader, Mladenov, promises free elections in May and the abolition of the communist party's leading role. On 12 December, two days before the death of Andrei Sakharov, the same subject is on the agenda in Moscow: The Congress of Deputies debates the abolition of the supreme dogma, the communist party's leading role. The proposal does not have the support of the majority, but the result, 1,138 votes against, 839 for, shows that it may well have a chance of succeeding in the future. Three months later it was to be so.

From 16 December a few thousand Romanian citizens of Hungarian extraction demonstrate in Timisoara. Despite, or precisely because of, the murderous reaction of the police, the protests spread to other sections of the population and to other cities, eventually reaching Bucharest on 21 December. The next day Ceausescu's dictatorial regime is overthrown, and the last leader of the former Eastern bloc disappears. Power is assumed by the National Salvation Front, whose members include former purged communist leaders, military men, and dissidents, with Ion Iliescu as their chairman. The fighting between members of the Securitate and the army continues, however, and costs even more lives. On 25 December the Genius of the Carpathians is executed with his wife, Elena. Three days later the Front decides to hold free elections, Petre Roman is appointed prime minister, and the word *socialist* is dropped from the official name of the country. The next day the Polish parliament votes for amendments to the Constitution, whereby the Polish Socialist People's Republic is similarly renamed the Polish Republic, and the leading role of the communist party is abolished.

The decade is brought to a splendid conclusion when, on 28 December, the architect of the Prague Spring, Alexander Dubcek, is elected speaker of the Czech parliament, and the next day the former dissident Vaclav Havel is unanimously proclaimed president and moves into the royal and presidential Hradcany Castle. History has taken its revenge in a very subtle way.

NOTES

1. Freddy de Pauw, "Poolse Perestrojka. Wil deze zwaar zieke patiënt onder het mes?," *De Standaard*, 19 November 1989, p. 5.

2. Jörgen Oosterwaal and Erik Brusten, "Oost-Europa in de ban van Gorbatsjov?," *Kultuurleven*, 55(2)1988, pp. 161–67.

3. Thierry de Montbrial, ed., *Ramses 89. Rapport Annuel Mondial sur le Système Economique et les Stratégies*, IFRI (Paris: Dunod, 1988), pp. 148–53, 175–77; "East Europe: A Special Report," *The Independent*, 26 January 1989.

4. Yves Cuau, "30 semaines qui ont changé le monde," *L'Express*, 29 September 1989, pp. 25–29.

5. Much of the factual material has been obtained from the chronological review that appears every two weeks in the German *Europa-Archiv* (on the Z pages) and monthly in the French *Le Monde* (on the second Sunday of each month).

6. Cuau, "30 semaines qui ont changé le monde," pp. 22–24.

7. "Poland: The sweet feeling of breaking free," *The Economist*, 16 September 1989, p. 28.

8. "Goodbye to Berlin," *The Economist*, 16 September 1989, p. 27.

9. Frederick Painton, "One Germany?" *Time*, 11 September 1989, p. 13.

10. "Die Bundesregierung richtet sich auf 'alle Eventualitäten' ein," *Frankfurter Allgemeine Zeitung*, 31 August 1989, pp. 1–2.

11. Günther Nonnenmacher, "Das Ende der Stabilität. Die deutsch-deutsche 'Politik der kleinen Schritte' in der Krise," *Frankfurter Allgemeine Zeitung*, 13 September 1989, p. 15.

12. "Deutschlandpolitische Konzepte gesucht," *Frankfurter Allgemeine Zeitung*, 16 September 1989, p. 3; "Ratlosigkeit in Ost und West," *Der Spiegel*, 18 September 1989, p. 14.

13. "Hier ist Engagement gefordert," *Der Spiegel*, 25 September 1989, pp. 25–26.

14. Theo Sommer, "Starrheit ist nicht gleich Stabilität," *Die Zeit*, 1 September 1989, p. 1.

15. Jim Hoagland, "Back to the Wall, Krenz Chooses All-Out Reform," *International Herald Tribune*, 9 November 1989, pp. 1, 4.

16. Yves Cuau, "La fin de l'après-guerre," *L'Express*, 17 November 1989, p. 44.

17. "Zehn-Punkte-Programm zur Überwindung der Teilung Deutschlands und Europas, vorgelegt von Bundeskanzler Helmut Kohl in der Haushaltsdebatte des deutschen Bundestages am 28. November 1989," *Europa-Archiv*, 44(24)89, pp. D728–34.

18. *Libération*, 4, 18, 23 November 1989; *La Libre Belgique*, 20 November 1989; *The Wall Street Journal*, 22 November 1989; *Le Soir*, 5 December 1989; *De Standaard*, 8 December 1989; "Conclusions de la Présidence," *Agence Europe*, 10 December 1989, p. 11; *Le Monde*, 21 March 1989.

19. "Allocution prononcée par M. Chevardnadze . . . devant la Commission Politique du Parlement Européen à Bruxelles le 19 décembre 1989," *European Parliament*, pp. 17–18; Pierre Briancon, "Moscou délivre un permis de réunifier à Kohl," *Libération*, 12 February 1990.

20. Painton, "One Germany?"

21. John Tagliabue, "German Events Give Prague the Jitters," *International Herald Tribune*, 9 November 1989, p. 4.

15

L'Histoire est Libre

Since the end of 1989 the history of Europe has accelerated at a pace that no one would have thought possible. The past four decades of history are now seen to have been an aberration, which was rectified just before the last decade of this century began. Following the example that Poland and Hungary had been setting for two years, the other communist countries of Eastern Europe succeeded in a matter of months, weeks, or even days in transforming themselves into potentially democratic states with a market economy. The idea on which almost half a century of foreign policy had been based, that the East-West division was one of Europe's natural features, was suddenly found to have been an illusion.

Germany, which for four decades lay not in Central Europe but half in Western Europe and half in Eastern Europe, regained the political place that matches its location, in the heart of Europe. The European Community, which until 1988 was largely ignored by the eastern part of the continent and tended to be regarded by the West and the rest of the world as synonymous with irrelevance and internal discord, became a force of attraction for the East and a dynamic force in the West. Another factor previously taken for granted, the American presence in Western Europe, is now no longer so self-evident. And above all, Moscow realized not only that the communist experiment launched in 1917 was not such a good idea after all, but also that its attempt at dominance over nations and peoples was becoming indefensible.

What is remarkable is that, while all these developments were described everywhere as "incredible" and "unforeseeable" at the time, they were subsequently considered normal and obvious, as if it could not have been otherwise. Even more remarkable is that all these rapid and radical political and geopolitical upheavals passed off relatively peacefully, Europe seemingly being able to turn its back on the old order without difficulty. Shifts in spheres of influence, changes of political regimes, the merging of states—all classical causes of bloody revolutions and acts of war—took place with little or no force being used.

The fundamental changes that characterized the turn of the decade were, however, made possible only by a whole series of prior minor events and symbolic acts, tactical political moves and stunning pronouncements, coincidences and protracted basic trends—minor events and major developments that help to explain how the turnaround in European history could apparently be accomplished so smoothly, and that also indicate that what happened in 1989 was not so incredible, nor yet so obvious.

One of these protracted trends was the growing acceptance by both superpowers that for various reasons the security system that they had established after the Second World War was no longer tenable. The Soviet leaders realized that fundamental change was essential if the USSR was to retain its superpower status. This also led the Kremlin to agree, with self-preservation in mind, to relinquish its dominance over Eastern Europe, thus satisfying the basic requirement for the recent changes.

The members of the Atlantic Alliance gradually sensed that the alliance was no longer appropriate in view of the change in their mutual relations and that its military strategy and security policy were no longer in keeping with the military-strategic situation and the European allies', and especially West Germany's, changed perceptions of security. The main threat was increasingly seen to be not the Soviet Union but the military power structure of the two blocs and East-West confrontation. Hence the pressure exerted principally by the Federal Republic to take advantage of the shifts in Soviet policy to bring about a fundamental change in the East-West relationship. Bonn was, moreover, virtually the only NATO member country to base its relations with the Eastern bloc and its attitude toward disarmament on a long-term political view. The western partners were gradually to adopt the West German policy during the disarmament negotiations. Little by little, the goals became extensive troop reductions and the structural inability to launch an attack, and the prospect of NATO's deployment of new short-range missiles on European soil was increasingly ruled out. The possibility of a different kind of European security system thus grew.

The change in the attitude of both superpowers toward disarmament and the progress consequently made at the disarmament talks helped to establish a framework suitable for the reforms in Eastern Europe. Had it not been for the close and friendly relationship between Moscow and Washington and the prospect of a further reduction of military potential in Europe, the developments in Eastern Europe, which were extremely destabilizing in themselves, would not have occurred so smoothly.

Another important development was that the *Deutschlandpolitik* had become a permanent feature of West German policy after the Kohl government took office and had taken on a dynamism of its own. Apparent internal stability and the conclusion that Bonn's recognition of the East German regime was growing had led to growing self-confidence among East Germany's leaders, which enabled the relationship between the two Germanys to be significantly extended and intensified. If this relationship had not developed as it did in the second half of the 1980s, internal pressure might not have built up and the conditions that ensured that the GDR was swept along on the wave of developments in Hungary and Poland would not have prevailed.

The growing number of meetings between the political and economic elites of the two countries had resulted in an extensive network of contacts at various levels in every possible area of policy. The ground was thus prepared. Though initially taken by surprise, the Federal Republic was therefore able to react quickly and efficiently to the fall of the Honecker regime, and the ties between the two Germanys were strengthened with exceptional speed. The same was true of the contacts that West Germany had established with the other Eastern European countries, giving Bonn a considerable lead over the other Western countries in Eastern Europe when the Iron Curtain was removed.

The pursuit of an active *Ostpolitik* as well as a *Deutschlandpolitik* had become generally accepted in Bonn, especially after the limitations of the *Deutschlandpolitik* had come to light. As an alternative to reunification, now abandoned as an immediate objective, Bonn began trying to overcome the division of Europe, which would also mean an end to the division of Germany. Bonn's support and subsequently the support of the European Community as a whole for the reforms in Poland and especially Hungary gave the process of change in both countries encouragement and a wider perspective, and the internal and external pressure on them ensured that they stayed on course. This not only further increased the internal pressure for change in the GDR but also eventually led Budapest to decide to open its borders to the West.

The spectacular rise in the number of East Germans visiting the Federal Republic, which the GDR permitted as a supposed solution to the internal pressure and as the quid pro quo required by the Federal Republic for the economic assistance it provided, was another of the basic factors that made the 1989 revolution possible. Personal experience of the major difference in prosperity between the two Germanys led to a further increase in the pressure for change in the GDR. After Hungary's decision to dismantle its section of the Iron Curtain, East Germans chose this route for a massive exodus to West Germany, and the East German regime was eventually obliged to remove its part of the Iron Curtain and the Berlin Wall and to launch radical political and economic reforms.

It can be said that the network of contacts that had previously been established between the two Germanys and the resulting growth in the feeling of *Zusammengehörigkeit*, or belonging together, along with the calming influence of the Soviets, helped to ensure that, at the height of the internal political crisis caused by East Germans seeking asylum in West German embassies and fleeing to the West through Hungary, the GDR made concession after concession rather than electing to try to resolve the crisis by force. It is clear that this option, which the East German leaders obviously considered, might have had far-reaching implications for the further process of change in Eastern Europe and thus for the European security situation. A mounting crisis such as this, with no outlet for internal pressure, could have assumed extremely dangerous proportions.

Even more important, had it not been for the repeated concessions made by the East German regime and thus the end of the GDR as the cornerstone of communism in Eastern Europe, "nonreformable" Czechoslovakia, Bulgaria, and Romania would presumably not have been dragged into the wave of reform so soon. The sudden changes in the GDR and the other countries also ensured that the often difficult process of change which had already been under way in Poland, Hungary, and even the USSR for some time, was no longer so isolated and could in fact continue in a more favorable political environment. It was given an additional boost by the often far more rapid and radical changes initiated in the last countries to fall, and it became easier for the reformers in these countries to overcome opposition and to risk more extensive reforms (cf. the tolerance with which the independent attitudes of the local communist parties in the Baltic States and, later, the reforms of the communist party in Moscow itself were initially treated).

Another development that was very important in preventing Bonn from pursuing its security interests in a political vacuum was the growth of Franco-German security cooperation. Initially, by strengthening the Bonn-Paris axis, France supported the Alliance, which was in difficulty at the time, and was to some extent able to compensate for West Germany's flagging confidence in the United States and NATO. A basis of military cooperation and consultations on security between the two countries also emerged and, though not enough to take NATO's place, it may prove useful in the development of a defense and security policy appropriate to the new situation in Eastern Europe and to the profoundly changed East-West relationship to which this situation has given rise. Later, Paris helped to ensure that, in seeking to promote its security interests, Bonn did not become isolated within NATO and that, in fact, the Alliance gradually accepted its views and began to respond to the changes in the Eastern bloc. An open split in the Alliance was thus avoided. Had there been such a split between the Federal Republic and the most important of the other NATO partners, the developments in Eastern Europe and their sequel might have taken a completely different turn.

The question is whether Moscow would have supported and accepted radical reforms in the Eastern European countries if the Federal Republic had gradually emerged as some kind of independent Central European power. A West Germany moving toward neutrality might, after all, have had a contagious effect on certain Eastern European countries, and this at a time when the neutralization of its allies would not have been acceptable to Moscow, given the East-West relationship as it was then. The reform movement in these countries could thus have assumed a dangerous dimension for the USSR. The reforms were possible only when the Kremlin was sure that each country would remain within the Warsaw Pact and that West Germany, though gaining in influence, was still controlled by and firmly anchored in NATO.

This brings us to a point that is also important for the future. The conventional wisdom is that the USSR has always advocated a neutral Germany (and, in return, would possibly agree to reunification), but it seems more likely that Moscow would consider a neutral Germany dangerous. It can be assumed that this is instinctively felt by the Soviet Union. The situation would certainly have its dangers if a political, economic, and military power vacuum were to emerge in Central Europe. With its growing power and influence, a neutral Germany would have a free hand in this power vacuum. Given the fear of a strong German power in Central Europe still felt in the Soviet Union because of historical events, Moscow may therefore have a greater interest in seeing Germany incorporated in a larger entity.

This is all the more true since, though perhaps fearing a strong Germany, the Soviet Union needs its help. The Federal Republic has already played a crucial role for the USSR by helping to ensure through its economic power and its influence both in Eastern Europe and in NATO and the European Community that the removal and dismantling of the communist regimes in Eastern Europe did not occur in an economic and political power vacuum or lead to total chaos. The reduction in the economic assistance these countries have received from the USSR has already been partly offset in recent years by the increase in the Federal Republic's influence. At the political level there has similarly been a shift from the USSR to West Germany and Western Europe, as was evident, for example, from the many contacts in 1988 and 1989 between the Eastern European countries on the one hand and the Federal Republic and the other countries of Western Europe on the other.

Western European political influence became even more important after Moscow had also relinquished its ideological hegemony, and the Western European countries offered a serious alternative model in the shape of their democratic system. This may prevent the political and ideological freedom that the Eastern European countries have gained from eventually assuming dangerous proportions for the USSR. It feared, for example, a revival of fascism in East Germany, a resurgence of nationalist and ethnic conflicts in

Central and Eastern Europe, and the emergence of anti-Soviet feelings. It must be remembered in this context that the USSR has lost most of its means of exercising control over the Eastern European countries by the wavering of the Warsaw Pact, COMECON, and the network of communist parties. Western European integration, and the mutual monitoring it brings, may provide an alternative for maintaining and increasing stability in the region. West Germany's influence within the European Community may thus be important to the USSR, since Bonn is a strong advocate of the inclusion of the Eastern European countries in the process of Western European integration.

In view of the crucial role that West Germany can play in all this, it is vital for the USSR that Bonn should remain firmly entrenched in a Western European entity, firstly because West Germany will be unable to perform these political and economic integrating and stabilizing tasks on its own and will need the support of its Western European partners and the European Community. Germany's unification and the cushioning and support of the process of economic reform in the Eastern European countries will require the backing of a stronger economic and financial entity than the Federal Republic, even though it is an economic superpower. The short-term implications of Germany's economic and monetary unification, particularly for the value of the Deutsche mark and inflation, may be such that the balance of power within the European Community shifts somewhat to the advantage of the other member states. It must be borne in mind in this context that the Federal Republic's strong position within the Community is closely linked to its stabilizing influence in the monetary sphere and the measures it takes to combat inflation. Secondly, Germany must also remain firmly entrenched in the Community to prevent Bonn from gaining too much and, above all, uncontrolled influence in Europe—in other words, to prevent German power and influence from filling a European power vacuum. Despite its initially positive role, this would eventually result in the USSR again seeing West Germany as a threat to the USSR.

This also points to another development that helped to ensure that the process of change in Europe was able to take place against a stabilizing background: the rapid strides made by the process of Western European integration, in which Franco-German relations have played an important part. This was very clear from the discussion at the summit meeting in Strasbourg (8–9 December 1989) on the convening of an intergovernmental conference on EMU, when Kohl, despite previous doubts and the opposition of the *Bundesbank*, agreed to the conference in return for the retraction by France and the Community of their reservations about German unification. That the two-plus-four formula (the four victors in the Second World War and the two Germanys) was chosen for the political discussions on the unification of Germany indicates that the Community is not yet the dominant force at the political level. Nonetheless, the inevitability of German unification, the need for a political settlement of the German question, and the special nature of the GDR's relationship with the Community were first recognized by the Commission through its President, Jacques Delors. This led the Commission to set up a special advisory group to prepare the Community for East Germany's entry. The political initiative was to remain with the Commission, resulting in the special summit meeting in Dublin (28 April 1990) to consider the German question. The Community was not, then, so politically immature, although a number of member states still have great difficulty in recognizing this.

The Community framework has the major advantage of being able to develop further and of also being flexible enough to adjust to new situations and requirements relating not only to new member states and associated countries but also to such new areas of policy as European security. The Community framework and the degree of integration that has been achieved mean that the Community can respond like no other body to the changed European environment, with the links between the monetary, economic, and external economic spheres and politics in the strict sense becoming increasingly important.

The various developments referred to above will help to determine the framework of the security system in Europe. There is little hope of accurately predicting what form this system will take in the future. Nor can it be said what course history will follow in the coming years and with what series of events it will surprise the world. The events of 1989 indicate the need for a large measure of humility in this respect.

An attempt can, however, be made to present a plausible scenario, a possible scenario based on a long-term view, which can also be regarded as an indication of the direction to be taken and the goal to be pursued, a scenario that can prevent Europe from being left unstable, neutralized, and weak once its and Germany's division have been overcome. The developments in Eastern Europe and the Soviet Union not only invite humility but also indicate that the course of history can sometimes be speeded up, adjusted, or even predetermined if an appropriate long-term policy is pursued and possible turning points are prepared and anticipated. Seen from this angle, developments in East and West in the past ten years become particularly relevant, and an attempt can be made on this basis to look ten years ahead.

The revolutionary phase that Europe experienced in late 1989 and early 1990 soon gave way to awareness that, while it might be possible to do away with the Yalta system in just a few months, designing an alternative was not so easy. A great deal of ingenuity and political insight as well as financial effort and the questioning of traditional premises are now expected of both the former Eastern bloc countries and Western Europe. The euphoric reports of the collapse of the Wall, of a dissident becoming president, of the abolition of decades of old power monopolies, of the first free elections for more than forty years were quickly followed by questions about the persistent flow of refugees from East Germany, the billions contributed to help the East German unemployed, the future European order, and a united Germany's place in it.

In Germany a specific course was charted: rapid transition to economic and monetary union, followed by political unification—which took place on 3 October 1990, less than eleven months after the Wall came down. The situation as regards international policy and the future peaceful order in Europe was and is very much less clear-cut. In this respect there has been a remarkable change. While the international context determined any relations between the two Germanys in the last 45 years, and until the end of 1989 the redefinition of international relations in the light of developments in the Soviet Union and the Eastern bloc was seen as a precondition for German unification, German unification became a fact to which international balances must adjust.

A European security system can take shape only if Germany's regained sovereignty and Franco-German cooperation are central to the larger entity that is the European Community. The restoration of sovereignty to Germany means more than the unification of its two parts. It also means this united Germany being able, without being treated with suspicion, to play the political role—in security as in other spheres—which is its due in view of its economic strength and geographical position. The Franco-German relationship is crucial to European cooperation in security and defense. This is evident from the combined economic, political, and military potential of the two countries, even though the suspicion that is a legacy of history has still not been completely overcome. The Franco-German axis also ensures a continuing balance between the reforms in Eastern European and the improvement in relations with these countries on the one hand and progress in the process of integration in the European Community on the other. Furthermore, placing the military component of the European security policy at the level of the twelve member states from the outset is unrealistic and perhaps not even necessary.

The question that arises in this context is how much "variable geometry" the concept of a Community evolving toward a Union can tolerate. It is therefore important for the security system, and little by little its military aspect, to be organically linked to the Community. It can then be influenced by the centripetal forces of the Community approach. Germany will, moreover, become the more firmly incorporated in the Community the more the latter takes on not only economic and monetary but also political and, by degrees, military tasks. Despite the initial hesitation, this may also reassure the USSR in the long term.

At this juncture a parenthetical comment needs to be made on the idea of a grand European confederation, which to some minds could be seen as an alternative to the existing Community. The idea is tempting and the concept generous, but is it not, in the final analysis, just a convenient solution and a smoke screen intended to obscure the lack of decisiveness?

Of course, the process of change in the former communist countries must have the active support of the Community and the individual Western European countries. The Western Europeans must be prepared to make the necessary financial and economic efforts, but without compromising their elementary security requirements and the basic principles on which their democratic system is based for the sake of the reforms in Eastern Europe or because of Soviet demands. That this fundamental position, to which the Community has adhered in the past, is worthwhile became apparent, for example, when the USSR was eventually forced by the Community's single-minded attitude to accept that it is not the relationship between the Community and COMECON that predominates but the relationship between the Community and the individual communist countries.

It is illusory to think that the level of integration among the member states of the Community can be transferred to a larger confederation embracing the new democracies in Eastern Europe, let alone that further integration would then be possible, and yet further integration is precisely what is needed if past achievements are to be consolidated. Thus monetary integration is needed for the consolidation of the planned single market, but can it seriously be contended that this would be possible within a larger confederation? It must also be remembered in this context that the process of integration will advance or decline. There is no middle course. A larger confederation would very soon degenerate into, at best, a discordant free trade area. Instead of the foundations being laid for a European peaceful order, these foundations would be undermined. A gradual approach, in which the Community, advancing toward economic, monetary, and political integration, remains a beacon, is then far preferable to the mirage of a pan-European confederation.

If the Eastern European countries are to benefit from this strong Community, growing cooperation will be needed. The European Community and the Eastern European countries must therefore conclude association agreements that provide for closer relations and become more comprehensive the more these countries transform themselves into states with a democratic political and market-oriented economic structure. When granting aid, the Community must urge the Eastern European countries to cooperate in the reform of their economic and political systems and to institutionalize this cooperation in one or more regional organizations, just as the United States urged the Western Europeans to do after the Second World War. In this way the European Community can ease the political tensions between certain Eastern European countries and increase the stability in this region.

As regards the accession of these countries, the Community should be honest and avoid arousing false hopes. The negotiations on the accession of Spain and Portugal, which already had democratic and market-oriented structures, took years and were very difficult. In every conceivable respect solutions had to be found to the problems posed by the major disparity between the two Iberian countries and the Community's member states in terms of economic development and economic and financial structures. Provision was made for long transitional periods in many areas. It must also be remembered that Spain and Portugal are just two countries and that they acceded before work began on the completion of the single market, which signifies a major qualitative leap forward in the process of integration. This indicates that, for practical reasons alone, negotiations cannot yet be held with the Eastern European countries on their possible accession, which does not, however, mean that accession to the Community cannot be offered as a long-term prospect. This is, moreover, the purpose of an association agreement. The great challenge that the existing Community faces is the completion of its economic and monetary integration and progress toward political union, so that it may then play its full role as the economic driving force and political stabilizer in Europe.

In this shaping of political Europe the balance created by the Bonn–Paris axis is particularly important. What is so specific about this balance? Both for reasons of economic strength and as a political guarantee, in view of the suspicion with which Germany is still treated, the support given by France (and the Community) is crucial, first to what was for the Germans above all emotionally important unification of their nation, and subsequently to the reconstruction of Eastern Europe through the PHARE-action (Poland/Hungary: Assistance to the Restructuring of the Economies) and the establishment of the BERD (Bank for European Reconstruction and Development). On the other hand, France realizes that, although the idea leaves it with a lurking feeling of uneasiness, it can play a major part on the European and world stage only if European integration continues, which presupposes Germany's support. Nor is there any alternative to the Franco-German marriage. Britain remains aloof, and Southern Europe is far from being Germany's economic or political equal. Marriage with Germany may well be a marriage of convenience, but France has at least made a good catch.

It is therefore no coincidence that European integration has made progress at times when France and West Germany were of like mind—though their premises usually differed—and stagnated when the unity of approach faded. An apt example is provided by the unexpected events at the intergovernmental conference in Luxembourg, which led to the Single European Act (1985). That it was possible for this conference to be held and a response was thus given to the European Parliament's proposals was very largely due to the agreement between Bonn and Paris on the need for progress in the establishment of the European Union. The sights were set high, and at first the conference proceeded apace. Then the peace was disturbed by a difference of opinion over Europe's response to President Reagan's SDI plans. France opted for a strictly European approach, through the EUREKA plan. West Germany did not want to exclude a bilateral relationship with the United States. The engine stopped, the conference came to a standstill, and the final outcome was less than expected. Of necessity, increasing the depth of the process of European integration is therefore bound to hinge on the Franco-German relationship.

In late 1989 and early 1990 this relationship was often turbulent, tempting many to refer to these difficulties as permanent. In itself it was not surprising that German unification aroused mixed feelings in France (and the rest of the continent). Mitterrand's "*bonne chance à l'Allemagne*" speaks volumes on the subject. But the cooperation that had developed over four decades and the realization that, as German unification was inevitable, political answers were needed, gained the upper hand and emerged as the catalyst of the process that may lead to the Community's political union.

This process of giving the Community added depth is taking place at three levels, each of which influences the other two positively (or negatively) and drives them on (or causes them to stagnate). First, there is the satisfactory conclusion of the 1992 operation and the establishment of the Economic and Monetary Union. The speed with which the Community is transforming its economic legislation and the way in which the industrial and service sectors are responding to these changes are in themselves astonishing. Monetary union as a precondition for the proper functioning of the single market has become an attainable objective. Although Germany will be fairly occupied with itself, it will support the efforts to establish a European central bank. Political commitment to the process of monetary integration is high, and the traditional theory advanced by the Germans that economic convergence should be achieved before thoughts turn to monetary integration has been eroded both by progress in the completion of the single market and by the inter-German monetary union—where the cart really was put before the horse.

Second, there is still some considerable room for maneuvering within the present institutional structure, particularly at the political level, if the will exists. We have already referred to the possibility of a broad interpretation of the Single European Act on the question of security. European Political Cooperation and the workings of the General Affairs Council could be brought closer together within the existing structure. In this respect, the Irish presidency took the lead in early 1990 by convening a meeting of the foreign ministers, the permanent representatives, and the political directors of the foreign ministries. However, the progress that can be made within the existing structures has its limits and is possible, moreover, only because the participants see it as a prelude to a fundamental debate on the Community's ultimate political goal. Being well aware of this, Margaret Thatcher preferred not to take part in this courtship display. If the fundamental debate does not come, these "overtures" are likely to die a quiet death.

Third, the Community had therefore at last to give shape to "political Europe." A number of factors have made it necessary for thought to be given to the Community's political unity for a long time now. The Community has long been an economic giant with political feet of clay. The need to give the Community added depth before further enlargement existed before the upheaval in Eastern Europe, the potential applicants being Austria, Malta, and Turkey.

What factors will lead to real decisions being taken on progress toward political union?

Stability in Europe in the postwar period was determined by the Pacts. Essentially, this stability has two facets: stability in the relationship between the two superpowers as reflected in Europe, and stability among the European nations. Now that the race between the USSR and the United States has slowed and is no longer the driving force behind political and military thinking in East and West, the problem of stability among the European nations, including the USSR, arises. Here the picture is dominated by the prospect or fear of an overly powerful German nation, the resurgence of Central Europe, ethnic tensions, the Balkanization of Europe, the shifting of Europe's epicenter to the East, and the disintegration of the USSR with all its destabilizing consequences.

To this the Pacts have no answer. But who does? The new unified Germany perhaps. That idea must make the French and Polish shudder. An entente among medium-sized European countries, perhaps. A glance at European history is bound to lead any responsible statesman to cast this idea aside without further ado. And, what is more, which medium-sized countries, and in what combination?

Renewed stability on the European continent is impossible without a reference point and a beacon, a core from which a power of persuasion and a centripetal force emanate. At the moment the Community is this point of attraction, this beacon. And it has a unique prospect of remaining so and thus making a lasting contribution to stability in Europe. This, however, presupposes the early establishment of the European Union. From long-term developments in NATO, France, Germany, and the Community itself it seems likely that the Community will take this course. It is also possible to find in these developments elements that can give the political union real substance in the areas of external policy, security, and defense.

During the construction of this political union the question of the defense aspect is bound to arise, because it happens to play a part in every known model. For the issue we are considering this is primarily a question of phasing, which the direct approach to the subject need not impede. For the moment, there is no general military problem in Europe that calls for an immediate solution, there is no potential aggressor in the short term, and our political reflections do not need to be based on infernal scenarios. In other words, a start could be made on building the political union, which would also encompass, by degrees and not necessarily embracing all the member states, the military aspects at a rate that matches the USSR's and United States' disengagement and might be accelerated by nationalistically inspired troubles in Europe and the European part of the USSR.

Two mutually reinforcing trends will result in the gradual absorption of the military aspects into the political union. First, there is the Community axis, the establishment of the political union leading not only to the formal disappearance of the lines separating the various policies but also to these policies becoming an organic and cohesive whole. The Twelve will be increasingly explicit in their views on security questions, a tendency that has, moreover, been growing in recent years. As the Twelve would take a growing interest in the nonmilitary aspects of security, the links between all the various aspects of security will mean their also considering with increasing frequency problems relating strictly to defense. As the military component would become just another aspect of the general security policy, the reservations of certain member states about this subject being discussed by the Twelve will diminish. General political declarations will tend to give way to increasingly specific positions concerning Europe's military security. At Community gatherings more informal discussion of more operational military aspects will take place. The confidential discussions on these aspects will at first not be translated into official positions, but they will influence the policies of the member states, which will slowly begin to coordinate certain aspects of their defense policies.

Second, it can be assumed that some member states of the Community would come under growing pressure to take the necessary precautions where their own defense is concerned and to seek cooperation and, progressively, integration in the military sphere too. The pressure will increase because the existing alliances will continue to crumble despite the attempts of NATO to remain in command. It will further be realized that, one way or another, account must be taken of the presence of the Soviet superpower in the European continent—its behavior still unpredictable because of its internal problems—and of the possibility of conflicts both in and outside Europe. France could be expected to take initiatives in this direction, motivated not only by the factors referred to above but also by a desire to tie Germany to itself. Germany is over time likely to react positively to this European defense cooperation because, with the diminishing impact of NATO, it will feel an even greater need than other countries for continued military protection. To ensure that Germany turned to France first for this protection, France should be unequivocal about security guarantees for Germany and include them in its defense policy. This would also mean France taking account of German interests and sensitivities in its nuclear strategy.

Other factors will also play a part in overcoming any reservations Germany might have about this option. The structural impossibility of launching an attack is to emerge as a basic concept of a European approach to the defense problem, since this concept dominates German thinking on the subject and has also formed a latent part of the French strategy since the time of de Gaulle. Furthermore, the "Europeanization" of defense, with the eventual disappearance of foreign troops, particularly from German soil, would give Germany absolute sovereignty over its territory. The demise of the Forward Defense concept also points in this direction. Finally, the option described above will be attractive to Germany because it would preclude the renationalization of military defense in Europe, which would have a destabilizing effect, especially in Central Europe.

The question of the relationship between the European Community and WEU arises in this context. An increasingly close relationship would be a major step in the establishment of a European Union with an independent security and defense policy, provided that WEU gradually become part of the EC structure and decision-making process. This would remove two limitations of cooperation within the WEU: its exclusively military approach of security and its intergovernmental character. Linking WEU to the EC framework would ensure that the military and non-military aspects of a security policy were progressively merged, and that while the military cooperation might initially remain intergovernmental, it would eventually form part of an institutional framework in which growing importance was attached to majority decisions and democratic control by the directly elected European Parliament.

It is not certain, however, that one of WEU's main limitations can be overcome through a close relationship with the European Community: the widely differing views among the WEU countries on European cooperation and integration in the security and defense sphere. As the United Kingdom and some other WEU countries are wary of more extensive European cooperation in this sphere, they may regard WEU even in the longer term as just another part of NATO, which would not be a realistic option for Germany and France. It is indeed to be feared that any attempt by WEU to transform itself into a genuine European forum would cause years of futile discussion on relations between WEU and the Atlantic Alliance.

The chances of more substantial cooperation and integration would therefore continue to be remote, despite growing links between the European Community and WEU. To overcome a possible impasse, there must be an alternative solution capable to generate, if necessary, its own dynamism in addition to the developments within the European Community and the ever closer EC-WEU relationship.

If further moves toward more substantial security and defense cooperation and integration proved unacceptable to all EC or WEU countries, a separate European Security and Defense Council should be created by the countries willing to accept major new steps in this direction, thus anticipating the possibility of general agreement within the European Community and WEU. This council would consist of the ministers of foreign affairs, the ministers of defense, and the commanders-in-chief of the participating countries, assisted by various specialized committees. As the security and military cooperation and integration proceeds, the Council's authority would be increased, as in the European Community, through periodic meetings at the level of the heads of states or government of the countries concerned. The meetings of the Security and Defense Council would preferably take place just before the normal EC meetings. EC countries that did not join the Security and Defense Council would be permitted to attend its meetings as observers. The Council would be accountable to the European Parliament, which would include for these issues the Members of the European Parliament elected in the member states participating in Security and Defense Cooperation.

The Security and Defense Council would gradually approximate the various national defense concepts and develop a joint security and defense concept, which might be slowly converted into a coordinated and joint policy. Like military cooperation, which would initially be rather limited and modest in scale, the responsibilities and authority of this European Defense Council would grow as the initiatives already taken made progress in practice, and as circumstances made this psychologically possible. The Council would seek to harmonize positions on the disarmament negotiations and to adopt a common position; it would encourage a higher degree of interoperability of the armed forces and closer cooperation in arms production.

The Security and Defense Council would have the authority over the joint military units that would gradually be created. These multilateral forces should include both operational units that could be deployed in and outside Europe and units used for verification and peacekeeping purposes. The existence of this second category of troops might facilitate the future involvement of EC countries reluctant, for whatever reason, to participate in military integration or military actions. The Council could gradually take political and military charge of part of its member countries' armed forces, which would be greatly reduced in size after the East-West negotiations. The growing irrelevance and/or disappearing of the pacts and the progressive withdrawal of foreign troops from German and European territory would not then lead to the renationalization of the European countries' military apparatus or to recourse to equally destabilizing bilateral military agreements.

The Council might become the forum for deliberations on the nuclear aspects of European defense, and for consultations between the Western European nuclear powers and the other member states. The former should increasingly attune their nuclear strategies to general Western European security interests, taking particular account of the position Germany occupies because of its specific geographical location. The non-nuclear countries should be increasingly involved in the formulation of the policy. Only then, moreover, will it be possible to close the gap between France and Germany that is due to the difference in their nuclear status and their views on the role of nuclear weapons.

Even though only some of the Community's member states would participate in Security and Defense Cooperation, the Security and Defense Council should ensure that its initiatives were commensurate with the EC Council's security policy and that this resulted in a close relationship between the military and non-military aspects of security policy. At meetings of the EC Council the Security and Defense Council's decisions and consultations could be informally explained to the countries that had not joined the Security and Defense Council. The inevitable linking of the various security aspects would thus enable policy within the EC/EPC, the WEU, and European Security and Defense Cooperation to be progressively coordinated. This might eventually make integration seem more normal to EC member states not participating in the Security and Defense Cooperation. The Security and Defense Council and Cooperation could then eventually be extended to include the other member states. A Security and Defense Council of this kind would be a form of "variable geometry" leading to the ultimate objective: the European Union.

With the existence of a European defense authority and with NATO's dominance weakened as a result of the East-West changes, it would become politically and psychologically easier for France to strengthen its relationship with NATO. This could be achieved by seeking indirect cooperation between the European Security and Defense Council and NATO's Defense Planning Committee (of defense ministers), in which France does not participate, by making more extensive use of NATO's North Atlantic Council (of foreign ministers), to which France does belong. For the issues where a need for consultation and military cooperation between the European Security and Defense Council and the Defense Planning Committee was felt, the defense ministers could join the foreign ministers at the meetings of the North Atlantic Council and help make the relevant decisions. France would not then be faced with the choice of formally rejoining the Defense Planning Committee and the integrated military structure of the Alliance. For the relevant issues, NATO's technical committees, which normally report to the Defense Planning Committee, would come under the authority of the North Atlantic Council, thus making consultation and cooperation with the European Security and Defense Council's specialized committees possible.

The link between the European and NATO structures would enable European military cooperation to be prepared for more extensive forms of cooperation and integration and for a gradual, initially perhaps implicit, transfer of responsibilities and powers from the Atlantic to the European level, without the NATO structure, however, being unnecessarily undermined by the member countries themselves before a credible European alternative could be installed. European Security and Defense Cooperation would gradually take on the stabilizing function which the existing structures are finding increasingly difficult to perform.

Once European Security and Defense Cooperation has developed sufficiently, the present North Atlantic Treaty could be supplemented by or replaced with a new treaty between, on the one hand, all the Member States of the Community militarily integrated within the Security and Defense Council, and on the other hand, the other NATO member countries, among which the United States would occupy a central place. This treaty would have to be based on the continuing possibility of rapid military intervention by the Americans in European territory, even if the bulk of American forces would already have left Europe. A supplementary or new treaty of this kind would also ease the growing pressure in the United States for adjustment of the Atlantic relationship to the new international economic, political, and military situation.

The establishment of a Security and Defense Council closely related to the European Community would thus permit a gradual transition both from a primarily Atlantic to a primarily European security and defense system with an American guarantee; and from limited European security and defense cooperation among a limited number of member states to more extensive cooperation and integration within the European Union.

The Conference on Security and Cooperation in Europe would be the forum where the United States, Canada, the European Community, the democracies in Eastern European, and the USSR would meet, conclude disarmament agreements, and ensure that they were observed. Through European Political Cooperation and the European Security and Defense Council the Community would play a growing role in, initially, conventional disarmament negotiations. Through the CSCE forum the influence of the European countries on the disarmament process would increase, which would be in keeping with a tendency for the negotiations to be conducted less between two military blocs and more among the European countries (and the United States and Canada) within the CSCE.

Its three baskets also make the CSCE the appropriate forum for maintaining a link between the disarmament process, political and social reforms, respect for human rights, and economic aid and cooperation as relations between Eastern and Western Europe improve. Like the Community, with which the Eastern European countries would be closely associated, the CSCE forum could help to ease nationalist tensions in the east of the continent. The CSCE forum will not be enough on its own, however, since integration is not yet sufficiently advanced and, unlike the European Community, the CSCE does not have its own executive structure. Hence the need for a Community that plays a central role, since it could also assume responsibility for many of the executive aspects.

The broad lines of an evolution from an Atlantic to a European security system with an American guarantee are thus revealed. Efforts must be made to establish a differentiated structure of European contacts, cooperation, and integration as a prelude to a European security system that takes account of all aspects of security and ensures a coherent and global view of European security, a system that includes different institutions and decision-making levels so that the member states can be involved in decisions on security to varying degrees. The centripetal force of European integration will, however, ensure that more and more countries are involved at a growing number of decision-making levels, which will in turn reflect the growing intensity of the process of integration. This security system will permit both the division of Europe to be completely and finally overcome and the goal of the European Union to be achieved.

These centripetal forces of European integration have a far greater impact than such spectacular events as the Gulf crisis of 1990–91 that, with its overemphasis on the military dimension and the dominance of the United States, was in essence an *accident de parcours* rather than an indicator of future developments. The Gulf crisis did not, indeed, do anything to alter the fundamental long-term developments described above. The crisis was not "resolved" in the way in which international conflicts are normally resolved, and the methods used can therefore be seen as an experiment that cannot be repeated.

If the scenario outlined above materializes, European Security and Defense Cooperation is likely to be eventually absorbed into the European Union. The way in which monetary cooperation has grown within the European Community conforms to the premises of the blueprint we advocate for defense cooperation. After more than fifteen years of patient development, the Monetary Union is now within reach, even though monetary policy too forms a quintessential part of national sovereignty.

Epilogue

The evolution toward a genuine European security policy described above is a feasible scenario. Past developments indicate that the various steps that must be taken to this end are quite possible. If this scenario is to be implemented, certain decisions and measures will, however, have to be taken, with developments taken in hand rather than being allowed to continue uncontrolled. In other words, a European security system can be developed, but political steps have to be taken now. *L'histoire est libre.*

This also implies, however, the possibility of all the steps that have been described not being taken. If we look ten years ahead and ask ourselves how the European scene will look if the steps described earlier are not taken, it becomes clear that the scenario we have outlined is not optimistic or idealistic but in fact necessary if Europe wants to control its own future.

The Europe revealed by a laissez-faire, laissez-passer scenario is a sophisticated free trade area in which, whatever happens, the two superpowers still have considerable influence, the Europeans are divided among themselves, and nationalist tensions threaten the security and stability of Europe.

Before the 1992 project is completed and before the European Community is given new, solid foundations in the shape of an economic and monetary union backed by institutional reforms, new member states would be admitted to the Community. The difficulties this would entail would mean accepting the completion of the single market in diluted form and deferring work on the most delicate but most essential aspects of the whole project. The plans for the Economic and Monetary Union would also be weakened, given the need to avoid making the accession of the new member states more difficult. The Community's further institutional development would also be delayed. Power within the Community would shift from the central European institutions back to the member states, resulting in these institutions no longer having the same authority and no longer being able to play the same coordinating and creative role as they did in the last few years of the 1980s. It would be impossible for the Community to have more power and to play a more active part in foreign policy, if only because this would be irreconcilable with the position of the future new member states. Growing competition among the member states in their efforts to establish good economic and political relations with the USSR and the Eastern European countries would lead to increasing departures from the basic principles that governed relations with these countries. The Community would not be a real economic power, and it would forfeit the prospect of becoming a political power equal to the United States and the USSR with an appropriate military substructure.

The fact that the Community would be no more than an economic grouping would reflect on relations with Eastern Europe. The requirements relating to human rights and the further development of a democratic and market-oriented system would be tempered, partly because the member states would be more rather than less likely to pursue their own individual *Ostpolitik*. With the removal of pressure from the Community the Eastern European countries would be under no obligation to take certain difficult and painful decisions, and in countries such as Romania the heirs of the former regime might continue to exercise control in an albeit changed form. As the process of political and economic reform in the Eastern European countries would be weakened and the USSR would no longer be faced with a European bloc whose strength in political, economic, and security terms it must take into account, the pressure for reforms in the USSR would also wane.

As a few unstable and dubious regimes would remain in place in Eastern Europe, as the Community would have less influence and power over the Eastern European countries, and as they would not be required to consolidate their mutual relations through cooperation in return for Western European aid, the tensions among them would grow. Problems with minorities would lead to divisions within Eastern European countries, and countries would disintegrate without an influential European structure being in a position to cushion the adverse effects this would have. Stability in Europe would decline. As there would be no European security and defense system and the Europeans would not have even a minimum military apparatus of their own to show that the European institutions must be taken seriously, the Europeans would be unable to take action or to exert a deterrent influence if nationalist tensions in Eastern Europe threatened to erupt into violent conflict.

European stability would also decline because united Germany would not be part of a strong political European structure forming the basis of a comprehensive European security system. As the Community would no longer be an important political structure, there would also be less chance of effective action being taken within the Community and through talks between the Community and associated Eastern European countries to prevent and settle possible conflicts and misunderstandings and to coordinate and reconcile divergent interests and objectives. Given its economic power, its central geographical position, and its traditional links with the whole of Europe, Germany would gain most from the rivalry among the various European countries. It would become even more powerful economically and politically. This and the consequent revival of the traditional view that Germany poses a threat would lead surrounding countries to treat it with growing suspicion. This in turn would prompt a negative reaction in Germany itself, where the criticism from abroad and the psychological restrictions imposed would no longer be found acceptable.

As the development of European integration and the European institutions would cease, the Community would not play the stabilizing role that is needed in Europe. To maintain stability in Europe, the superpowers and what was left of the Pacts would still be needed. Such stability would, however, depend on the security and interests of the two superpowers, not on specifically European interests and security. The USSR and the United States would continue to determine the run of affairs in Europe, despite having less power and having lost their grip on events at the turn of the decade. A new kind of non-military Yalta, with the USSR and the United States deciding the fate of Europe in discreet but intensive consultations between themselves, would come into being. *L'histoire se répète.*

Selected Bibliography

Asmus, Ronald D. "Die Zweite Ostpolitik der SPD. Mit Perspektiven aus den USA," *Aussenpolitik*, 38(1)1987.

Baylis, John. "NATO Strategy: The Case for a New Strategic Concept." *International Affairs*, 64(1)1987/88.

Bel, Jacques. "Les relations entre la Communauté et le Conseil d'assistance économique mutuelle." *Revue du Marché Commun*, no. 318, June 1988.

Bertram, Christoph. "Europe's Security Dilemma," *Foreign Affairs*, 65(5)1987.

Brzezinski, Zbigniew. "The Future of Yalta," *Foreign Affairs*, 63(2)1984/85.

———. *Game Plan: How to Conduct the U.S.-Soviet Contest*. Boston and New York: The Atlantic Monthly Press, 1986.

———. "Postkommunistischer Nationalismus," *Europa-Archiv*, 44(24)1989.

Calleo, David P. *Beyond American Hegemony: The Future of the Western Alliance*. New York: Basic Books, 1987.

Dean, Jonathan. "How to Lose Germany," *Foreign Policy*, (55)1984.

Deibel, Terry L., and John L. Gaddis. *Containment: Concept and Policy*. Washington D.C.: National Defense University Press, 1986.

Flanagan, Stephen J., and Fen Osler Hampson, eds., *Securing Europe's Future*. London: Croom Helm, 1986.

Freedman, Lawrence, ed. *The Troubled Alliance: Atlantic Relations in the 1980's*. London: Heinemann, 1983.

Genscher, Hans-Dietrich, ed. *Nach vorn gedacht . . . : Perspektiven deutscher Aussenpolitik*. Stuttgart, Germany: Bonn Aktuell, 1987.

Gorbachev, Mikhail. *Perestroika: New Thinking for Our Country and the World*. London: Collins, 1987.

Groth, Michael. "Fortschritte im KSZE-Prozess. Das dritte Folgetreffen in Wien," *Europa-Archiv*, 44(3)1989.

Guérard, François. "Le débat sur l'identité allemande," *Problèmes politiques et sociaux*, no. 578, 19 February 1988.

Harrison, Michael M. *The Reluctant Ally: France and Atlantic Security.* London and Baltimore, Md.: Johns Hopkins University Press, 1981.

Hassner, Pierre. "L'Allemagne dans les relations Est-Ouest." *Revue Française de Science Politique,* June 1987.

Heisbourg, François. "Europe/Etats-Unis: le couplage stratégique menacé." *Politique Etrangère,* 52(1)1987.

Hoffmann, Stanley. "The U.S. and Western Europe: Wait and Worry." *Foreign Affairs,* 63(3)1985.

Howard, Michael. "1989: A Farewell to Arms?" *International Affairs,* 65(3)1989.

Howorth, Jolyon. "Resources and Strategic Choices: French Defense Policy at the Crossroads." *The World Today,* 42(5)1986.

Kaiser, Karl, and Pierre Lellouche, eds., *Le couple franco-allemand et la défense de l'Europe.* Paris: IFRI, 1986.

Kelleher, Catherine M., and Gale A. Mattox, eds., *Evolving European Defense Policies.* Lexington, Massachusetts and Toronto: Lexington Books, 1987.

Kennedy, Paul. *The Rise and Fall of the Great Powers, Economic Change and Military Conflict from 1500–2000.* London: Unwin Hyman, 1988.

Kissinger, Henry, and Cyrus Vance. "Bipartisan Objectives for American Foreign Policy." *Foreign Affairs,* 66(5)1988.

Kolboom, Ingo. "Ostpolitik als deutsch-französische Herausforderung." *Europa-Archiv,* 44(4)1989.

Krepon, Michael. *Strategic Stalemate: Nuclear Weapons and Arms Control in American Politics.* London: Macmillan, 1984.

Lafontaine, Oskar. *Angst vor den Freunden: Die Atomwaffenstrategie der Supermächte zerstört die Bündnisse.* Hamburg, Germany: Spiegel-Verlag, 1983.

Leisler Kiep, Walther. "The new Deutschlandpolitik." *Foreign Affairs,* 63(2)1984/85.

Lellouche, Pierre. *L'avenir de la guerre.* Paris: Mazarine, 1985.

Lieven, Dominic. "Gorbachev and the Nationalities." *Conflict Studies,* (216)1988.

McAdams, A. James. "Inter-German Détente: A New Balance." *Foreign Affairs,* 65(1)1986.

Medvedev, Zhores. *Gorbachev.* Oxford, England: Basil Blackwell, 1986.

Mitterrand, François. *Réflexions sur la politique extérieure de la France.* Paris: Fayard, 1986.

Montbrial, Thierry de. "Sur la politique de sécurité de la France." *Commentaire,* 40(10)1987/88.

Plock, Ernest D. *The Basic Treaty and the Evolution of East-West German Relations* Boulder, Colo., and London: Westview Press, 1986.

Racine, Bruno. "La France et les FNI." *Politique Etrangère,* 53(1)1988.

Record, Jeffrey, and David B. Rivkin. "Defending Post-INF Europe." *Foreign Affairs,* 66(4)1988.

Ruyt, Jean de. *L'Acte Unique Européenne.* Brussels: Editions de l'Université de Bruxelles, 1987.

Schmidt, Helmut. *A Grand Strategy for the West.* New Haven, Conn.: Yale University Press, 1985.

Schmidt, Peter. "The WEU—A Union Without Perspective?" *Aussenpolitik,* 37(4)1986.

Schneider, Heinrich. "Über Wien nach Gesamteuropa? Der KSZE-Prozess nach dem dritten Folgetreffen." *Integration*, 2(12)1989.

Schoutheete, Philippe de. *La coopération politique européenne*. Brussels: Editions Labor, 1986.

Sécurité et défense de l'Europe—le dossier Allemand, Les sept épées, no. 36, 1985.

Sharp, Jane. "After Reykjavik: Arms Control and the Allies." *International Affairs*, 36(2)1987.

Simonian, Haig. *The Privileged Partnership: Franco-German Relations in the EC, 1969–1984*. Oxford, England: Clarendon Press, 1985.

Sloan, Stanley R. *NATO's Future: Toward a New Transatlantic Bargain*. Washington D.C.: National Defense University, 1985.

Teltschik, Horst. "Die Reformpolitik Gorbatschows und die Perspektiven der West-Ost-Beziehungen." *Aussenpolitik*, 40(3)1989.

Tourrain, Raymond. *De la défense de la France à la défense de l'Europe*. Besançon, France: Cripes, 1987.

Ullman, Richard H. "The Covert French Connection." *Foreign Policy*, (75)1989.

Wettig, Gerhard. "Osteuropa in den Ost-West-Beziehungen." *Aussenpolitik*, 37(1)1986.

Yost, David S. "La coopération franco-allemande en matière de défense." *Politique Etrangère*, 53(4)88.

———. "France's Deterrent Posture and Security in Europe." *Adelphi Papers*, nos. 194 & 195, 1984/1985.

Index

ABM Treaty, 49, 100
Adamec, 188, 205–6
Adelman, Kenneth, 70
Adenauer, Konrad, 5, 47, 94
Ad Hoc Committee on NATO in the 1990s, 76
Afghanistan, Soviet invasion in, 8, 28, 69, 66, 163, 166, 191
Air-land battle doctrine, 25, 51
Andropov, Yuri, 173–74
Arbatov, Georgi, 72
Armenia, 184, 192–94
Arms control. *See* ABM Treaty; CDE; CFE; European Community, and arms control; INF; MBFR; NATO, and arms control; SALT; SNF; *names of specific countries*
Arms race, 21–22
Aron, Raymond, 83–85
Austria, 189, 191, 197
Azerbaijan, 192–94

Bahr, Egon, 44, 199
Bailer, Seweryn, 174
Baltic states, 182–85, 189, 191–94
Bangemann, Martin, 9
Belgium, 97, 161
Benelux, 96

BERD (Bank for Reconstruction and Development), 218
Berlin, 6–7, 9, 122, 139, 141; crisis, 20, 35
Berlin Wall, 9, 136–38, 142, 201–4. *See also* Iron Curtain
Brandt, Willy, 40. *See also* Ostpolitik
Brest-Litovsk, Peace Treaty of, 185
Brezhnev, Leonid, 14, 56, 173–74, 191
Brezhnev doctrine, 15
Broszat, Martin, 3
Brussels Treaty (1948), 96
Bulgaria, 195, 204–7
Bundy, McGeorge, 49
Burt, Richard, 74
Bush, George, 67, 155, 204; and NATO, 125
Brzezinski, Zbigniew, 62, 73

Calfa, Marian, 188, 206
Canada, 120
Carlucci, Frank, 67, 74, 115, 118
Carter, Jimmy, 8, 24, 65–66
Caucasian region, 184–85
CDE (Conference on Confidence- and Security-Building Measures and Disarmament in Europe, Stockholm), 37, 162

CDU/CSU (Christlich-Demokratische Union/Christlich-Soziale Union): and Eastern Europe/Soviet Union, 135, 145–47, 149; and German identity/self-confidence, 3, 43; and Inter-German relations, 5–8, 41, 133–36, 145–46; and security policy, 41–44, 122, 133, 149

Ceausescu, Nicolae, 187–89, 192, 205, 207

CFE (Conventional Armed Forces in Europe, Vienna), 120, 124–25, 163, 190

Chemical weapons, 23

Chernobyl disaster, 51, 58, 195

Chirac, Jacques, 84, 116–18

COCOM (Coordination Committee for Multilateral Export Control), 139

Cold war, second (1979–85), 8–9, 31, 36–37

COMECON, 147, 150, 168, 214

Commission on Integrated Long Term Strategy, 61–62

Communism, 177–78, 180, 188, 198, 214

Conference on Confidence- and Security-Building Measures and Disarmament in Europe, 37, 162

Conference on Disarmament in Europe, 37, 162

Conference on Security and Cooperation in Europe. *See* CSCE

Conventional forces, disarmament. *See* CDE; CFE; MBFR

Cruise missiles. *See* INF

CSCE (Conference on Security and Cooperation in Europe): 27, 31, 39–40, 120, 152, 162, 195, 225; follow-up conference (Belgrade) 163; follow-up conference (Madrid) 163; follow-up conference (Vienna) 40, 163–64, 190, 195

Cuba crisis, 58, 71

Czechoslovakia, 5, 9, 192, 201, 204–7; Prague Spring and Warsaw Pact, intervention in, 188, 196, 205–6

Davos, World Economic Forum, 39

De Gaulle, Charles, 54–55, 82–83, 94, 128–29

Delors, Jacques, 11, 150, 161, 167, 169, 215

Denmark, 158

Détente, 7, 21, 27–28, 31–32

Dienstbier, Jiri, 206

"Discriminate deterrence," 61–62

Dregger, Alfred, 42–43, 113

Dubcek, Alexander, 205, 207

Dumas, Roland, 203

Eastern Europe: and COMECON, 147, 150, 168, 214; and the European Community, 150–51, 163, 167–70, 194, 216–18; the fall of communist regimes in, 179–80, 204–5, 210–14; opening of the borders, 148, 197–98, 201–2; reforms in, 140, 178–80; and the Soviet Union, 178–80, 183, 213–14; and Warsaw Pact, 134, 206, 214. *See also* FRG, and Eastern Europe, policy towards; Franco-German relationship, and Eastern Europe; *names of specific countries*

East Germany. *See* GDR

Eisenhower administration, 53

Elysée Treaty (Franco-German, 1963), 93–94, 115–16

Erhard, Ludwig, 94

Estonia, 191. *See also* Baltic states

EUREKA, 98–99, 139, 219

Eurogroup, 76

European Coal and Steel Community, 95

European Commission, 166–70. *See also* Delors, Jacques

European Community, 215; and Afghanistan, Soviet invasion in, 166; and arms control, 159, 161–64; and COMECON, 150, 168; and the CSCE, 162–64, 168, 225; Dooge Committee on Institutional Affairs, 158–60; Draft Treaty on European Union, 158–59; Eastern Europe, association agreements with, 170, 217–

18; and Eastern Europe, reforms in, 150–51, 163, 167–70, 194, 216–18; enlargement of, 170, 217–18; and European peaceful order, 217; and external relations, 166–68; and EPC, 158, 160, 165–67, 219; Franco-German relationship and, 83–84, 126, 203–4, 214, 216, 218–19; Genscher-Colombo initiative, 158; and German unification, 168–69, 203–4, 214–15; and the Group of 7, 167–68; and NATO, 159–62, 224–25; and "1992," 150, 157, 212, 217, 219; and Poland, crisis in, 167; Presidency of, 76, 149–50, 165–67, 203, 219; and sanctions, 166–68; and security and defense issues, 76–77, 157–65, 169–70, 216, 220–26; Single European Act, 157–61, 170, 218; and Solemn Declaration on European Union (Stuttgart Declaration), 158; and the Soviet Union, 150, 161, 168–69; Treaty of Luxembourg, 158, 165; Troika, 167; and Western European Union, 160–61, 222–23. *See also* European Commission; European Council; European Monetary Union; European Parliament; European Political Cooperation; European Political Union; European Security and Defense Council/Cooperation; European Union
European Council, 161, 167; Stuttgart (1983), 158; Fontainebleau (1984), 158–59; Luxembourg (1985), 158, 165, 218; Rhodes (1988), 162; Madrid (1989), 164; Paris (1989), 203; Strasbourg (1989), 168, 204, 214; Dublin (1990), 169, 215
European Defense Community, 94–96
European Economic Community. *See* European Community
European Monetary Union (EMU), 165, 168, 214, 217, 226
European Parliament, 165, 203–4, 222; and European security, 77, 158–61, 169–70, 222; Galluzzi report, 160–61;

Haagerup report, 159–60; Hänsch report, 169; Penders report, 170; Spinelli report, 158
European Political Cooperation (EPC), 98, 158–67, 219; and the European Community, 158, 160, 165–67, 219; EPC Secretariat, 162, 164, 166
European Political Union (EPU), 219–21
European Security and Defense Council/Cooperation, 222–26; and defense cooperation, 223; and the EC, 223–25; and European military units, 223; and NATO, 224–25
European Space Agency (ESA), 149. *See also* Hermes project
European Union, 220, 222, 224, 226
European weapons procurement, 97

Fabius, Laurent, 113
FDP (Freie Democratische Partei), 149; and Inter-German relations, 5–7, 137, 145–46
Federal Republic of Germany. *See* FRG
Flexible response, 24, 48–50, 54–56, 88, 123
FOFA, 25, 51
Forward Defense, 25, 222
Fouchet Plan, 55, 94
France: and arms control (conventional), 120, 123; and the defense of Germany, 82–83, 86–88, 91–92, 105–9, 113–14, 117, 129, 221; and the European Community, 55, 83–84, 203–4; 218; and the "Force d'Action Rapide" (FAR), 91–92, 105–8; and German neutralism/peace movement, 84–85, 92–93, 104; and German unification, 83, 85, 203–4, 219; independence, requirements for, 83–85, 91, 104; and INF, 81, 84, 92–93, 99; and military strategy, 82, 86–89, 91, 104–8, 127–28; and NATO, 47, 76, 82–84, 86–88, 91–93, 106, 108–10, 114, 118–20, 123–25, 128–29, 224–25; NATO withdrawal of, 50, 51, 82–83, 128; nuclear forces,

French, 55, 59, 82, 84, 92, 104, 107–
9, 118–19, 123–25, 127–28; and SDI,
98–99, 103; and technological developments, 85–86, 88, 93, 104; and the
United Kingdom, 75, 129; and the
United States, 70–71, 82, 125, 128–
29; and U.S. presence in Europe/
Germany, 83, 85, 92–93, 103; and
WEU, 87, 96–100. *See also* European
Defense Community, Franco-German relationship.
Franco-German relationship, 93–94,
97, 98–100, 105–9, 113–17, 121, 123–
26, 149, 203–4, 212; and Eastern Europe, 115, 118–19, 126–27, 150, 218;
and European Community, 83–84,
126, 203–4, 214, 216, 218–19;
Franco-German brigade, 113–15,
120; Franco-German Defense and
Security Council, 113, 115–16; and
French nuclear forces, 104, 107–9,
113, 117–19; institutionalization of,
93–94, 105, 113, 115–16; joint arms
production, 94, 99, 116; military
maneuvers, 107–10, 113–15; and
NATO, 106, 108–9, 212; and SDI,
98–99; and short-range nuclear
weapons (SNF), 118–19, 123–25,
150. *See also* European Defense
Community; Elysée Treaty
FRG (Federal Republic of Germany):
and arms control, 22–25, 44 (*see also*
INF; SNF); CDU/CSU-FDP government, 6–7, 13, 36; CDU/CSU-
SPD government (Grand Coalition,
1966–69), 5; and the "comprehensive
concept," 43, 125; and CSCE, 40,
203; and Czechoslovakia, 5, 38; and
détente, 7, 21, 28; and division of
Europe, 127, 136—37, 145–47; and
Eastern Europe, policy towards
("Second *Ostpolitik*"), 133–35, 137,
146–49, 211–12; and Eastern Europe/
Soviet Union, changes in, 148–49,
151, 154; elections, March 1983, 6;
elections, January 1987, 3, 7, 39, 41,
134; and the European Community,
138, 149–50, 154, 203–4, 214, 216;

and "European peaceful order," 27,
32, 37, 39–40, 137, 204; and the
GDR *Deutschlandpolitik*, 5–8, 36–37,
148, 198–99, 210–12; *Historikerstreit*,
3; and Hungary, 147–48, 196–98;
and INF, 7–9, 23–26, 36–37, 41–44,
60, 113, 133; and NATO, 7, 19–26,
43, 77, 121–22, 153–55; and "neu-
tralism," 22, 28, 32, 104, 149; Poland, 5, 203–4; and SDI, 8, 98–99;
self-confidence, 1–5, 43–44, 121,
149, 153–55; singularization of, 43,
60, 121; and SNF (short-range nuclear forces), 25–26, 33, 39, 41–44,
60–61, 73, 118, 149, 154; and the
Soviet threat, 20–21, 56; and the Soviet Union, 104, 151–55, 185, 204,
213—14; SPD/FDP government
(1969–82), 7, 13; and the United
States, 20, 23–26, 28, 38, 113, 121–
22, 154–55; and Western European
Union, 97; and *Westpolitik*, 149–50;
World War II, legacy of, 1–5, 121–
22. *See also* CDU/CSU; European
Defense Community; FDP; Franco-
German relations; GDR; German
unification; Inter-German relations;
SPD

Galvin, John, 118
GDR (German Democratic Republic),
8–15; and détente, 12; erosion and
fall of communist regime, 11–15, 34,
38, 136, 138–43, 148, 152–53, 198,
200–202, 211–12; and Eastern Eu-
rope/Soviet Union, reforms in, 140,
142, 148; and Inter-German relations, 8–14, 133–34; and internal
(in)stability/pressure, 12–14, 140–42;
protest movements in, 142, 148,
199–201, 205; reform in, 201, 205–6;
self-confidence, 12–15, 135, 143; and
the Soviet Union, 14–15, 140, 200–
201, *See also* Inter-German relations
Geneva summit (1985), 106
Genscher, Hans-Dietrich, 6–7, 35–41,
99, 137, 139, 155, 158, 199; and
Eastern Europe, 146–49; and SNF

(short-range nuclear forces), 122, 124; and Inter-German relations, 37–38; and the Soviet Union/Gorbachev, 39, 134

Georgia, 184, 193–94

German Democratic Republic. *See* GDR

German unification, 5–6, 10, 139, 145–46, 168–69, 198–99, 202–4, 214, 216; France and, 83, 85, 203–4, 219; Soviet Union and, 202–4; and two-plus-four talks, 204, 214. *See also* FRG, and the GDR (*Deutschlandpolitik*)

Giscard d'Estaing, Valéry, 81, 83–84, 113

Gorbachev, Mikhail, 15, 48, 173–77, 184, 193, 196; and arms control, 106; and Germany, 151–53, 200; Western attitude, 23, 39

Great Britain. *See* United Kingdom

Greece, 158

Gromyko, Andrei, 195

Grosz, Karoly, 146, 187–88, 195

Gulf crisis, 226

Gysi, Gregor, 206

Habermas, Jürgen, 3

Hager, Kurt, 142

Hallstein doctrine, 5, 134

Harmel report, 27, 31, 203

Havel, Vaclav, 188, 192, 195, 205, 207

Helsinki process. *See* CSCE

Hermes project, 94, 99, 149

Hernu, Charles, 87, 89

Hillgruber, Andreas, 3

Honecker, Erich, 6, 9, 14, 119, 134–37, 140–42, 187–88, 199–201, 204

Horn, Gyula, 197

Human rights/freedoms, 23, 34, 39–40, 164, 168, 195

Hungary, 40, 147–48, 179; and German refugees, 196–98; reforms in, 140, 179–80, 187, 191, 195–98, 201, 204–6; and Romania, 189, 195, 207; and the UNC, 195, 197

Husak, Gustav, 187–88, 206

IEPG. *See* Independent European Programme Groupe

Iklé, Fred, 28, 62

Iklé-Wohlstetter advisory committee, 61–62

Iliescu, Ion, 188, 207

Independent European Programme Group (IEPG), 76

INF (Intermediate-range nuclear forces), 21–24, 26, 70, 169–70; double-zero option, 25, 41–43, 60, 103, 120; dual-track decision (1979), 21, 23, 49, 51, 54, 56–57; and third zero option/short-range nuclear weapons, modernization of, 26, 38, 41–43, 103, 118–19, 122–25; Washington Agreement (1987), 44, 57, 60–61, 103–5; zero option, 48–49, 59–61, 106. *See also* France, and INF; FRG, and INF; SNF; Soviet Union, SS–20 missiles; United States, and INF

Inter-German relations, 133–41, 148; Basic Treaty, 5; Berlin Wall, 6–7, 9, 122, 136–39, 141–42, 201–4; and "common responsibility," 9, 14, 32, 36–37, 85; division of Germany, and NATO, 26–27; and Eastern Europe, 134–35, 148; and east-west relations, 8–9, 14, 134; economic relations, 6, 8, 11, 137–40; *Deutschlandpolitik*, 5–8, 36–37, 148, 198–99, 210–12; Iron Curtain, 142, 189, 195, 197–98, 202; political contacts, 6, 9–10, 135–37, 139–40; and refugees, 141–43, 192, 196–98, 200–202; Soviet Union and, 14–15, 134, 151–52; SPD and, 5, 33–34; visits, 10–11, 134, 138–43; and the West, 36. *See also* Berlin Wall; German unification; Germany, and the GDR

Intermediate-range nuclear forces. *See* INF

Ireland, 158, 164–65

Iron Curtain, 142, 189, 195, 197–98, 202. *See also* Berlin Wall

Italy, 96–97

Jakes, Milos, 187–88, 205

Jaruzelski, Wojcich, 187, 194, 196

Kadar, Janos, 187–88, 190
Kennan, George, 26, 49, 78
Kennedy, Paul, 68–69
Khrushchev, Nikita, 175
Kissinger, Henry, 57, 62, 69, 73
Kohl, Helmut, 36, 41–44; and Eastern
  Europe, 146–47, 149; and Franco-
  German relations, 92–93, 97, 107,
  113, 124–25, 203; and German iden-
  tity/self-confidence, 2–3, 7; and the
  German unification, 168, 198, 202–3;
  and Inter-German relations, 6, 10,
  41, 134, 136–37, 140–41, 147, 198–
  99; and military strategy, 42, 44; and
  NATO, 154–55; and short-range nu-
  clear weapons, 118, 122, 124, 133;
  and the Soviet Union/Gorbachev,
  41, 151–54, 204
Korean war, 94–95
Kosovo, 189, 192
Krenz, Egon, 200–201, 206
Kristol, Irving, 22
Kuron, Jacek, 196

Lafontaine, Oskar, 4, 26, 34
Leisler Kiep, Walther, 10
Lellouche, Pierre, 60, 89
Lenin, Vladimir, 184–85
Lithuania, 191. *See also* Baltic region

McNamara, Robert, 49–50, 54, 56, 58
Mansfield amendments, 72–73, 100
Marshall Plan, 68, 78
Martens, Wilfried, 161
Massive retaliation strategy, 24, 53
Mazowiecki, Tadeusz, 188, 205
MBFR (Mutual and Balanced Force
  Reductions), 23, 31, 120, 190
Milosevic, Slobodan, 189
Mischnick, 9
Mittag, Günter, 10
Mitterrand, François, 71, 84, 88; and
  European military cooperation, 94,
  97, 161; and Franco-German rela-
  tions, 93–95, 107, 115–17, 119–21,
  123–26, 203–4; and NATO, 119,
  123; and nuclear weapons, 118–19,
  124, 127–29

Mladenov, Petur, 205–7
Modrow, Hans, 10, 188, 201–2
Moldavia, 183
Montobello agreement, 42–43
Mutual and Balanced Force Reduc-
  tions, 23, 31, 120, 190
Mutual Assured Destruction (MAD),
  53

Nagorno-Kharabakh, 183, 192–94
Nagy, Imre, 189–90
NATO (North Atlantic Treaty Organization): arms control, 22–23, 104,
  161; Brussels Summit (March 1988),
  118–19, 150; Brussels Summit (May
  1989), 121–25; burden sharing, 72–
  73, 75; changes in, 62, 65, 75, 221,
  224–25; "comprehensive concept,"
  43, 125; conventional strategy/
  forces, 25, 50–51; détente, 27, 31–32;
  division of Germany/Europe, 26,
  204; and Eastern Europe, 77, 148;
  and the EC, 76, 149–50, 165–67; and
  the Eurogroup, 76; European contribution to, 75; and European pillar/
  Europeanization, 76–77, 222–26; and
  Franco-German cooperation, 76; future of, 220–21, 224–25; Harmel report, 27, 31, 203; and IEPG, 76;
  nuclear strategy, 21–25, 48–53, 77;
  origin of, 20, 26, 68, 77–78; United
  States–European problems, 69–72;
  and WEU, 76, 96. *See also* Flexible
  response; France, and NATO; FRG,
  and NATO; INF; SNF
Nemeth, Miklos, 188, 195, 197
Netherlands, 97
Neutron bomb, 24
Nixon, Richard, 128
Nolte, Ernst, 3
Norstad, Lauris, 82
North Atlantic Assembly, 76–77
North Atlantic Treaty Organization.
  See NATO
Norway, 120
Nuclear Planning Group (NPG), 55
Nunn, Sam, 72–74, 76

Nunn amendment, 72–73
Nyers, Reszo, 195, 201

Ostpolitik (1970s), 5, 7, 10, 12–13, 31, 35, 56, 70, 135. *See also* SPD, "second *Ostpolitik*" of

Paris Treaty (1954), 96
Peace movement, 21–22, 35–36, 97, 99, 106
Perle, Richard, 73
Pershing Ia missiles, 42
Pershing II missiles. *See* INF missiles
PHARE, 218
Pleven Plan. *See* European Defense Community
Plumb, Lord, 161
Poland, 5, 40, 189, 203–4; reforms in, 140, 179–80, 187, 190, 194, 196, 198, 204–5, 207; 1980–82 crisis, 8, 13, 28, 69, 85, 163, 167
Pompidou, Georges, 83, 128
Pozsgay, Imre, 191, 194, 201

Rakowski, Mieczyslaw, 190
Rau, Johannes, 4
Reagan, Ronald, 3, 32, 65–66, 73–74, 118, 129, 191; Irangate, 66; and military strategy, 48–49, 51; and the Soviet Union, 25, 52, 58, 66, 106
Reykjavik summit (1986), 48, 51, 59–61, 103
Rogers, Bernard, 103, 109
Roman, Petre, 188, 207
Romania, 179, 204–5, 207; and Hungary, 189, 195, 207
Roosevelt, Franklin, 53
Rühe, Volker, 42, 44
Rusk, Dean, 71

Sakharov, Andrei, 193, 207
SALT (Strategic Arms Limitation Talks), 23, 100
Schmidt, Helmut, 2, 8, 13, 19–21, 34–35, 56, 83, 85, 93, 135
Schroeder, Pat, 75
Schultz, George, 71

SDI (Strategic Defense Initiative), 48–49, 51, 74, 98–99, 219
Serbia, 189, 192
Shevardnadze, Eduard, 146, 204
Short-range nuclear forces. *See* SNF
Skubiszewski, Krzysztof, 196
Smith, Gerard, 49
SNF (short-range nuclear forces), 25–26, 33, 38–39, 41–44, 60–61, 73, 103, 118–19, 122–25, 149–50, 154
Solzhenitsyn, Alexander, 195
Soviet Union: arms control proposals, 23, 60, 106, 161; Brest-Litovsk, Peace Treaty of, 185; and China, 181, 190–91, 200–201; and COMECON, 147, 150, 168, 214; and Eastern Europe, 178–79, 183; Eastern Europe, changes in, 14–15, 150, 153, 168, 183, 196, 213–14; and the European Community, 150, 161, 168–69; foreign policy, reasons for the change in, 177–81, 183; and the FRG, 104, 151–55, 184, 204, 213–14; and GDR, 14–15, 200–201; and German unification, 202–4; Glasnost, 176–77, 184; and the Helsinki Final Act, 152; and Inter-German relations, 14–15, 134, 151–52; internal problems in, 175–76; military strategy, 58, 61; and the nationality problem, 182–85, 189, 191–94; Perestroika, 176–77, 184; political reforms in, 176–77, 184, 192–93, 200, 207; Soviet empire, 65–66, 177–84; SS–20 missiles (INF), 21, 23, 36, 56, 93, 181; Western attitude toward changes in, 72, 103–4, 147–51, 154, 161. *See also* Afghanistan, invasion in; INF
Spain, 115
Späth, Lothar, 10, 41, 147
SPD (Sozialdemokratische Partei), 137; and France, 92; and German identity, 4; and Inter-German relations, 5, 13; military strategy, 31–33, 44, 77; Nuremberg-congress of, 31–35; "parallel foreign policy," 33–34;

"second *Ostpolitik*" of, 31, 33–34,
39, 145–47, 149. *See also Ostpolitik*
Sputnik, 53
SS–20 missiles, 21, 23, 36, 56, 93, 181.
See also INF
Stalin, Josef, 54, 95, 184
Strategic Arms Limitation Talks
(SALT), 23, 100
Straub, Bruno, 187
Strauss, Franz-Josef, 3, 6, 8–9, 36, 42,
44, 146–47
Strukturelle Nichtangriffsfähigkeit, 33,
39, 44, 222
Stürmer, Michael, 3, 36

Technological changes (military), 25,
51, 85–86, 88
Thatcher, Margaret, 115, 118, 219–20;
and Germany, 43, 122; and the
United States, 69
Tindemans, Leo, 161
Todenhöfer, Jürgen, 146
Transylvania, 189, 195, 207
Truman, Harry, 52, 54, 77

Ukraine, 182, 185, 196
Ullman, Richard, 129
United Kingdom: and the European
Community, 97, 161, 165; and the
European military cooperation, 74–
75, 95–98, 222; and Franco-German
cooperation, 109, 115; and German
defense, 96, 105; nuclear forces, 59;
and short-range nuclear weapons
(SNF), 122
United States: and the *Achille Lauro* affair, 69; and arms control (conventional), 22–24; and Central America,
66, 69; Congress, 53, 66–67; and
CSCE, 27; decline of, 65–69; defense
budget, 67; and détente, 28; "discriminate deterrence" report, 61–62;
economic and budgetary situation,
66; and the European Community,
74; and European military cooperation, 73–74; foreign policy, 52–53,

71–72, 180–81, 183; and Franco-German military cooperation, 73–74,
115; Gramm-Rudman-Hollings Act,
66; Grenada, invasion in, 58, 66; and
INF, 22–26, 41, 59–61; Iran, hostages in, 52, 65; and Lebanon, 66;
and Libya, 58, 66, 69, 71, 73; and
military strategy, conventional, 50–
51; and military strategy, nuclear,
48–54, 56–58, 60–62; security/nuclear
guarantee, 20, 24, 47–49, 53, 56–59,
60–62, 65, 70, 93, 103, 105–6; and
short-range nuclear weapons, 122,
125; and troop withdrawal, from
Europe, 67, 72–73, 100, 103; Vietnam War, 52, 56, 65; and Watergate,
56; and WEU, 74. *See also* FRG, and
the United States; INF; NATO;
SDI; SNF
Urbanek, Karel, 205
USSR. *See* Soviet Union

Vaclav, Klaus, 206
Vance, Cyrus, 69, 73
von Hapsburg, Otto, 189
von Weizsäcker, Richard, 4, 41, 134–
35, 202

Walesa, Lech, 190, 194
Warnke, 146
Warsaw Pact, 134, 206, 214
Washington Agreement (1987). *See*
INF, Washington Agreement
Weinberger, Caspar, 67
West Berlin. *See* Berlin
Western European Union (WEU), 76,
87, 93–94, 96–99, 161, 222–23
West Germany. *See* FRG
Wilms, Dorothee, 145–46

Yalta, 32, 53, 126, 202, 215, 229
Yeltsin, Boris, 193
Yugoslavia, 189, 192

Zhivkov, Todor, 135, 187–88, 205

About the Authors

KAREL DE GUCHT has been a member of the European Parliament since 1980, representing Belgium. A published author and lawyer by profession, he is a managing partner of a development capital investment company.

STEPHAN KEUKELEIRE is a researcher in the International Relations section of the Department of Political and Social Sciences at the University of Louvain, Belgium. He is the author of numerous articles in scholarly journals.